FULL SPECTRUM DISORDER

STAN GOFF
U.S. ARMY (RETIRED)

FULL SPECTRUM DISORDER

THE MILITARY IN THE NEW AMERICAN CENTURY

STAN GOFF

U.S. ARMY (RETIRED)

Soft Skull Press | Brooklyn, NY | 2004

© 2004 by Stan Goff
Cover © 2004 Kayrock and Wolfy, Kayrock Manual Screenprinting

Design: David Janik

Published by Soft Skull Press
71 Bond Steet, Brooklyn, NY 11237

Distributed by Publishers Group West
www.pgw.com I 1.800.788.3123

Printed in Canada

Library of Congress Cataloging-in-Publication Data
Goff, Stan. Full spectrum disorder : the military in the new
American century / Stan Goff p. cm.
    ISBN 1-932360-12-3 (pbk. : alk. paper)
    1. United States—Military policy. 2. United States—Armed
Forces. 3. World politics—1989- . 4. Goff, Stan. 5. United States—
Foreign relations—1945-1989. 6. United States—Foreign relations—
1989-. 7. United States—Social conditions—1980-. 8. United
States—Moral conditions. I. Title.
    UA23.G653 2003
    355'.033573—dc22
                        2003027360

TABLE OF CONTENTS

for Jaydin Amari Hobbs
the heart is a muscle
it loves
and struggles

INTRODUCTION

If a frog had wings, he wouldn't bump his ass every time he hops.

Folk wisdom from my Army career. This word "if" is so very often used as an excuse, an evasion, and a denial of hard realities.

Chief among those realities, I think, is that the universe refuses to hold still.

It's a tough thing for people to accept because of our existential dread, our adrenal desire for some kind of safety, some rebuttal to mortality that just doesn't exist. If things did hold still there wouldn't be anything, because everything rides time's great arrow in one direction.

As quick as we think we've got hold of something, it has somehow changed because whatever "it" is doesn't exist in a vacuum, but amidst a vastly complex and shifting set of relations to everything else. That includes society, so-called human nature, all of it.

Somewhere under all that change, there are some rules—physical laws and various species of tendential laws—if anything approaches knowable in the traditional sense, it's these, and many of these uncloak themselves as surprises along our way.

Even scientists and academics are frequent prey to the delusion that reality is reducible. Fear, deep and wide, is the secret motive force of much human behavior, and I think reduction is often rooted in fear. Passing over fear, I think, is the beginning of every liberatory project.

That lack of reducibility is my excuse for not writing something as conclusive as an English paper or a master's thesis here. Consequently, this book is not being developed along the same lines as that kind of writing. *Full Spectrum Disorder* is an unapologetic composite of the personal, the political, and the praxic, mined from experience, study, and reflection over the past few years, particularly since my first book. It doesn't conform very well to a "genre." It will change its tone and standpoint. In fact, it began as a series of essays during the build-up to the March 2003 military aggression against Iraq.

With the invaluable guidance of Nick Mamatas, who as my editor has thankfully again consented to discipline my amateur pen, I have edited out much of the polemic. These essays began in the heat of a remarkable international antiwar struggle, and that tone was appropriate then. Now I want them to be think pieces. I have argued with several people about my colloquial tone and the evocative character of much of this. That's just me. Academics are obliged to use a barrage of citations and other appeals to authority to buttress their case, and in that process risk becoming so arcane no one wants to deal with it. I'm not anti-intellectual, or even anti-academic, but I am not an academic. I do not have to legitimize my assertions—especially the more iconoclastic ones—through bogus appeals to authority because they are challenges for debate and thought.

On the other hand, I'm not falling off some pomo cliff here and challenging reality as a set of competing narratives, though competing narratives certainly form one aspect of social reality. But scholasticism (sometimes disguised as scholarship, which I value very much) as a core standard completely misses my point in this book. I don't want to write a book that "proves" itself. I want to write a book that shakes up people's thinking, and if it provokes debates or even attacks, so be it. I don't mind being proven wrong, if that's what happens. If the book were meant to support some overarching conclusion, it would be different, more confined within a genre. It's not that kind of frog. It doesn't have wings. It will bump its ass.

I have some things to say and a unique standpoint from which to say them. And I think they have some value. The only thing that unifies the themes in this book is my own experience with war and the military and my now atypical perspective as a Special Operations veteran who seeks to suggest—in the way of a small contribution—how this experience might be examined using the insights that have grown out of resistance struggles against capitalism, patriarchy, and ecocide.

Those are sometimes insights that appear to stress ugliness and harshness. But in my own experience, each of these is irrevocably combined with its opposite.

In beloved Haiti, one can see plenty that is ugly, much that is harsh and often terrible. It is the heroism of everyday people in surviving, the tenacity of those who consciously struggle, that gives Haiti its intense beauty. That simultaneous refusal to either deny reality or to quit struggling within it had much to do with my eventual drift into a politics of resistance, and if there's an orientation in this book that's it.

I am a monist and a universalist. I believe there is one reality, and here we are, and that it includes us all.

I make some rather catastrophist prognostications about U.S. power and U.S. society, without trying to predict exactly how they will come to pass. For those of us in the metropoles, who don't understand that *this collapse has already happened all over the world*, we will probably see its first form as deflation. But I can't be sure. We just need to understand that it is real, it is here, and it is now. Just not for us, yet. We are not the norm. We are not the center of the universe.

Do white Americans have to be reduced to dollar-a-day subsistence before dollar-a-day subsistence is a real collapse?

There will certainly be those who say, "Oh hell, we heard it all before. Another doomsayer, back from the sixties." That may be an effective strategy of fallacies, and we have all witnessed how effective fallacies are as ideological weapons in these days of political huckster-ism gone mad. But saying someone said something like this before does not confront the assertions. It evades them. These arguments are based on some very specific and researchable trendlines—and my cata-strophist calculations are no more than extrapolations of them. I des-perately wish I were wrong, that social transformation could happen painlessly, that we could all drink from the fountain of youth, and that the lion would lay down with the lamb.

Generalization and conflation will not erase the facts of water short-ages, postcolonial social wreckage, climate change, the organic compo-sition of capital, fossil fuel depletion, AIDS, nuclear waste, deforesta-tion, white supremacist patriarchal capitalism or its wars to defend itself from its own consequences. Those who would say this is a replay of the sixties need to do some simple math. Count heads, count water, count trees, count debts. What is the planet's human population right now compared with 1970? What is the status of, say, the Oglala Aquifer right now compared with 1970? How many hectares of forest were there in 1970 worldwide and how many are there now? What were the debts of the Third World then, and of the U.S.? What are those debts now? These simple questions suggest the scope of change since 1970 and the direction of change since 1970, but they simultaneously fail to grasp the complexity and the simplicity of that change. And these are not and cannot be merely quantitative changes.

When you inflate a kid's balloon, the pressure in the balloon steadily increases. The instant before it explodes, it appears that you are simply increasing quantities of air and pressure. Then the step-change happens that releases all that latent disequilibrium. My argument is not that the balloon will explode tomorrow. It is that it will explode.

The complexity of our era is in the social dynamics that underwrite these changes, and in this book I want to start a thought process about one piece of that dynamic—the military, global to personal. The simplicity is that these trends are aimed at endpoints. Aquifers do run dry. Land is converted from forest to desert. Civilizations do collapse. Refute me if you will on any assertion I make. I am not afraid to be wrong. But simply saying someone cried wolf thirty-five years ago won't do. It's not 1969. Things have changed, a lot. We are not living at the end of history, and we never will. But we could die at the end of it.

A good deal of what you read here will surely already be outdated. If the universe won't hold still for anything else, it sure as hell won't hold still for a little book. That's just the nature of writing about events as they happen. They will change. In a sense, it will be an opportunity for anyone who is so inclined to test the validity of much of what I say and to identify the assumptions that led me astray. I prognosticate from time to time. I've lost the fear of being wrong in much the same way I've lost the fear of being homely, the fear of aging, and the fear of authority. It just passed, like a bad fever, and I am relieved.

Someone asked me to explain why I refer to African Americans and others as "oppressed nationalities." Fair enough. That explanation affords me an opportunity to preface the book a bit and append my last book, *Hideous Dream: A Soldier's Memoir of the U.S. Invasion of Haiti* (Soft Skull Press, 2000). That book pivoted on struggles around race. In being exposed to the work and ideas over the past few years of Black activists like Cynthia Brown of Southerners for Economic Justice, Gary Grant of the Black Farmers and Agriculturists Association, Saladin

Muhammed, Ajamu Dillahunt, Ray Earqhart, Shafea M'Balia, Ashaki Binta and Rukiya Dillahunt of Black Workers for Justice, and many others, I became interested in better understanding the contradictions presented by the issue of "race." I became interested in understanding how the biological myth of race was outweighed by the social reality of it, how that weight still presses down on all of American society and traps the terrible biological myth inside it. I wanted to understand the phenomenon of negrophobia that I observed in the Special Operations community—a special form of discrimination aimed in an exclusive way at Black soldiers. I also began to read Fanon, Du Bois, Malcolm X, Mab Segrest, Eric Foner's *Reconstruction*, Rod Bush's *We Are Not What We Seem*, Joy James, David Roediger's *The Wages of Whiteness*, Angela Davis, and anything else I could get my hands on. I became convinced—especially by feminists like bell hooks, Chandra Talpade Mohanty, and Maria Mies (referring to Fanon)—that many collective oppressions were not merely characterized by inequality, but by a relation that was qualitatively "colonial." That is, these oppressions were historically organized to exploit and control a whole people to the overall benefit of another whole people. And when a people, like African Americans or Chicanos, have been forged in a historical process that creates the objective and subjective experience of separateness in development, their struggles against the dominant people have the character of both a class struggle and a national liberation struggle, because they exist in the larger relation as an oppressed nation.

So I will refer to "oppressed nationalities," and that is why.

There are certainly complexities here that have been explored elsewhere, and "oppressed nationality" is at least as inadequate a term as "capitalist patriarchy," for example. "Patriarchy" by itself—dehistoricized—is a great descriptor but a poor theoretical category, because it's extracted from history as if it stands alone as some universal category, a reification. Situating it within a specific system that we can define at least gives it an historical context with which we can perform some calculations. It doesn't describe the difference between women in a Shanghai sweatshop, women in the Haitian countryside, and white middle-class women from North Carolina, but it at least grounds the notion of male supremacy in the real world, and thereby gives us a real point of departure. "Oppressed nationality" is the same. Race and racism describe much but explain little, and to make a fight, we need to do more than name a problem; we have to understand it.

Language itself reduces what is irreducible. But there is the reason I have used this term, oppressed nationalities. It is better than "minorities" and infinitely better than "race." The ideology of American racism is white supremacy, but the reality is one of collective political domination similar to that forced on many nations in the global periphery, and this term at least acknowledges that it has an identifiable form.

Behind the militarism of our current period, there is a heightening struggle in the periphery—including oppressed nationalities here—to break free of a history imposed on them and restart the process of building their own histories. Alongside this struggle for self-determination, there is a dwindling ability of hegemonic power to prevent it.

The U.S. is in over its head. But humanity is in many ways in over its head, too. So it won't bother me much to be in over my own head with this book. Or that I'm likely to be wrong from time to time.

This year, three skulls were found in Ethiopia that proved our species has been around for at least 160,000 years. So the notion that anything I write is somehow original would be an egoist fallacy. All of us are standing on the shoulders of our ancestors, going all the way back to these newfound grandparents with the etched skulls in Ethiopia. This book will bear my name, with only my little point of view having a gram of originality.

I also want to ensure a few other living folks get their due. The folks at Freedom Road convinced me at one of the many marches in Washington last year to start writing about a good deal of what's here, and the folks at Soft Skull continue to take admirable risks with anti-genres. The members of the A-List, an international discussion forum, have done much to advance my consciousness, particularly Mark Jones, who is quoted several times in this book. He was an intellectual mentor of the first order and a man with a great, stern compassion that I valued more than I can say.

Mark died on April 9, 2003, at fifty-five years old. His contributions to my own thinking and to humanity are woven through every letter and punctuation mark in this book. He gets much credit for its strengths, and I reserve credit for its weakness to myself. I am one of many who acutely miss him. Mark now looks over my shoulder and will continue to do so until I join him in whatever condition it is that we revert to when that personal Armageddon comes.

There are comrades too numerous to list with whom I am blessed, with a special emphasis here on queer women—whom I am convinced will be a significant part of any future revolutionary vanguard in this society. And I am one who still stubbornly believes in the necessity of vanguards. Through some inexplicably good fortune, I have had the opportunity to befriend many lesbian activists, and I am intensely grateful for that. You (Aimee, Akiba, Alyce, Beth, Celia, Chelsea, Inga, Kim, Latoya, Melissa, Pat, and Sheila) have all been marvelous teachers, comrades and friends. My next book on sex and war will rely much on the experience and insight of fierce, no-bullshit, woman-centered radicals.

I thank Barbara and Nancy for plain old supportive friendship.

There are my four children and one grandchild; Elan, Jessie, Jayme, Jeremy, and Jaydin, respectively, without whom I could not struggle and without whom I could not know myself—and my terrible fallibility. I cherish them all.

And while I wrote this, there was someone who acted as the designated driver for all of our lives, who made sure things worked while I was staring into a tunnel. She was there before I began writing these things down. She was there going through that turbulence with me, and still is. And I'm not easy to live with. My partner in every sense, Sherry Goff has consented to a life sentence with me, which may be the epitome of heroism. I have not been untouched or undamaged by my own experience as either a metropolitan white man or a soldier, and I am not easy to live with. An unshared life is not worth living, and she still makes my own worthwhile, as I hope I do hers.

HAITI:
THE OCCUPIER AND THE ROCKS

the enemy
are imperfect men . . .
—Layle Silbert

For a brief time in 1994 I acted as the shadow de facto dictator of a portion of northeastern Haiti. With the possible exception of my first marriage, I have never been more ill-prepared for any task, nor has any endeavor so beaten me down—physically, mentally, or psychologically. When it was all over, I ended up in meetings where I would introduce myself by saying, "Hi, I'm a drunk named Stan."

I dodged a court martial and disappeared into a troop medical clinic where I reverted back to my Special Forces Medic role and saw patients all morning. And I wrote.

At the end of every day at Ft. Bragg, I would go home, do my family chores, then line up behind my primitive laptop and vent. This was part of my decompression strategy. Some days I would write five pages, some days ten, some days two. I took a copy of the journal Captain Mike Gallante had made for me and went through it day by day, diving straight back into all that muck and rage, trying to make a little sense of it. In a few months I was all better (right!) and set aside over six hundred pages of these therapeutic notes to myself.

In late 1998, Nick Mamatas, an editor with Soft Skull Press, asked to see them. Two years later, with a couple of light rewrites, these therapeutic notes became a book, and presto, I was an author. I received better reviews than I deserved, in my opinion, but sales have been slow.

It occurs to me now, after two and a half years of anemic sales (many American book buyers don't want to read about Haiti unless they can idealize it, exoticize it, or reinforce their racist preconceptions), I finally might have a market for it: the U.S. military in Iraq and Afghanistan. They are now experiencing what I did—the role of an occupier.

It took me 107 pages just to cross the frontier into Haiti on a CH-47 helicopter. I found that I couldn't get at the root of all those things that happened there without going back to my childhood, because that's when the odyssey that landed an eighteen-year-old in the Army began; that went through Vietnam where illusions were shattered, then launched a small boat on a huge, unfamiliar sea of race, death, sex, class, and a 24-7 preoccupation with the possibility of armed combat.

It took me another 148 pages to get to Ft. Liberte, Haiti, because—as the troops in Iraq and Afghanistan can probably tell us now—the hardest part is usually getting there. Everyone wants to focus on that luminous adrenaline Eucharist when the "game" is on, when tomorrow is inscrutable—the delicious dread of chaos, of not knowing when or how that next bifurcation will hit.

These periods of operations are the stuff of Hollywood. They're also what our militarist society rewards with deference and honor. But honest soldiers know that operations are just a high-adrenaline interlude. Soldiers who can't understand that will spend the rest of their lives trying to re-enter that luminous time, and they will become mentally ill.

Some will exploit the operations mystique for all it's worth, especially when it's all they have to hang onto, but they know the banal, tedious, bumbling, backbiting, one-foot-in-front-of-the-other reality of before and after. Getting there is before. Occupation is after.

I read a story in April 2003—just a passing news story a couple of weeks after Baghdad fell—about Iraqi kids throwing rocks at soldiers in Baghdad. I have a couple of rock throwing stories myself, one described in *Hideous Dream*, that I'll share here.

The first happened early in the invasion, when my Special Forces team and six other teams were jammed together inside the Haitian Army caserne in Gonaives, every day dealing with scenes of wild jubilation that bordered on riotous. These were not the staged scenes with special recruiting and tight camera angles that we saw pumped into our living rooms by the Central Command (CENTCOM) news network when the statue of Saddam Hussein was pulled over by an Army tracked vehicle.

The perception in Haiti during the opening days of the invasion was that the U.S. was reinstating the rightful leader of the nation, Jean-

Bertrand Aristide, even though the U.S. had worked diligently behind the scenes to discredit and defang Aristide before they brought him back in the saddle of a U.S. military occupation. The celebrations—with a latent undercurrent of sullen revenge in the tributaries—were the real thing. We, the American occupiers, found ourselves in the paradoxical position of being perceived as a (suspect) liberation force, even as we were directed to work jointly with the Haitian military police. I had personally queered that pitch on Day One in Gonaives when I led my team to arrest four Haitian soldiers and two of their collaborators for menacing a crowd with M-1 rifles.

It was the next day during one of the turbulent demonstrations/celebrations in front of the Force Armee d'Haiti (FAdH) caserne, that some well-drilled marksman of the stone pitched a rock half the length of a football field and knocked the cowboy shit out of a FAdH NCO.

The Haitian sergeant, long accustomed to ruling over the locals with a sidearm and a baton, blood running down the side of his head while the crowd cheered madly, snapped. And his rage began to infect his fellows. Within moments, the suppressed fear and resentment of the FAdH boiled to the surface, and the chatter indicated they were about to say, Fuck the Americans, we are going to kick some civilian ass!

Reacting to the sudden outburst, my team, followed by other teams, shouldered its weapons, but our eyes were fixed on the FAdH themselves, some of whom noticed and some of whom were too agitated to understand that they were in imminent danger of being shot. Only the panicked ministrations of a FAdH commander, himself a mass murderer of wide repute, calmed his troops and prevented them from being slaughtered in their own caserne by their new cohabitants. We then had to pull additional guard shifts to keep an eye on our new friends.

This happened in seconds. This was triggered by a rock.

So what is the significance of rock throwing here, and what does it have to do with the occupation of Iraq and Afghanistan?

Rock throwing is the ultimate asymmetric warfare. It erases all the markers of combatants that formalize warfare. It is completely democratic. It is a first step across an invisible line between obedience and resistance, across the boundary of the taboo against physical resistance.

It is unabstracted combat, combat that stays close to its cause, like Palestinian kids hurling stones from behind their own demolished houses. It is agile. It provokes, then moves. It requires no technology. It catalyzes dramatic changes with minimal effort. It destabilizes.

The metropolitan left today will undergo a transformation and reclaim its place not when we merely learn the lessons of the collapse of the Eastern Bloc, yada yada yada. Those things are important. But we will be transformed into leaders when we learn the lesson of rocks.

Our actions at Gonaives had made temporary heroes of us and created profound resentment and suspicion among the Haitian soldiers toward us. That was contrary to the intent of the Task Force commanders, and by and by it was "corrected." The "liberation" turned into an occupation.

In Iraq and Afghanistan, the situations are substantially different.

No more than a handful of the most venal opportunists from Iraq supported the invasion, given that the United States military slaughtered and maimed tens of thousands of Iraqi civilians in the first invasion, killed untold numbers of retreating Iraqi military, then proceeded to subject hundreds of thousands more to a slow death by malnutrition, disease, and medical neglect via sanctions. In Afghanistan, the U.S. attacked an already shattered society, killing thousands of civilians, because Saudis and Egyptians had flown airplanes into U.S. buildings.

That's not to say the U.S. government didn't assist the installment of the Cedras-Francois junta by engineering the coup d'etat against Aristide in 1991.[1] The U.S. did exactly that, and one of their co-collaborators—Emmanuel "Toto" Constant—is a fugitive from justice in Haiti who is being harbored by the United States in Queens, New York, "where he lives with his auntie, sells phone cards, goes nightclubbing, and collects McDonalds Happy Meal toys."[2] Toto is also reputed to have a recurring taste for cocaine.

The direct brutality of U.S. bombs and sanctions had been part of everyday life for twelve years before the latest U.S. invasion of Iraq. So there was no welcome mat laid at the feet of the invaders.

It's different. Here's what's not different though.

Every day, the troops responsible for carrying out these occupations are executing seemingly contradictory directives based on political maneuvering to which they are not privy. This begins as confusion. Then it develops into frustration. Then comes an indescribable psychic fatigue, and finally a seething hatred of the place and its people.

Those who have no desire to collaborate with the occupiers will keep their distance—or attack them. (Not many attacked us in Haiti, but in our case, those with firearms were the same people who were confident that after our "liberation" show was over, they would be safely reinstalled.)

Those who did approach the American troops had agendas. Lots of agendas, and all hidden. After every revolution, there is a Thermidor period. After every occupation, there is a scam period.

It was a time to settle scores. A time to brown-nose the new rulers. To maneuver for jobs and positions. And every time there is a conflict of interest between occupation grifters, they compete for the attention and credulity of the occupying troops. This begins to leave the impression among the troops that the whole society is a pack of scheming, pathological liars. They are, after all, being approached by the most unethical sectors of that society.

When I was in Haiti, I had a couple of advantages over the troops in Iraq and Afghanistan. First, there were clear class lines drawn there in an otherwise homogeneous society. Haitians are not divided into several ethnic and religious groups. There is some diversity of religion because of the plague of evangelist proselytizers there, but the culture of Haiti is distinct and all encompassing, even among the Protestants who, in a real crisis, will head over to the nearest Voudon temple for a *ti loa*, just to hedge their bets.

Another advantage was functional Spanish, since I was largely in an area adjacent to the Dominican border. A great number of local folk spoke Spanish.

Hardly any GIs speak Arabic, Farsi, or Pashtun, so they remain thoroughly dependent on interpreters who themselves may nurse agendas.

In Haiti, Iraq, and Afghanistan, there was another common denominator. Military Intelligence. Yes, there is such a thing. Sort of . . .

The U.S. military does nothing to correct the yawning cultural ignorance of the troops, or the officers for that matter, who have been trained in Huntington's Model, about which I will speak later in this book). A typical military Intelligence Summary (INTSUM), which presumably sweeps away ignorance, serves primarily to amplify ignorance. To the initiated, these INTSUMs are rib-rocking collections of error, innuendo, stereotype, and idiocy, worthy of burlesque. In preparation for Haiti, we were warned of "voodoo attacks."

No lie. Voodoo attacks . . . with secret poisonous "powders."

INTSUMs cannot be satirized.

I have little doubt that troops in Iraq and Afghanistan have been forced to sit through many of these perfidious sideshows, and even less doubt that, barring any counternarrative, the majority believed them. Troops preparing for Haiti largely accepted the reports of magic powders, cannibalism, and all the rest. The most tragic thing that many of them were told and many of them believed, and that will disabuse them of their naïve faith in officialdom, was that they were liberating somebody. Now they all know better.

By June of 2003, Robert Fisk was reporting conversations with occupation soldiers in Iraq, noting that the now battle-hardened and edgy troops—undergoing a Somalia-like habituation to daily rocket propelled gernade (RPG) and rifle attacks—would sniff at you like you were an idiot if you talked about liberation.[3]

It is a combination that the television-stoned U.S. civilian populace is incapable of understanding—terminally fatigued machismo, paranoia, racism, homesickness, official stupidity, confusion, and the contempt for each other that only a long occupation can breed among soldiers—that translates into occasional outbursts against the local populations, like shooting up crowds, which the military then has to justify or cover up.

A small handful of independent-minded soldiers identified with some locals, and that has led them directly into a role conflict. The refusal to dehumanize the Iraqis and the Afghans will not immediately convert our soldiers into conscientious objectors or—like me—leftists, but it will begin an irreversible process that separates them, first from many of their fellows, then from their old selves.

In Fisk's account, some soldiers attempted to respond to rocks with candy. Some deeply ingrained religious impulse, perhaps, some finely developed sense of morality . . . and it will be met with more rocks, until the denial is overcome. Then comes the sadness. Then comes the acceptance, or the breakdown.

This is painful, like molting.

In the Army, we called it "going native." This is the implicit us-ver-sus-them dichotomy. If you begin to identify in any way with the occupied population, you have flipped, gone native, and you will be stripped of your identity. I heard it the first time when I gave a Vietnamese girl a stick of gum. "Gook-lover." Ridicule is a policeman.

In 1994, one of my men would write in a statement against me that I had "turned Haitian."

The crux of it is this. There *are* sides. If you assume the role of occupier, no matter how much you rebel against it emotionally, that role exists objectively against the occupied. That conflict, along with a host of others, can be brought to the surface with a few rocks.

Haiti was an easy occupation, and quite probably the culmination of a priceless education I received from the United States Army.

Those in Iraq and Afghanistan will have more to contend with than I did. The Haitians waited us out. There's hardly a drop of oil in Haiti. Nor does Haiti sit, like Afghanistan, between the Gulf states, the Caspian Basin, and China—the worst geographic luck in the world today.

These new occupations are for keeps, and they will be played for keeps, like my first occupation—Vietnam.

VIETNAM:
TRANSGRESSION

> When I have considered the enormity of the
> white man's crimes . . . I think in perfect
> harmony—with my sister of long ago: Let
> the earth marinate in poisons. Let the
> bombs cover the ground like rain. For noth-
> ing short of total destruction will ever teach
> them anything.
>
> —Alice Walker, on Zora
> Neale Hurston, 1976

Vietnam, 1970–71:

I never actually saw any tigers in the Tiger Mountains. We walked into
them—the mountains, not the tigers—after an eight-day stay at an
eight-cubicle whorehouse on Loh Du Beach, where one of the prosti-
tutes called herself Pussycat.

A few days into our sojourn in the Tigers, we got word that the
November Rangers, our long-range reconnaissance guys, had just hit a
North Vietnamese Army (NVA) hospital, and we had to secure it for a
damage assessment.

The landing zone was an artillery crater on the side of a mountain,
and the choppers hovered over ten feet off the ground. When I leaped
out, I hit the ground and tumbled into a heap with around sixty pounds
of rucksack and radio pinning my head against mud and shredded veg-
etation, but to my credit I never let go of my weapon.

We'd all taken a few hits off the DXs, Kool cigarettes with some
heroin sprinkled into them, before the helicopter assault, so I didn't
really feel the latest knots on my head and was able to walk off the
funny sensation in my ankle.

When the November Rangers had pulled back, a CH-47 Chinook
helicopter had come in with a sling load of thickened fuel, called Phugas,
that was dropped and ignited by a spotter plane with a little rocket.

The whole place was on fire when we got there. A great wide column of opaque, oil-black smoke boiled into the sky. The burning forest crackled in the distance like gunshots and made us flinch.

Some of the guys from First Squad linked up with us. I was in Second. We sat and smoked while we watched and waited for instructions. They told us they'd found the bodies of four NVA nurses.

Since it was an NVA hospital, the women there had to be NVA nurses, you see. They'd been lined up in a row, all on their backs, and they were pretty burnt from the Phugas, but the First Squad guys had scoped them out up close anyway. All of the bodies had sharpened sticks thrust into their cunts. Each had a bullet hole in her head. There was a little laughter at this report.

"Fuckin' rangers."

I laughed a little, too. The most dangerous thing I might be was a pussy or a gook lover. Laughter was cover and concealment. When I had first arrived in the country, I watched members of my platoon go into the ville to murder on old woman hoeing her potato patch. My spirit was enclosed like the eye of an alligator behind its nicitating membrane. That was when I learned about laughing.

Boy to man, male to Alpha male. Soldier, teenager, now nihilist, each and all were the pieces of something I was becoming as I learned to laugh at new things. At wet work. Have a DX after.

I was nineteen. I was afraid. I was a boy, afraid, involved in wet work, with a little heroin in my lungs and my blood and my brain. So I laughed.

Memory is a funny thing. When my dad died, and that was only a dozen years ago, the grief cascaded out of me when I saw him there in the box with his funny hat on (a family sense of humor). I "remember" that, but I can't get that feeling back. We closed the lid, loaded him into a long car, and buried him in a rocky little oak stand outside Hot Springs, Arkansas.

I seem to remember when I was very young, every sentient being I encountered was worthy of something that might be love. Step by step, being by being, parents and relatives, strangers and associates and the black and white television in our living room all taught me to stop loving. I didn't stop, but the totality of it was crippling my capacity for love. My sister was encouraged in her loving, but once she started to grow tits, she was encouraged to stop thinking.

I wonder, if I had a choice to go back and start over, would I choose to live with thinking distorted by crippled loving, or with loving distorted by crippled thinking? Maybe love is the wrong word. Maybe care is the right one. I'm still not sure.

My father taught me to fish when I was very young, and he hunted and brought home the corpses of animals. He taught me to clean the fish and the quail and the rabbits. I learned to cut into their bodies and remove their skins and eviscerate them, and my father would smile and pick me up and squeeze me. And I learned that I could win approval by "crossing over" my reticence and fear and loathing. The truth is, too, that this cutting was a thrilling, sensual thing.

I was a boy who delighted in the flight of quail, and I was a boy who delighted in the approval of his father. And I ate the fish and the rabbit and the quail and the deer as just one part of pledging the vast patriarchal fraternity.

I don't really remember the original boy. I just remember the memory, so that's all I can grieve for now, and I don't remember really deep grief, so the grieving is removed from itself.

I am rootless now, with no sense of place, no friendships that reach between my long past and short present; so in many ways I am a man ahead of my time. I think we are all about to become rootless. It may be time. The soil has grown poisonous.

I didn't know it when I was a child, but I was being shaped for a career in the Army.

I was very small for my age, and I remain a fairly diminutive person today—never a very imposing physical presence. In the world of boys becoming men, this can be a terrible liability, and the source of a paralyzing fear.

One day in junior high, where I was the smallest person male or female in the whole school, our science class had recruited a volunteer—me—to have his finger pierced with a sterile medical lancette for a drop of blood on a microscope slide.

I had the girls' attention, because the bigger boys had emphatically refused, and I swelled inside at my little victory over them when I didn't so much as blink.

Later in the cafeteria, after stealing several of the lancettes, I sat down and ate lunch, then pulled out the lancettes, opened one, and systematically lanced all ten of my fingertips, nursing a drop of blood from each one. Several people paled, and some of the biggest, most aggressive boys in school—boys who had entertained themselves closing me in my gym locker—gave me a look of pure terror. I had cut into my own body. I began to understand the psychology of power, risk, and transgression. They never locked me in that locker again.

I found that whatever I couldn't be, I could construct myself now as "weird." That's an identity, too. And it keeps a lot of people off of you.

A friend asked me not long ago if I had ever been diagnosed with post-traumatic stress disorder (PTSD). I haven't, not officially, but I picked up a book about trauma after she asked that. Here's what it said:

> trauma destroys our fundamental assumptions about the safe-
> ty of the world; trauma destroys the positive value of the self;
> trauma destroys the belief in a meaningful order of creation.

The Army sent me to a kind of two-decade school, and in school I learned something.

The world is not fundamentally safe.

The first time I felt like I was universally validated was when I joined the Army and went to Vietnam. People couldn't stop praising me, even after I'd burned down poor peoples' homes and barns and killed their livestock and their dogs, even after I became one of thousands of accomplices in the mass murder and ecocide that we now reduce to something called the Vietnam conflict.

I've heard the stories about the poor, spat-on Vietnam vets, which is more urban legend than reality. No one ever spit on me when I got back from Vietnam. They didn't spit on me when I came back from other exotic places either—El Salvador, Guatemala, Grenada, Colombia,

Peru, Somalia, Haiti . . . I got a chest full of fruit salad ribbons, free drinks in airports, and people just admired the fuck out of me. I got *paid* for my trauma. A lot more than our victims did. Pass the DX.

And there is *no* meaningful order in creation. There's *order* aplenty. Something holds things together and ensures that there is something and not nothing. But trauma or no trauma, you can look as hard as you want for meaning there in all that infinite externality, and you still have to lie to make it happen.

A lot of the people I ran into in the process of securing Uncle Sam's favorable investment climates around the world never had any assumptions about the safety of this world. Moreover, I can drive fifteen minutes from where I'm writing right now and find people who can't assume safety.

In the bigger scheme of things, there is no such thing as safety, of course. It's a grotesque and debilitating illusion.

That's why September 11 took America from mourning to rage in an instant. Comfortable white America will kill to protect its illusions.

So the world is suffering from PTSD.

There is no meaning without a consciousness to invent it. Once that subject is gone, and all of us certainly *do* disappear, meaning is gone with us. There was a kind of responsive mantra in the boonies of Vietnam.

"It don't mean nuthin'."

"What don't mean nuthin'?"

"Nuthin'."

People think we're all damaged, the vets. A lot of that is hype. A lot of that is attention-getting from veterans who never humped a rucksack, who never heard supersonic ammunition crack around their ears, and who are copping a tragic pose for a credulous, war-worshipping public. Many of the combat veterans are the healthiest people left. No patience for hypocrisy. They understand the guy in *All Quiet on the Western Front*, who goes back to the front to escape the safety and hypocrisy of "home." Shit is honest there. Some of us can be *what* you wanted us to be—"men"—but not *like* you wanted us to be—men who will prop up your most treasured lies.

Militarists won't soon describe to you how homoerotic combat is, bent as they are to the task of de-feminizing boys so they'll be "good" workers, "good" husbands, "good" fathers, "good" soldiers, "good" men.

Get with your significant other some time and do something that cheats death. Jump out of an airplane. Get into a fight with firearms. That luminous feeling lasts for hours. It's like an orgy, like going into the haunted house, like murder, like giving up your religion. It keeps everything immediate and fresh, like being born again.

It's transgression, and in a culture like ours that simultaneously inhibits and stimulates, transgressions become our way of knowing we are real. I wanted to see things when I was young, even things I wasn't supposed to see, especially things I wasn't supposed to see; even things that frightened me, especially things that frightened me; things that broke up my safe, comfortable universe, because in that suburban postwar neighborhood where I spent several formative years leading up to my enlistment, where everyone worked at the same plant and their insular vanilla lives were about acquiring appliances and sharing factory gossip, I felt like I couldn't fucking breathe.

I saw people who were supposed to be my enemies practicing transgression.

Not out of fear and alienation, like me. They did it when there were no options left open to them. They did it because their families had been burned out or murdered or had sharpened stakes driven into their cunts. They did it so a next generation might not have to live under someone's heel. They did it out of hate, because they did it out of love. Some were older than soldiers and some were younger; some were women and some were children.

They fought not to dominate but to defend and liberate. We rotated back to the States, where we could nurse our post-traumatic stress disorders, but they were there for the duration.

I don't know how to explain because after fifty-two years, two marriages, five continents, and after more than two decades in uniform, the voices in me are as numerous as they are contradictory. I was slow to find my way back from that phallocentric, shattered little world after Vietnam, but in retrospect, it was the beginning of the most superlative education imaginable. You know what they say about school. You get out of it what you put into it.

Now I am the Vietcong.

LATIN AMERICA:
AQUÍ HAY LOS INDIOS AMIGOS

> *If we do not want to fall into the trap of moralism and individualism, it is necessary to look below the surface and to come to a materialist and historical understanding of the interplay of the sexual, the social, and the international division of labour.*

—Maria Mies, 1988

1992:

Tolemaida is hot. The whole Sumapaz River Valley is hotter than hell.

Steep, semi-arid, with plenty of thorns and mosquitoes, it's the perfect place for the Lancero School, where the Colombian military runs its toughest training and assessment course.

About seventy miles south of Bogota, Tolemaida is also home to Colombian Special Forces, kind of like the Fort Bragg of Colombia. I'd been married for the second time only ten days when 7th Special Forces sent me there on October 22, 1992.

Bill Clinton was campaigning for the presidency against George Herbert Walker Bush, and I remember the Delta guys who were billeted alongside us shrieking and carrying on when the election results came through, "Faggot lovin' draft dodger!"

Delta was there training a select group of Colombian soldiers for "close-quarter battle," which means fighting inside buildings, often using precision marksmanship and nanosecond target discrimination. Our team was training two battalions of Colombian Special Forces in night helicopter operations and counterinsurgency tactics.

The official story was that the embassy wanted to relieve the Colombian government in its defense of democracy against leftist guerrillas. We would do that by assisting in the fight against narcotics traffickers, from whom the guerrillas were supposed to be getting all their support.

Colombian democracy is a lot like U.S. democracy. Only a tiny fraction of the population has the means to recruit and promote candidates. It's different, for now, in that there is a civil war in Colombia, and the government works with paramilitaries who stalk and murder leftists, trade union organizers, and peasants who are on land their patrons want. They don't murder many guerrillas because they fear them. The guerrillas generally stalk and murder the paramilitaries. Fair's fair.

During high school, I lived in a neighborhood where everyone worked in the McDonnell-Douglas plant, which built the F-4 Phantoms that provided close air support for the troops in Vietnam. My dad and mom both riveted on the center fuselage assembly.

In 1970, I enlisted in the army, volunteering for the airborne infantry and a tour in Vietnam. I seem to recall that I wanted to impress a girl with whom I'd just broken up. And of course I bought the "domino theory," a Cold War relic now, that blood-drinking communists were taking over the world, one country at a time, and that if we didn't stop them in Vietnam, we'd be fighting these furious demons in places like Rolla, Missouri.

That sounds stupid, but people have to understand that being raised a white male in the U.S. in the fifies and sixties, for most of us, meant being raised stupid. George W. Bush, while he had a lot more money and opportunities than the rest of us baby boomers, was raised just as stupid as the rest of us. He was just stupid in color while the rest of us were still stupid in black and white.

Not being altogether stupid, I did see that my future was either joining the army or working in an aircraft factory like my folks. For an eighteen-year-old, the reasoning is that at least with the army I might get to do some hero shit that people could adore me for.

Vietnam took some of the naiveté away, but not all of the stupidity. Stupid can mean learning all sorts of good technical stuff, and it means acting like we know something even when we can't find our asses with radar. Michael Moore just made a lot of money pointing that out in a book called *Stupid White Men*. I, like totally, get it. Great at solving immediate practical and technical problems while stubbornly resisting any thought of long-term consequences or systems. We need to build some more cars.

So being a stupid white baby-boomer American male, I got out of the army for four years, went to college off and on, and got into a dysfunctional relationship that I consummated with a dysfunctional marriage.

And we had a daughter, so economic necessity took me back to where I could find some security—the army.

Long story short, I got to be pretty good at what I did and drifted into something called Special Operations, where I proceeded to work all over the world.

I don't really know where expediency turned into a career. It just happened.

In the army, there is garrison soldiering and field soldiering. Everyone does some of each. Most people have a preference. If you place a very high value on daily hot showers, comfortable routines, and don't mind marching and saluting and shining boots, then garrison soldiering is your cup of tea. If you don't mind smelling bad and sleeping outside, and if you hate shining boots, saluting, and marching, and if you take a special masochistic pleasure in sometimes extreme physical challenges combined with sleep deprivation, bad food, and the chance to test your wits in a very multidimensional way, then field soldiering is your racket. Some jobs have lots of garrison with occasional field exercises, and others stay in garrison only to prepare for the next field exercise or actual operation.

I despised garrison soldiering and I wanted to travel. So, it was inevitable that I ended up in Special Operations, first with the Rangers and later with Special Forces.

1980:

I went to Panama. High fences separated us from the slum dwellers that lived in the Canal Zone—very colonial. After that, I went to El Salvador, Guatemala, and a host of other dirt-poor countries.

Over and over, the fact that we as a nation seemed to take sides with the rich against the poor started to penetrate—first my preconceptions, then my rationalizations, and finally, my consciousness.

1983:

Posing as a political officer, former Special Forces sergeant Seamus O'Donnell (not his name), posing as a political officer didn't even try to hide his real job from me at the U.S. Embassy in Guatemala.

"You with the political section?" I asked.

I knew what he did. I was trying to be discreet.

"I'm a fuckin' CIA agent," he responded.

Seamus adopted me out of friendship for a mutual acquaintance, one of my Delta buddies with whom he had served in Vietnam. He told me where to get the best steak, the best *ceviche*, the best music, the best martinis.

He liked martinis.

We stopped off one afternoon at the El Jaguar Bar in the lobby of the El Camino Hotel, a mile up Avenida de la Reforma from the U.S. Embassy. He drank eight martinis in the first hour.

Seamus began blurting out how he had participated in the execution of a successful ambush "up north" two weeks earlier. "North" was in the Indian areas Quiche and Peten, where government troops were waging a scorched-earth campaign against Mayans considered sympathetic to the leftist guerrillas. He was elated.

"Best fuckin' thing I got to do since 'Nam."

"You're talkin' kinda loud," I reminded him, thinking this must be pretty sensitive stuff.

"Fuck them!" he shot a circumferential glare. "We own this motherfucker!"

The other patrons looked down at their tabletops. Seamus was big and manifestly drunk.

I should have known better, but I mentioned a Mayan schoolteacher who had just been assassinated by the *esquadrones de muertos*. It had been in the newspapers. The teacher had worked for the Agency for International Development (AID), a U.S. agency operating out of the embassy that oversaw dozens of little projects designed to contain resistance, co-opt local leaders, and provide intelligence to the CIA. My naïve point to Seamus was that it made the United States look bad when these loose cannons pulled stunts like that. The impression was left that the U.S. government tacitly *approved* of assassinations by continuing to support Guatemala's government.

"He was a communist," stated Seamus, without even pausing to toss down his twelfth martini. His eyes were getting that weird, stony, not-quite-synchronized look.

So that's how it was. I never thought to thank him for peeling that next layer of innocence off of me.

I had to take Sean's car keys from him that night. He wanted to drive to some whorehouse in Zone 1.

When we left the bar, he couldn't find his car in the parking lot, so he pulled his pistol on the attendant and threatened to shoot him on the spot. He accused the attendant of being part of a car theft gang.

"I know these motherfuckers," he glared.

The attendant was almost in tears, when I coaxed the pistol from Seamus's hand.

We found his fucking car in the lot one block away. That's when he started talking about driving to his favorite bordello. I grabbed his keys out of his hand. He was wall-eyed, piss-on-his-own-feet, fucked-up drunk.

"Gimme the keys!" he bellowed as I danced away from him.

"I can't."

"I'll kick your ass," he said.

I reached into my pocket and grabbed three coins. When he lunged at me again, I tossed the coins into a street drain with a conspicuous jingle.

"There's the keys," I said.

He peered myopically into the drain for a moment, then tried to train his eyes on me. I dodged his staggering assault like he was a child. He almost fell, and I found myself wondering how I could possibly carry him. If I left him in the street, he'd be dead by morning.

He turned abruptly, like he'd just forgotten something, and tottered quietly away.

I dropped his keys off at the political section the next day, with a note explaining where his car was.

Fred Chapin was the U.S. ambassador in Guatemala. He was famous for his ability to drink a bottle of Scotch and still give a lucid interview in fluent Spanish before his bodyguards carried him up to his room at *la residencia* and poured him into bed.

Chapin was credited with coining a quote well known in Foreign Service circles: "I only regret that I have but one liver to give for my country."

Embassies are collections of these idiosyncratic characters. Mauro, another such individual, was the chief Guatemalan investigator assigned to work with the security section at the embassy. He was dissipated to a fault, and even the thugs on bodyguard detail gave him a wide berth. His reputation as a sociopathic former death squad member was well known. His history was on him, too, like an aura of ruthless decay, like a cadaver whose appetites had outlived him. Make the hair stand up on the back of your neck.

"If you need to find something out, just send Mauro," was the provincial wisdom at security.

Langhorn Motley, Reagan's special ambassador to Central America, came to Guatemala to see what was being done with U.S. money, other than aboriginal genocide and the elimination of Bolshevik school teachers, of course. I was assigned to his security detail for a trip to Nebaj, a tiny Indian hamlet near the Mexican border. We were going to inspect a hospital. There were no roads into Nebaj, so a helicopter was arranged.

When we finally arrived in Nebaj, the pilot and crew chief were in an animated conversation, both referring again and again to the fuel gauge. Out of the helicopter, we were escorted through the dirt streets to an open-bed, two and a half ton truck by a corpulent, European-looking Guatemalan lieutenant colonel.

The villagers stood in silence as we passed. Two small children, maybe three years old, burst into hysterical tears when I walked too close with my CAR-15 assault rifle. I tried not to speculate about their reaction.

The truck took us to a dusty stone foundation. Nothing more. No rooms, no walls, no nothing. This was the hospital.

Motley turned to me and said, "This is a fuckin' white elephant."

Later, the white Guatemalan lieutenant colonel sat us in a room at his headquarters and trotted in two "former guerrillas." Indians. One was a skinny old man. The other was a pregnant woman, around twenty-five years old. They told us dutifully that they had been reformed by their newfound understanding of the duplicity of the communists and by the humanitarian treatment they had received at the hands of the soldiers.

It was a flat-eyed, canned recital, but it seemed to please the lieutenant colonel who sat there with a benevolent half-smile, glancing from them to us and back, judging their performance, assessing our reaction.

The skin of the two demonstration Indians almost moved from underneath with an arid, copper-tongued terror. The whole place smelled like impunity and murder.

1985:

Reporters in El Salvador tended to hang out at the pool in the Camino Real Hotel with transistor radios pressed to their ears. They drank and scribbled, and talked warily, regarding one another like rattlesnakes.

I was chatting up a member of the press corps one day. She was having lunch at the Camino. Around thirty, she worked for the *Chicago Tribune*. She was terribly excited because she had been allowed aboard a helicopter the week before that flew into Morazan, a stronghold of the leftist guerrillas. She got to see some "bang-bang" and was sooo fucking grateful to the embassy for arranging it for her.

Would I mind, she asked, taking her out for coffee or a drink somewhere in the barrios sometime? She would never think of doing it alone.

I was disillusioned. Her anemic weariness annihilated my idealized preconception of journalists as eccentric, fearless salts, obsessed with getting at the real story.

Bruce Hazelwood was a member of Milgroup, the embassy military liaison section at the U.S. Embassy in El Salvador. He was a former member of my unit, Delta, the counterterrorist unit at Fort Bragg. Hazelwood oversaw training management in the *Estado Mayor*, army headquarters. Over the past five years, he had earned an enviable reputation as a productive liaison with the Salvadoran military. He told me off the cuff once that his biggest problem was getting the officers to quit stealing.

Good-looking, strawberry-blonde, freckled, and charming, Hazelwood was a favorite of the young women in the press corps. I went with him and an embassy entourage to visit an orphanage at Sonsonate. The women from the press pool absolutely doted on him. He rewarded them with tons of mischievous magnetism.

Billy Eschen (pseudonym), another ex-Delta fellow with Elvis-like looks, who was with Milgroup, did the same thing at a party. The women from the press would sidle up alongside him, asking how he thought progress was coming with the human rights situation.

He would ask them how it seemed to *them*.

Well, they'd say, *there were only a few battlefield executions of prisoners still taking place, according to rumors, but they'd heard nothing else. We can't expect them to come around overnight, now, can we?*

Would you like to go dancing at an all-night club later?

You know where one is?

I know where they all are, he'd tell them.

Eschen—the dangerous downrange fuck fantasy of roving reporters—told me at a bar once that he was training the finest right-wing death squads in the world.

We first heard of "embedding" reporters during the full-scale invasion of Iraq. But they've been getting embedded for a long time.

The reporters at the Camino Real hired rich Salvadoran kids as informants and factotums. It was very important that they be educated, English-speaking kids, twenty to twenty-five years old, who could keep the reporters abreast of rumors and happenings in the capital. But the rich kids were as far from the lives of average Salvadorans as were most of the reporters.

In the street, I could see an old woman dragging herself down the sidewalk with a gangrenous leg, a crazy man shriveled in a trash-littered corner, bone-skinny kids who played music for coins with a pipe and a stick.

On the bus one day in downtown San Salvador, a blind man came begging and people who could ill-afford it gave him a coin. These people were calloused, very modestly dressed, with Indian still in their cheeks. To the slick, manicured, round-eyed well-to-do, the poor and the beggars were invisible, as invisible as the blackened *carboneros*, the worm-fattened market babies, and the brooding teens with raggedy clothes, prominent ribs and red eyes glaring out of the spotty shade on street corners.

If they are invisible, they can be ignored. If they are less than human, they can be killed. If they see a chance, they may fight.

I was reminded of the goats at the Special Forces medical lab.

When I was training to be a medic, we used goats as "patient models." The goats would be wounded for trauma training, shot for surgical training, and euthanized over time by the hundreds for each fourteen-week class. The Special Forces "goat lab" is sometimes called Caprine Auschwitz. Nearly every student upon arrival would begin expressing his antipathy for the caprine breed.

"A goat is a dumb creature, hard-headed, homely," we'd say.

A few acknowledged what the program was actually doing without seeking these comfortable rationalizations. A few even became attached to the animals and grew more depressed with each day. But most developed an anti-caprine ideology as conscience balm.

1991:

As a member of 7th Special Forces, I went to Peru. The reasons we went there were manifold and layered, as are many of our rationales for military activity.

We were committed, as a matter of policy, to encouraging something called IDAD, or Internal Development and Defense, for Peru—a nominal partnership in the "war on drugs."

Peru was in our "area of operational responsibility," and we (our "A" Detachment) were performing a DFT, meaning Deployment for Training. So, we went to Peru to assist in their internal development and defense, to improve their "counterdrug" capabilities, and to train ourselves to better train others in our "target language," Spanish.

Those were the official reasons. No briefing mentioned another part of the mission: unofficial wars on indigenous populations. The course of training we developed for the Peruvians was basic counterinsurgency. Drugs were never discussed with the Peruvian officers. It was a sensitive issue, if you get my drift.

We were quartered in an ammunition factory outside the town of Huaichipa for the first few weeks. Later, we moved into *Jefe de la Direccion de Fuerzas Especiales* (DIFE), the Peruvian Special Forces complex at the edge of Barranco district in Lima.

During the middle of the mission, we camped at the edge of an Indian village called Santiago de Tuna, in the sierra four hours outside the capital. *Tuna* is the Spanish word for prickly-pear cactus fruit. "Blessed with Cactus Fruit" would be the direct translation. Local Indians welcomed us with two sacks full of cactus fruit, which is delicious and makes you shit like a goose. We became very chummy with the Peruvian officers, some of whom were easy-going gents and some of whom were aggressively macho. They stuffed us full of *anticuchos* (spicy, charbroiled beef heart) and *cerveza Krystal,* the Peruvian national beer, every night. Sometimes the combat veterans would get shitfaced and spit all over us as they re-lived combat experiences. One major couldn't shut up about how many people he had killed and how the sierra was a land for real men, *una tierra por machos.*

A lot of drinking went on. Beer with the officers and soldiers. Cocktails in the bars; *pisco* with the Indians, who the soldiers tried to run off because they were considered a security risk.

One Indian man, in particular, toothless and dissipated, his blood-red eyes swimming with intoxication, astonished me with his knowledge of North American Indian history. He even knew the years of several key battles in our wars of indigenous annihilation. Geronimo was a great man, he said. A great medicine man. Great warrior. A lover of the land.

A Peruvian captain said a strange thing to me as we walked past an Indian cemetery during the eighteen-mile gut-check march out of Santiago de Tuna.

"*Aquí hay los indios amigos.*" Here are the friendly Indians. He opened his hand toward the little acre of graves.

1992:

When I was training Colombian Special Forces in Tolemaida in 1992, my team was ostensibly there to aid the counter-narcotics effort.

We were giving military forces training in infantry counterinsurgency doctrine. We knew perfectly well, as did the host-nation commanders, that narcotics was a flimsy cover story for beefing up the capacity of armed forces who had lost the confidence of the population through years of abuse. The army also had suffered humiliating setbacks in the field against the guerrillas.

But I was growing accustomed to the lies. They were the currency of our foreign policy. They were part of the job. Security clearances are promises to protect lies.

1999:

Drug tsar Barry McCaffrey and Defense Secretary William Cohen were arguing for massive expansion of military aid to Colombia. Already, Colombia was the third-largest recipient of U.S. military aid in the world, jumping from $85.7 million in 1997 to $289 million in 1999. Press accounts said about three hundred American military personnel and agents were in Colombia at any one time. Private military contractors like SAIC, MPRI, and Dyncorp weren't counted. The Clinton administration was seeking $1 billion over the next two years. The Republican-controlled Congress wanted even more, $1.5 billion, including forty-one Blackhawk helicopters and a new intelligence center.

The State Department claimed the widened assistance was needed to fight "an explosion of coca plantations." The solution, according to the State Department, was a 950-man "counternarcotics" battalion. But the request was strangely coincident with the recent military advances of *Fuerzas Armadas Revolucionarias Colombianas–Ejercito del Pueblo* (FARC-EP), the leftist guerrillas who controlled forty percent of the countryside.

In the United States, there was a different kind of preparation afoot: the preparation of the American people for another round of escalation.

McCaffrey—not coincidentally the former commander of the theater for the U.S. armed forces in Latin America (SOUTHCOM), and a war criminal—was already "admitting" that the lines between counternarcotics and counterinsurgency were "beginning to blur" in Colombia.[1]

The reason? The guerrillas were involved in drug trafficking, a ubiquitous claim that was repeated uncritically in the press. There was no differentiation between the FARC and a handful of less significant groups, nor was there any pressing need to cite evidence.

When this construct first began to gain wide currency, former U.S. Ambassador to Colombia Miles Frechette pointed out that there was no clear evidence to support McCaffrey's claims. His statement was soon forgotten.

Americans—white, patriarchal, and stupid in our manner of knowing everything—were to be prepared. In Colombia, it is well known that the Colombians who profit the most from the drug trade are members of the armed forces, the paramilitaries, and police; government officials; and the "big businessmen" of the urban centers.[2]

The FARC taxes coca (the buyers, not the *campesinos*), a far cry from trafficking. Coca also is the only crop left that keeps the *campesinos*' heads above water. The peasant who grows standard crops will have an average annual income of around $250 a year. With coca, they can feed a family on $2,000 a year. These are not robber barons. They are not getting rich.[3]

Once the coca is processed, a kilo fetches about $2,000 in Colombia. Precautions, payoffs, and the first profits bring the price to $5,500 a kilo by the time it reaches the first gringo handler. The gringo sells that kilo, now ready for U.S. retail, for around $20,000. On the street in the United States, that will break out to $60,000. There are some high rollers at the end of the Colombian chain, but as with cheap manufactured goods from overseas sweatshops, the real markup winners are the American dealers.[4]

Drugs can fill in for the World Communist Conspiracy only so far. Drugs alone wouldn't justify this vast military build-up. For that, the Clinton administration had to convince America that it was defending democracy and protecting something called "economic reform." The rationales had become more sophisticated since I was in Guatemala in 1983, way more sophisticated than the blunt instrument of open war in Vietnam. Democracy wasn't the goal then. We were stopping communists. Drugs are a great rationale, too. But with the FARC, we could have our drug war and our war against communists together, like rum and coke.

Nowadays, of course, the insurgents are terrorists. This one can simply be decreed.

Behind the now crumbling democratic facade in Colombia are the most egregious and systematic human rights violations in this hemisphere. The exception, until it was dissolved in a government betrayal in 2001, was the geographic forty percent of the country where the FARC held sway.

Right-wing paramilitaries, supported and coordinated by the official security forces and U.S. Department of Defense contract-mercenaries like Dyncorp, are involved in a process that would have made Roberto D'Abuisson or Lucas-Garcia or Rios Montt proud: torture, public decapitations, massacres, rape-murders, destruction of land and livestock, forced dislocations, and defoliation (a form of chemical warfare). Favored targets have been community and union leaders, political opponents, and their families.

In July 1999, the commander of the Colombian army, Jorge Enrique Mora Rangel, intervened in the Colombian judicial process to protect the then-most powerful paramilitary chief in Colombia, Carlos Castaño, from prosecution for a series of massacres.

Castaño's organization was directly networked for intelligence and operations with the security forces. That network was organized and trained in 1991, under the tutelage of the U.S. Defense Department and the CIA. This was accomplished under a Colombian military intelligence integration plan called Order 200-05/91.[5]

The cozy relationship between the Colombian army and Castaño raised another little problem for the drug-war rationale. Castaño was a known drug lord. Not someone who taxes coca growers, but a drug lord.[6]

There is also the U.S. government's troubling history of fighting alongside—not against—drug traffickers. Indeed, the CIA seems to have an irresistible affinity for drug lords. The Tibetan *Chushi Gangdruk* (*Four Rivers Six Ranges*, the traditional name of the Tibetan province of Kham) trained by the CIA in the fifties became the masters of the Golden Triangle heroin empires. In Vietnam and Cambodia, the CIA worked hand in glove with opium traffickers. The contra war in Nicaragua was financed, in part, with drug profits. The CIA's Afghan-

Pakistani axis employed in the war against the Soviets was permeated with drug traffickers. Most recently, there were the heroin traffickers of the Kosovo Liberation Army.[7]

It might have made more sense for McCaffrey to find $1 billion dollars to drop a neutron bomb on Langley, Virginia.

MORAL IMPERIALISM & THE IRON LOGIC OF WAR

> *A revolution is not a dinner party, or writing an essay, or painting a picture, or doing embroidery; it cannot be so refined, so leisurely and gentle, so temperate, kind, courteous, restrained and magnanimous. A revolution is an insurrection, an act of violence by which one class overthrows another.*
> —Mao Zedong, from *Report on an Investigation of the Peasant Movement in Hunan*, March 1927

> *Unfortunately, the class struggle does not always pit a plucky guerrilla band in white hats against a villainous Uncle Sam, in some kind of latter-day version of Robin Hood. Far more often you end up with a much more complex drama involving shades of gray. If your sole criteria for offering solidarity to those struggling against imperialism is morality blended with esthetics, it is very easy to lose your way.*
> —Louis Proyect, 2003

Acteal, Mexico, 1997:

It began in a church. The quiet tension of the occupied territory was broken by automatic weapons fire. Lives were extinguished, and lives next to them were changed forever with the instantaneous absence of friends, relatives, parents, children. Life was reduced to the inescapable right-now and the necessity to run. Mourning was slammed into a box in the heart, deferred until survival was secure. Running blindly down the dirt streets, between houses of clay and straw, with the dry metal taste of terror in their mouths, one after another fell from the physical shock of tissue cavitation, shattered bone, shredded organs, the personal Armageddon of high velocity ammunition.

The Chiapas Rebellion entered a new phase in Acteal on December 22, 1997.

Since the uprising of Mexico's southern indigenous peoples in 1994, around five hundred murders had been committed against rebels, rebel sympathizers, and those suspected of being sympathizers. But the massacre at Acteal was a qualitative escalation. Foreigners were expelled to rid the terrain of witnesses.

The relative circumspection of the rebel operations, the astonishing initial successes they had against shocked government troops, and the gnome-like, charismatic spokesperson for the rebels, known as Subcomandante Marcos, had given the rebellion a mystique. Chiapas had become a cause célèbre in left-liberal circles in the United States and around the world. The David-and-Goliath tenor of the conflict is partly responsible for the popularity of the rebellion. But another reason the rebellion has been embraced by many has been the ability of the rebels to defend a certain moral high ground, refraining from the more brutal and repugnant activities of war. They shed little blood, and thereby avoided the kinds of crossfires, military and political, where everyone is transformed into a combatant.

Until Acteal.

The last century was filled with examples of what happened in Chiapas in 1998, the marriage of violence and capital. The forty-five massacred Tzotzil civilians represented a deliberate escalation of hostilities designed to attain the objectives of the Mexican political patriarchs who ordered the attack. Much attention would be paid to the phony investigation that the federal government conducted, and to Jacinto Arias Cruz, mayor of Chenalho, who was accused with twenty-three others of perpetrating the action.[1] Little attention was paid to the net result of this and smaller actions; the land that produces the wealth, and which the rebellion was designed to preserve for its original inhabitants, was then "willingly" vacated. Mission accomplished.

The government had agreed in 1996 to refrain from sending government representatives or armed forces into Acteal and environs. Pure fraud. Government-tolerated death squads did the job much more efficiently with terror, terror sponsored by the economic elite that needed to liberate the capital locked in the rich coffee lands upon which these bothersome Indians resided. History should have taught us, and the Zapatistas, that a belief that the invisible captains of the land grab might be reformed or contained is a pious fantasy. They would destroy the indigenous rebels or the rebels would destroy them.

The action of December 23, wherein the forty-five terrified residents of Acteal met their extinction, was the next logical step for the ruling class in Mexico. And their logic was as clean and cold as a scalpel. That is why the Zapatistas could no longer afford circumspection and restraint, except at the service of a logic as cold and calculating as their enemy's. The struggle had moved to another level. They would make war, real war, or they would be systematically dismantled as a viable force.

Hesitation under these circumstances would be fatal. The rebels had to fight. To fight, they would need weapons, many weapons, and ammunition, and communications equipment . . . all the luggage of war. There is only one way for an isolated force with no outside sponsorship to acquire that material. When I worked in Special Forces, it was called "battlefield recovery." They would have to wage frequent, audacious, and deadly assaults on small police and military elements simply to seize their weapons and equipment.

The people they would have to destroy would have families, parents, grandparents, spouses, and children. The starkest reality of war is that the enemy is never really a monster, never inhuman. Warriors have often tried to reduce their foes to sub-humans to prop up their denial, but the fact is the enemy is someone who dreams, someone who loves, someone who just needed a job, someone who is just waiting for a break to take a leak or eat his supper: a full-fledged human just like us.

To conduct such operations would require central coordination and the refinement of a general staff to both direct operations and determine the disposition of new troops and equipment. They needed to become an even more disciplined, secretive, decisive, vigilant force. The only principles they would be capable of embracing in every situation would be the principles of war. They would cease looking like pastoral heroes and begin to gain the hard edges of soldiery.

They would encounter spies, collaborators. Those would have to be dealt with summarily and ruthlessly. Failure to do so would result in loss of security and therefore the loss of precious combatants. Mistakes would be made. If and when victory approached, seasoned combatants would have committed excesses. Every soldier is the same fallible breed of human that we are. The making of war, even the most necessary and "just" war, hardens human hearts. War has its own internal logic, one that is icily cruel and impervious to refinement. These warriors would have no nation to which they might appeal for aid. The Soviet Union and the Cuba that provided support for African national liberation fights and the Soviet-Chinese-Vietnamese partnerships that supported the latter's anti-colonial struggle are no more.

The rebels of Chiapas now depended upon the outside world, in the most critical way, for solidarity in their political struggle. More than anything, they needed us to understand the necessity of what they would have to do. They needed international recognition and unwavering support for the ultimate justice of their fight, a solidarity that would weather the brutality into which they were being inexorably pulled to secure that justice.

And they choked. Neither they nor their international base had the will for what was necessary.

The paramilitaries were organized by *Grupo Aerotransportado de Fuerzas Especiales* (GAFE), a Mexican Special Forces group trained at the School of the Americas and the JFK Special Warfare School in Ft. Bragg, and were materially assisted by members of the Guatemalan military—maintain close ties to the U.S. foreign policy establishment as well. The massacre was portrayed as "senseless," but my point is that military operations, when they are successful, are anything but senseless. Acteal had a purpose. The purpose was to accelerate the depopulation of key terrain in the conflict area, and it worked very well.

The tiny, ineffectual remains of the Zapatista military force are now confined in the Lacondon (forest), cut off from all outside lines of communication, encircled and effectively neutralized. This cannot be romanticized away. It is a fact on the ground.

Just to remain fair, however, it is important to point out that military success is not measured in linear ways. It's not a football game. It has to be measured against political objectives, and the Zapatistas have always been a reformist movement. They never sought military victory or state power. This accounts for their popularity even in some chic metropolitan coffee houses where class war is anathema.

It also accounts for their incremental destruction as a guerrilla movement.

An interesting read on this comes from the 1995 U.S. Army Command and General Staff College publication, *Insurrection: An Analysis of the Chiapas Uprising*, by Major Grady G. Reese, U.S. Army. It is an extremely well-documented account of the insurrection up to the time of the report with a great deal of detail, albeit with a scrupulous evasion of the informal connections between landowners, political structures, the *guardias blancas*, and the Mexican armed forces. The U.S. military hates talking about political stuff. We all hate talking about our weaknesses.

From the executive summary:

> The Zapatista Army of National Liberation (EZLN) limited its objectives to the betterment of the Indian condition. The desired end-state was an Indian community with a greater share of the national wealth. Not wanting to necessarily overthrow the central government, the Zapatistas were deliberate in designing their strategy to force the government into negotiations. Their military operations supported the strategic objectives until they made the error of trying to capture Rancho Nuevo. The EZLN leadership timed the campaign well. The greatest strategic error was to underestimate the readiness of the government to negotiate. At the point that the government declared a unilateral cease-fire, the EZLN lost the strategic initiative.

The Mexican government, under the *Partido Revolucionario Institucional* (PRI) and now Vicente Fox, played a decade-long game of diplomatic and military bait-and-switch with the Zapatistas. Repeatedly, political concessions have been made then abrogated, and with each high-publicity withdrawal of the official Mexican armed forces from Chiapas, Guerrero, and Oaxaca, more substantial and less legally constrained paramilitary forces—composed of former *guardias blancas* and PRI paramilitaries, among others, now integrated with the armed forces—have filled the void. The Zapatistas are allowed to march by the thousands on *Distrito Federal* unmolested, and the *chi-*

langos welcome them as folk heroes; but in Chiapas, they have been slowly squeezed into the mountains and encircled. Viable Zapatista military forces have been cut off from their popular base, and that base, subjected to intense military and economic pressure including forced dislocation, has broken out into a series of interethnic rivalries. All that remains for the Mexican government now is to seize the moment when international political support for the EZLN is diverted or neutralized.

Armed struggle has to be weighed carefully against political objectives. As the Reese paper indicates, without fully grasping its own implications, a political objective short of the seizure of state power can fence in combatants and cause them to lose the intangible that has the greatest material force in war—initiative.

There is a naive and dangerous faith among people of good will in the churches and coffeehouses and campuses of America and Europe that "righteousness" will win out. Failing to grasp the full context of the nonviolent struggle against British colonialism in India and against Jim Crow in the U.S., where neither could have happened except against the backdrop of a well-armed socialist bloc, there is an ahistorical faith in nonviolent resistance combined with moral imperialism that leads progressives to distance themselves from aggressive armed resistance. Support for the Zapatistas has been so broad precisely *because* the EZLN has limited its objectives and avoided combat. Liberals and many anarchists are down with that. For entirely different reasons, each of these constituencies opposes any contest for state power. This is lethal when it is the state that is bent on your extermination. And it's why I'm not and never will be a progressive.

The charm of the Zapatistas has been their refusal to engage in any but defensive operations and their scrupulous avoidance of Marxist rhetoric. They have become the "good guerrillas," as opposed to the *Fuerzas Armadas Revolucionarias Colombianas–Ejercito del Pueblo* (FARC-EP) in Colombia, who are now seen by limousine liberals and parlor socialists as the "bad guerrillas."

The Zapatistas' refusal to engage in offensive operations, to ramp up their political objectives from reform to revolution and with it all the implications regarding military objectives, is the central error that is leading to their political defeat—no matter its PR value, no matter the *moral* high ground it gains them.

One cannot defend oneself against an unleashed army from "moral" high ground. One needs *real* high ground—as in key terrain—and one needs cover and concealment, well-covered avenues of approach, well-appointed automatic weapons, appropriate tactics, and reliable logistics. The Mexican government has all but won, and Zapatista allies here can do little but wail and fume and cling to their denial.

When any conflict, regardless of its social and political content, escalates to war, war itself asserts a stark logic. All other objectives are sublated into the choice between destroying the enemy's capacity and will to fight or perishing as a viable military force. Military operations are shaped and directed by political objectives—a fact the U.S. military has yet to grasp in all its complexity—but the conduct of war is brutally physical. It is the desolate and hideous application of physical laws to the project of open and absolute destruction. When a people or a movement is the target of that destruction, it must employ the same cold pragmatism in its defense, or it will drown in its own blood.

I once saw a little plaque in English on the desk of a South Korean general. It said, "God favors the strong." Those who are strong can be patient. But strength in war is not solely determined by mass or technology. The great guerrilla leaders have shown that *initiative* is the key. When you have it, you are ahead, and when you lose it, you are behind.

Reese again:

> The military performed well in supporting the national strategy. It mobilized and deployed rapidly. It used combined arms in joint operations and quickly gained the initiative. The success of operations in the field allowed the government to pursue a negotiated settlement from a position of relative strength.

Warfare is a temporal process. Time matters. Speed matters. Getting inside your enemy's decision-making cycle and seizing the initiative matters. Taking the offensive matters. There is no due process. There are no time-outs.

And there is no perfection.

Armed forces, both oppressive and liberatory, are organizations that, once committed to active combat, must administer themselves, supply themselves, train themselves, protect themselves, and replace themselves . . . by any means necessary, *while in the conduct of inherently chaotic conflict*. With what is available. Here is where an established state military is different from the guerrilla. The guerrilla cannot go to the state with its hand out. The guerrilla has no recognized courts or well-funded press with which to legitimize itself in the eyes of well-fed foreigners. And the guerrilla, once committed, cannot stop.

Failure to escalate quickly and to consolidate and expand guerrilla control in the wake of Acteal has spelled a complete loss of battlefield initiative. The Zapatistas are no longer a viable military force. Their "armed struggle" is now utterly symbolic.

Let me compare that to the FARC-EP.

Like the Zapatistas, the FARC-EP began in a struggle for land. After World War II, Colombian liberals supported the development of several peasant self-defense militias that clamored for land redistribution and limited autonomy. By the FARC-EP's own account, they employed a strategy that is eerily similar to that of the EZLN: an armed resistance combined with appeals for national and international solidarity.[2] The war became far more brutal, on both sides, and the Colombian government offered a negotiated settlement in 1952. This offer of diplomacy was accepted by the Liberal Party and by their followers among the insurgent militia.

But a small group of peasants led by peasant communist Pedro Antonio Marin refused to stand down. Marin had none of the gnome-like coffeehouse charm of Subcomandante Marcos, but he had a hard head for military matters. He would have understood Mao's little essay on Hunan peasants very well.

When you do what is necessary, you will be called "terrible," and you will have "gone too far." "No revolutionary comrade should echo this nonsense," said Mao.[3] Yet many still do.

Marin was convinced of the duplicity of the government, including the Liberals, and he continued to organize self-defense units among the peasantry. So effective did these militias become that the government began to refer to peasant communities as "independent communist republics," and in 1964—with urging from the U.S. government—

launched a sudden and unprecedented attack against the peasant militia at Marquetelia.

Marin, who had since changed his name to Manuel Marulanda Vélez, led the successful resistance to this massive military assault *with forty-eight guerrilla fighters.*

Thereafter, this guerrilla band took the name *Feurzas Armadas Revolucionarias Colombianas* (FARC). Marulanda, who put a high premium on marksmanship as a core skill for guerrillas and who was himself legendary for his skill with a rifle, became affectionately known as *Tiro Fijo*, or Sureshot.[4]

The FARC recognized that the battle had been decisively engaged and that there was no quarter asked or given. The struggle would now end with state power or defeat. They launched one audacious attack after another and perfected the ability to quickly concentrate and then diffuse their forces, massing for quick strikes, then disappearing in small teams back into the countryside; delivering one pinprick tactical victory after another; acquiring material and recruits along the way.

I have been questioned as to whether I really believed the FARC is winning. I do. From this forty-eight-person core, they have grown into a twenty thousand strong political and military organization, on seven regional fronts, in more than sixty independently maneuverable military organizations. In the past two years, they have decimated the paramilitaries, destroying at least ten percent of their forces (probably substantially more). They have survived and counterattacked one of the most well-financed military offensives in this hemisphere, even after losing the *despeje*, or autonomous demilitarized zone, when the Pastrana government was pressured by the right wing in Colombia (and the U.S. Embassy) to scrap peace talks.[5]

Without U.S. aid to the ever more-fascistic Colombian government, the FARC would achieve state power in less than five years, and that's conservative. The paramilitaries are neither the FARC-EP's equal on the battlefield nor do they command any loyalty from the rural population. And the Colombian armed forces are largely conscripts, led by a venal and corrupt officer corps suffering the daily stings of class resentment and blistering racism. The FARC-EP is racially diverse, and thirty percent female.

Without air support from the U.S. and its surrogates there, the Colombian armed forces could not match the FARC's military prowess, nor do they have a popular base outside the urban petit-bourgeois and ruling classes.

The metropolitan anticommunist left are now claiming that the FARC has evolved into some kind of authoritarian monstrosity that oppresses the people just like the government, or that it has become some criminal enterprise, or that it fails to bargain in good faith. They are now "terrible" and have "gone too far." This is a classic case of the left falling for the slanders of the mainstream press, assisted in their fall by the "bourgeois right" (as opposed to wrong, not left), or moral imperialism—the convenient morality of the fed and the fat in the imperial cores who've never known war and who never tire of telling all those brown people what the right thing is to do.

The FARC stood down from the armed struggle in 1984, forming an electoral wing called the Patriotic Union (UP), calling a truce, and agreeing to engage in electoral politics. Four thousand UP members were summarily assassinated by death squads. This was their one flirtation with the "bourgeois right." They are in a war and they understand the iron logic of war, especially after 1984.[6]

In 2002, after the Colombian military was ordered into the *despeje*, where their offensive fizzled out, paramilitaries began a savage campaign against civilians around Bojaya. The Colombian armed forces secured passage of the parmilitaries into the area. The paramilitaries were met by a surprise counteroffensive from the FARC, who killed over five hundred paramilitaries and lost approximately one hundred and thirty guerrillas, mostly due to support from the Colombian military in the form of an attack helicopter and a fixed-wing aircraft. Paramilitaries fell back on the pueblo of Bojaya, taking up positions around a public health center and a church. The FARC fired an expedient mortar that fell short onto the church, where civilians had taken refuge from the fighting, and killed dozens of those inside.

When this was reported, it was not reported by the mainstream press as a battle between the FARC and the paramilitaries. It was not reported that the paramilitaries were bent on violence against the civilians there. Military complicity was not reported. The huge tactical defeat of the paramilitaries was not reported. The FARC mortar attack that destroyed the church and killed the civilians inside was reported, not as the unintentional loss of civilian life in combat, but as a FARC massacre.[7]

The FARC admitted the terrible error, as they have consistently done. They have studied the assassinated Cape Veredean revolutionary, Amilcar Cabral, who warned comrades to "mask no difficulties, mistakes, failures."[8]

Weapons, equipment, and the "luggage of war" might be provided to the imperial soldier, but it must be gained through "battlefield recovery" by most insurgents, and in some cases improvised like the propane mortars used by the FARC. They will not be perfect or standardized weapons and equipment. Frontline soldiers, logicians, medical cadre, commanders, and staffs all are recruited (or conscripted) from the finite pool of people in areas of operation; all are trained with the resources and skill sets available; and all of those lost to attrition must be replaced. Combatants will inevitably be people of varying native ability, varying consciousness, varying motivations, varying character, and they will perform in variable and unpredictable ways. They will not operate with perfect oversight from top to bottom. And the situations at the bottom will never be clear to the top, and far less clear to those who are outside the armed conflict altogether.

Over time, including the coherence of the political program behind the organization, the strategy, the discipline, the agility and flexibility, the resources, the quality of intelligence, the soundness of the tactics, the leadership skills, and, last but certainly not least, the sheer size of the organization, will emerge through these other daily doses of overdetermination and leave a victor.

So when we judge the armed struggles of the left around the world, we need to be mindful of Sherman's statement that "war is cruel and cannot be refined." No commander worth a damn can ever measure decisions using the ethical tools of peacetime. Either the struggle is worth a war or it is not. We can't have it both ways. The political goal is paramount, not the accolades of pacifists in the imperial centers, not the approval of liberal media, not the blessing of those who should be allies but are not there and cannot comprehend the urgency that sometimes leads to terrible mistakes, sometimes even crimes.

So I will say this about the Zapatistas and the FARC-EP. At the end of the day, the difference between the two, aside from which is condoned or condemned by those outside the conflict, is that one is winning and one is losing . . . because one understands the iron logic of war, and the other does not.

SOMALIA:
THE MEANINGS OF BAKARA

For want of a nail, the shoe was lost;
For want of a shoe, the horse was lost;
For want of a horse, the rider was lost;
For want of a rider, the battle was lost;
For want of a battle, the kingdom was lost!

—Anonymous

In simultaneously making sense of a military career dominated by Special Operations experience, attempting to integrate that experience with radical social theory, and trying to understand the whole post-9/11 conjuncture, I find myself constantly reminded of my experience in Somalia, where I participated as a member of the ill-fated Task Force Ranger (TFR). That experience and some of the conclusions that might be drawn from it can begin to tell us something about the indeterminate declaration of war by a political faction of the U.S. ruling class that seized power in 2000 through a crypto-fascist judicial fiat.[1]

In addition to lying to the public, the military often lies to itself.

The American public now knows who Task Force Ranger was. The unit was lionized by Colombia Pictures in the hugely successful propaganda piece *Black Hawk Down*.[2] The real Task Force Ranger, however, was emblematic of the knotty state of U.S. Special Operations and the larger doctrinal context of Special Ops in this period. The *actual* debacle at Bakara in 1993, which the film purports to describe, can tell us much about the military failures in Afghanistan, where none of the putative reasons for the invasion have been met, where the Taliban is already re-infiltrating, where occupying forces are now bunkered into tightly contained bases to avoid incessant pinprick attacks, where opium production has already reached pre-Taliban levels, and where Pakistan may soon be threatened with civil war on its own Afghan border.

It also tells us much about a similar situation evolving in Iraq. Together, they are historically unique, in that we are now seeing two simultaneous failed military occupations by the United States.

I might be challenged on the claim that these are military failures, yet we must bear in mind—again—that battlefield success, by whatever measure, is not military success, because military operations are never conducted for their own sakes, but for some political objective.

I reviewed a paper archived with the U.S. Army Command and General Staff College with the cumbersome title, *Critical Analysis on the Defeat of Task Force Ranger Subject: A Clausewitzian Critical Analysis on the Military Defeat of Task Force Ranger in Mogadishu, Somalia during Operation RESTORE HOPE.* It was authored by Majors Clifford E. Day and Ralph P. Millsap Jr. For brevity, I will hereafter refer to this paper as simply "the Day paper."

The Day paper is accompanied by a disclaimer. That disclaimer states that the paper is not an official position taken by the Department of Defense, which is interesting on its own merit. The Department of Defense, as far as I can tell, does not take "official positions" with regard to past operations. However, the fact that it was authored by a student at the Command and General Staff College (CGSC) and his faculty advisor, and that it has been published by the United States Department of Defense, indicates that, at least in its assumptions, it conforms to the same analytical framework as existing military doctrine in the USA. Students and faculty at the CSGC are not in the habit of proposing doctrinal heresies.

By identifying key elements of the doctrinal framework, we can identify further evolved systemic weaknesses in U.S. military doctrine in Afghanistan and Iraq. We might also speculate about how military consequences can feed back into the political establishment as legitimation crises.

Military operations have become the new linchpin of U.S. policy, and, I believe, are now among the disparate winds swirling toward some synergistic combination to form a perfect storm of generalized social and political disorder.

The substance of the Day paper's conclusions are contained in a section called "Alternative Courses of Action." The very title of this section is instructive, in that the study of military science, to this day, is seen as an exercise in academic compartmentalization, reflecting the dominant epistemology—analytical as opposed to synthetic, atomized as opposed to relational, mechanical as opposed to dialectical.

The sub-paragraphs of the report critiquing TFR's mission are:

Adequate Political Support to Field Commanders
Construction of Viable Intelligence Gathering Systems
Employment of Decisive Force
Taking Advantage of Superior Technology
Ensuring Unity of Effort

I do not want to spend more time than is necessary on the details of this report, and I recognize that summary always leads to a certain amount of distortion. Nonetheless, I'm offering highly editorial translations under each sub-heading to combine brevity with critique. The paper itself is available on the internet.[3]

Adequate Political Support to Field Commanders is a backhand delivered to Les Aspin, then secretary of defense, who vetoed the introduction of heavy armor with the Task Force. Many of the senior Special Operations officers also expressed doubts about the use of armor, largely because these conventional units are not easily integrated with a Special Operations task force, and also because they tend to inhibit tactical agility.

But it is traditional in the military for civilian oversight to be scapegoated in the wake of tactical failures. Sometimes it is justified, and sometimes not.

Construction of Viable Intelligence Gathering Systems is similar to what we see now as more and more revelations emerge with regard to exactly what the government did and did not know in advance of September 11. The conclusion in the Day paper, presented in circuitous and obscure English, is that "if we'd known more, we could have done better." This kind of mental masturbation is also very common in the military, whose officers generally constitute the dustbin of the American intelligentsia. The irony now is that they are the occasional voice of reason *against* our political rulers, who (with the neocon clique) actually exceed the military in their intellectual mediocrity.

Employment of Decisive Force is a kind of Monday-morning-quarterback version of the Powell Doctrine of overwhelming firepower, which says, in a manner similar to the preceding conclusion, "if we'd have had more combat power on hand during the battle, we would have fared better." It is a conclusion based on quantity, not quality. The Day paper also takes this opportunity to again blame the lack of adequate combat force (adequate to what *contingency* they don't say) on Les Aspin and the civilians.[4]

Taking Advantage of Superior Technology concludes, mistakenly, that Task Force Ranger failed to use its night vision equipment to full advantage, and that had the raid in Bakara been conducted at night, the technological advantages of U.S. night vision equipment might have carried the day.

This is both inaccurate and stupid.

TFR conducted numerous raids at night during its stay in Mogadishu, but those raids were launched based on real-time intelligence, however inaccurate it might have been, about the current (and constantly shifting) location of Mohammed Farah Aidid, whose capture was the mission of TFR.

Moreover, night vision equipment does much more than merely magnify ambient light. In my personal experience, it often creates disadvantages just as problematic as the lack of visual acuity associated with unaided night combat. The equipment is noisy and cumbersome. It drastically limits and channelizes the operator's field of vision. It produces a kind of indescribable hypnotic and isolating psychological effect on the operator. It causes severe headaches at times. And it creates a profound night blindness for the operator for up to fifteen minutes after the operator quits using it, for whatever reason, like when the equipment malfunctions.

Ensuring Unity of Effort refers to the compartmented nature of the operation itself, wherein multinational forces and U.S. conventional forces were not "read in" on the operation. The Day paper concludes that coordination would have increased the efficacy of both intelligence, by combining collections and interpretations efforts there, and the response to Bakara, where conventional aid was very slow in coming. But the reality is that sharing information on the nature of the mission would as likely compromise the mission as it would assist it, and there was quite simply neither the time nor the capacity to coordinate this "special operation" with all units in Somalia.

With this peek at the military mindset in hand, let me resume the critique of the underlying doctrine.

The Day paper's forty-six pages allocate the majority of space to the technical and chronological facts of the defeat at Bakara. The United Nations Operation in Somalia (UNOSOM) mission, Operation Restore Hope (ORH), set the stage for October 3.

Whatever its political motives, the UNOSOM mission metamorphosed from a putative, multinational humanitarian-civic action (HCA) mission with a military security component, into a military operation to "stabilize" Somalia. One can already hear the echoes in Afghanistan and Iraq.

The HCA, contrary to what the Day paper stated, was essentially over the moment "stabilization" became the prime directive. These are often antithetical missions—humanitarian assistance and stability—and cannot be carried out simultaneously with equal emphasis on both, unless the military actually arms, lives with, and shares hardship with the "protected" population.

This is true even if there is a coherent state as a singular enemy. There was neither in Somalia, and so the contradictions of applied doctrine were compounded by the political and military paradox that was Somalia.

Tactically, once the United States/United Nations occupying military forces in Somalia became directly engaged in precombat operations, that is, adopted a more ready-for-combat posture, their actions triggered preparatory countermeasures on the part of every warring faction. The balance of forces in Somalia was in a constant state of flux anyway, and the introduction of this major new direct military player (U.S./U.N.) inevitably increased the social entropy of an already chaotic milieu.

The number of possible tactical combinations *increased* and inversely *decreased* the predictability of an already unpredictable situation. The initial success of the U.S./U.N. military insertion was based on the lack of preparedness, and consequent lack of response, by indigenous militias, who were obligated to busy themselves with vying for positions in the reshuffled strategic deck.

This was precisely the situation in Afghanistan after the alleged defeat of the Taliban in October/November 2001. As this is written, the Taliban has re-entered the realm of military operations against the Americans and their surrogates, beginning eighteen months after their "defeat." It is increasingly the same in Iraq, where a unified state was destroyed and the factions it suppressed have re-emerged, paradoxically unified in their desire to expel Americans. The key difference between Iraq and Afghanistan is the level of social integration that had been achieved in the former through modernization—a process that was interrupted in Afghanistan when the Soviet-aligned Taraki regime, supported by a massive Soviet military intervention, was defeated by Islamist factions unified, trained, and armed to a large extent by the United States.[5]

In Somalia, all parties significantly, and predictably, strengthened their defensive postures to ensure they held onto the terrain they already controlled.

A Pakistani attack in June 1993 against Mohammed Farah Aidid's Somali National Alliance (SNA) in Mogadishu met that well-prepared defense, and the SNA delivered them a decisive tactical defeat that pivoted on a very well-prepared anti-armor ambush—which the Day paper refers to, demagogically, as a "massacre." The SNA's next major ambush would be against the Americans in Bakara.

There is another inherent weakness for outside forces in this situation, and that is the necessity to develop fixed installations and then supply them. The airport had to be secured to maintain an airhead. The roads from the airport to Sword Base (the main U.S. installation), a good forty-minute drive by armored convoy—past a miniature Maginot line of 10th Mountain Division roadside bunkers, each themselves vulnerable to small attacks—went all the way around Mogadishu to avoid the ubiquitous mining and mortar/sniper attacks. These two installations and the corridor that linked them were all "fixed."

Against a highly mobile, lightly equipped enemy, this translates into a total loss of battlefield initiative, like timber wolves taking down an elk. The mobile indigenous force can pick away at the edges of the fixed positions, when they want and how they want, at minimal risk to themselves, especially in urban areas. Each mildly successful strike can inaugurate a whole new set of policies, procedures, and countermeasures from the fixed force, keeping them perpetually in a state of reaction to the initiatives of their enemies. The U.S. political emphasis on "force protection" (that is, an obsessive avoidance of any U.S. combat casualties, an implicit component of the Powell Doctrine) only increases the vulnerability associated with loss of battlefield initiative.

This not only drains resources and decreases flexibility. It is very hard on troop morale. I point that out not only in passing, but because it is significant to discussions about operations in Afghanistan and Iraq.

There was a way out of this dilemma from a strictly tactical perspective, and that was to regain the initiative through audacious, aggressive, sustained ground action against the SNA. But the Powell Doctrine is one that seeks to avoid ground combat engagements unless there is overwhelming superiority in firepower and a low likelihood of American combat casualties. For the ground tactical commander, ever mindful of the priorities of his or her superiors, that translates into a powerful reluctance to engage in, or even risk, decisive combat, and an inordinate emphasis at every level of command on force protection.

Audacious, aggressive, sustained offensive operations against one enemy organization will yield tactical victories, but it will inevitably cost "friendly" lives, and thereby risks losing the unseen but essential element in all U.S. military operations—the support of the civilian population at home.

So regaining the tactical initiative (forcing your enemy to react to your plans and actions, instead of you reacting to your enemy's) depends on a type of action—one with a higher probability of "friendly" casualties—that could threaten domestic acceptance of the military action. This is one reason the Bush-Rumsfeld regime after 9/11 gave them their pretext for war, began to warn the public about the "costs" of the Infinite War. We were being inoculated in order to give the military more tactical flexibility.

An integral part of the Powell Doctrine—and still one of the predominant thrusts of current military doctrine in the U.S.—is information/spin control. Controlling the public's perceptions of operations is as important a part of military operations, under this doctrine, as logistics or intelligence. One of the primary difficulties for the U.S. military, for example, in Haiti was that Haiti's porous borders allowed swarms of uncontrolled international reporters loose across the country.[6] Not so in Iraq, and not so in Afghanistan. These actions were sifted, sanitized, and packaged for public consumption.

With the release of *Black Hawk Down*, we have seen the retrojection of this policy to past operations through a public-private partnership including the Department of Defense and Hollywood—another piece of Powell Doctrine image management.

The Powell Doctrine is named for Colin Powell, who is the former chairman of the Joint Chiefs of Staff, and as of this writing is the U.S. secretary of state.

Powell's first test as a young Black officer was as deputy assistant chief of staff for the Americal Division in Vietnam, where he was given the difficult and dubious task of damage control after revelations about the My Lai massacre—in which U.S. soldiers from the American Division division tortured, raped, and eventually slaughtered 347 unarmed civilians in a remote Vietnamese hamlet.[7]

He performed brilliantly in that role, showing a real talent for negotiating politically sensitive bureaucratic and diplomatic mazes, and was noticed by one Caspar Weinberger, who would eventually appoint him his deputy security adviser when Ronald Reagan appointed Weinberger secretary of defense. Powell was then personally groomed to become the youngest (and only Black) chairman of the Joint Chiefs.

Powell never forgot the "lessons" [he imagined] he'd learned from Vietnam:

> that the full weight of government and press influence should be mobilized to ensure public support of the military action

> that overwhelming and devastating force must be
> employed against the entire society with whom we are at
> war (as opposed to "proportionality,"8 the bugaboo that
> many—including Powell—incorrectly hold responsible for
> the U.S. defeat in Vietnam, which was resurrected to explain
> the defeat of Task Force Ranger)
>
> and that there is some clear "exit strategy."

Implicit in the Powell Doctrine, with its heavy public relations emphasis, is an obsessive minimization of U.S. casualties, which is directly related to the emphasis on maximizing offensive force. Holding down U.S. casualties and hiding the U.S. collateral damage resulting from the heavy-handed operations that keep U.S. casualties low are the two halves of the public relations issue.

While the Day paper gives a very detailed account of the debacle at the Bakara, it commits precisely the same error that militaries have been making for the millennia—looking at the details as they occurred, a view only accessible through hindsight; then playing a (futile) game of "what if" to change the outcome; then converting the what-ifs into recommendations and (eventually) changes in doctrine.

Though I was sent home after a conflict with a dull-witted captain named Steele several days prior to the Bakara defeat (a blessing in disguise, perhaps), I was there as part of the Ranger component. I had earlier served almost four years as an operator with Delta Force (one component of TFR), so I was familiar with their organization and their planning models.

We had launched ground patrols out of the airport after the first night, August 26, in response to mortar attacks—a tactic that, had it been pursued aggressively, would have regained some of the initiative. But the firing of a warning shot to halt a fleeing Somali spooked the command element and they halted the patrols.

Veterans of Special Ops blunders like Grenada began complaining early, especially after we accidentally "captured" several U.N. aid officials on an August 30 raid in yet another classic goat fuck. The next two raids were done in exactly the same way. Our complaints centered on the execution of one raid after another using the exact same tactical template, which some of us were convinced was giving the SNA and others an opportunity to analyze that template and prepare counter-measures. (We were right, but most officers consider enlisted men, even senior ones, to be stupid.)

Each time we raided another target, we would simply go back to the airport and hunker down for a day or two until we did it again—the same way!

Our grouplet of malcontents was privately saying that we should fire up the coffee pots and launch one raid on top of another, using a different template each time, as fast as we could re-arm and refuel until we were dropping out from exhaustion, then sleep for six hours and start again. But we were not in charge. And greater tactical efficacy would only have altered the superficial features of the overall situation, as the retaliation rousts in Iraq are now showing.

We were still American troops in Somalia. The only way we could change that was what we eventually did—leave.

The Powell Doctrine pushed "force protection" and overwhelming firepower. The Special Operations commanders were a generation removed from an earlier Special Ops establishment that made the soldier, the team, and creativity the centerpiece of its doctrine. This new lot had been raised under a regime that constructed its doctrine around its technology (instead of the inverse). And the political context was very poorly understood, if at all. This is a perennial problem in the U.S. military.

Humans were subordinated to technology by capitalism to increase production, but military matters are not determined by production. If the organic composition of capital will eventually lead to an overwhelming mass of dead labor, with an overwhelming mass of superfluous labor as a death rattle of the economy, this domination of dead labor over live in the military undermines in the two key intangibles of tactical success: leadership and initiative.

The cascade of disorder that was developing was foreshadowed at the K-4 traffic circle on one of the raids just before I was sent home.

I was with a vehicle strong point outside the stadium adjacent to the traffic circle, and it was pitch dark. The Delta teams were inside the target, a building two blocks away. The supporting MH-60 "little bird" gunships had pulled off to avoid drawing fire.

Then out of nowhere, we were probed with close-range machine-gun fire, very close—like across the street. The SNA knew where the outer edge of our security was—based on observation of prior raids—and they had come right to us.

The fire was directly in front of me and I shot the machine gunner, firing around ten rounds of tracer to designate the target for the rest of our strong-point defense team. The Rangers on the strong-point had .50-caliber machine-guns, MK-19 40-mm automatic grenade launchers, and a phalanx of small arms; and they cued on the tracer fire, pouring an apocalyptic volume of ammunition into the stadium wall.

Then we received fire from the opposite direction, further off, without tracers so we couldn't immediately orient on it. We could only hear the snap of the incoming rounds as they ripped among us in the darkness—little reminders that, at this point, whether you are a casualty or not is a matter not of Rambo-like skill but volume of fire and dumb luck.

There was a weird, short, silent interlude.

When the Somalis took one of the helicopters under fire with visible tracers, we identified their position and opened up again at a little structure on a low hill, shattering the night again with a wild arcing river of our own tracers.

As it turned out, our fire into the stadium, which was filled with homeless people in raggedy cloth huts, killed dozens of civilians in addition to the two or three SNA fighters who fired on us, and our fire at the hill arced across Mogadishu and rained down on a chagrined U.S. Sword Base. We were an elephant inside a gift store.

We had a couple of wounded. I was a medic at the time. To start an intravenous infusion on one of the wounded, I had to hold a glowing green Chem-lite in my teeth to see his vein, making my head look like a radiant jade moon in a black sky—a nerve-wracking experience.

When we got back to the airport, we found a .50-caliber bullet hole in the door of one of our vehicles.

We had the only .50-caliber machine guns out there.

This raid was called a success, because we pulled a couple of Aidid's lieutenants out of the primary target.

The impact of the dead civilians was never factored in. The danger we subjected Sword Base to was never factored in, nor was the failure of coordination. No commander stopped and said, hey, it looks like they have figured out this plan, let's change it. No, we had the firepower, and we killed the most people, so we fucking won.

That's partly because success is measured technically, and only from a tactical and not a political standpoint, in the same simple-minded way it was all the way back in Vietnam. Remember "body counts?"

I had eliminated one threat with the shots that hit the machine gunner and suppressed whomever might have been with him. I recruited a hundred new militia with the civilians I (and the rest of us) killed and wounded behind him. And our technology, far from affording us an advantage, was becoming a danger to ourselves.

There is a correlation between the generalized complexity of a system and its vulnerabilities.

In any case, U.S. forces will continue to be faced with these problems because all U.S. commanders are going to husband their forces, and conventional U.S. forces will not willingly be committed to the kind of sustained ground action discussed here. Instead, they will stumble into it, as they have in Afghanistan and Iraq.

Special Operations will continue to emphasize quick-strikes, based on surprise, speed, and violence of action, to minimize their exposure, and conventional troops will continue to bunker down into progressively hardened positions as glorified guards with diminishing morale.

Iraq was an anomaly. There was not supposed to be any real resistance. When it appeared during the initial invasion, the whole operation was put on hold until commanders could integrate heavy close air support with ground forces.

The Officer Personnel Management System in the military is one that is as unforgiving and competitive as any corporation, and cautious officers rise up, leaving all but a tiny handful of aggressive field commander-types in charge of anything. It's a recipe for bureaucracy, and it works superlatively.

U.S. forces, even the hardest of the hard core, cannot long sustain operations abroad without a huge logistical tail. At bottom, they are products of a pampered and pasteurized society, and they are very fragile. You can put all the muscles you want on a U.S. soldier, and a local *E. coli* will bring him crashing down like a tall tree. Bottled water only for these guys. This is a contradiction of imperialism, a kind of reverse social Darwinism that is seldom discussed or fully understood in its ramifications.

Four to five days is the longest troops can stay in the field without bringing in helicopters or ground cargo transportation and exposing the choppers, the trucks, and their own positions to resupply the line troops. This means they *must* have bases for logistics and stand-downs between missions. So the most agile forces available to the U.S. will in short order always bring with them a fixed installation.

The Day paper does accurately describe the command and control difficulties of the mission, which created yet another violation of a Principle of War: unity of command. But that did not influence the operational template, which was Delta's, approved by General Garrison (the Task Force commander) himself. Better unity of command might have hastened the rescue effort to get TFR out of their shit storm, but it would not have prevented it from happening in the first place.[9]

Even had TFR pursued a more tactically sound course of action—sustained ground operations against Aidid—a tactical success against the SNA would have only strengthened one or more other factions relative to the SNA. The fundamental problem would have remained. Stateless war is asymmetric. When a conventional state military like the Americans' enters a de facto stateless milieu, it finds itself surrounded by multiple armed actors—all potential or actual enemies. The conventional doctrine upon which the invading state-based military is organized is then stranded, because the raison d'être of a conventional state military is subjection of another centralized state.

In the absence of long-term, sustained ground actions—with significant U.S. casualties—the non-indigenous (U.S./U.N.) forces, battened down in their fixed installations, remained a static target, ceding the initiative to the more flexible, mobile, and variable forces that surrounded them, with no such misplaced sentimentality about the necessity to risk casualties.

The occupying forces in Somalia were destined to come to harm.

Those in Afghanistan and Iraq will too. No one can predict how, but we can predict that it will happen.

The key similarity between Afghanistan and Somalia is the lack of political coherence and the existence of multiple, well-armed, potentially warring factions. The Bush folks knew that, and that's why they made such a vain and ridiculous effort to cobble together a government. This is a tar baby for them. The American military has taken the ultimate responsibility for maintaining it. The bases have already been built. And if Afghanistan has the potential to be a little like Somalia, Iraq has the potential to become a lot like Palestine.

Both will require a lot of maintenance. Expensive, politically costly maintenence.

A key difference between Afghanistan and Somalia is that in the former the U.S. is conducting ground operations primarily in rural areas, where they enjoy many tactical advantages. In Somalia, they were concentrated in and around the highly dangerous urban terrain of Mogadishu. Iraq, on the other hand, has already become an urban quagmire.

By late June, there were reports of multiple attacks each day against U.S. and U.K. forces in Iraq at a tempo that was creating a steady stream of fatalities, almost one a day on average, and the international media were just beginning to uncover evidence of numerous factions carrying out the attacks. This was contrary to the stubborn U.S. claims that the attacks were merely being conducted by disorganized and resentful Ba'athist holdouts. One possible reason Rumsfeld and others constructed this narrative was to ensure that the public didn't begin to make the comparison between the situation developing in Iraq and that of Somalia, in which multiple combatant factions prevailed.

In Afghanistan, there is still no guarantee that the tiny island of tranquility that is Kabul, where U.S. and allied forces maintain that tranquility at great cost and effort, will not become, as Mogadishu did, a final and near-apocalyptic point of convergence at the end of a long series of internecine conflicts and rapprochements.

Karzai's bodyguards failed to stop the assassination of vice president, Haji Abdul Qadir, and had to be replaced by Special Forces, who had trained them in the first place. Department of Defense resident lunatic Paul Wolfowitz told the press that the U.S. has to prepare for the next Cold War. The U.S. cover-up of the deadly Special Forces-directed AC-130 attack on two villages and a wedding party in Uruzgan Province fell apart in the international press, as U.N. investigators, usually known for circumspection, started calling U.S. spokespersons bald-faced liars and pointing to evidence of a deliberate cover-up. Talk of civil war emerged from Tajik warlord Ismail Khan in Herat, Tajik warlord Ustad Atta Mohammed in Mazar-i-Sharif, Uzbek warlord Abdul Rashid Dostum in Mazar-i-Sharif, Pashtun jihadi Haji Abdul Qadir in Jalalabad, Paktika Pasthun warlord Pacha Khan Zadran, Paktika Hazara warlord Karim Khalili, and Pashtun warlord Gul Agha Sherzai of Kandahar. As this is written, even Kabul is being destabilized, factions in the countryside are killing at will, and the Taliban is back.[10]

An indigenous force fighting a foreign invader or an existing state can use military action as a first course of action, a catalyst, the centerpiece of its political struggle, because it is not fighting to retain economic and political control, but rather to disrupt or prevent that control by another force. Military actions are intrinsically better at creating instability than stability. Any one of these leaders, alone or in combination with others, has the capacity to introduce total disequilibrium into the situation in Afghanistan.

Whoever learns to make an ally of that disequilibrium, wins.

With no long-standing armed factions in Iraq except the Ba'ath Party and the northern Kurds, it is more difficult to see what might be on that horizon. From the standpoint of the U.S. occupier, nothing good.

The paradox growing directly out of the inherent myopia of an imperial occupier, and the basis of its strength turning into its opposite was already observable by May 2003, when Jonathan Steele of the *Guardian* wrote:

> They [the American occupying forces] seemed to be working from a one-size-fits-all Pentagon textbook. First "liberate", then move in and provide policing whether people want it or not. In Baghdad there were indeed security problems after Saddam's forces vanished, and many residents

asked why U.S. forces did so little to halt the looting of key buildings. Having failed initially there, the U.S. over-compensated elsewhere. It came down too hard in Falluja [where trigger-happy American soldiers killed 13 people and wounded almost 50 by firing into a crowd and other cities where people did not want a U.S. hand.[11]

The contrast with Afghanistan is sharp. For months Afghans pleaded for the U.S. to deploy international peacekeepers beyond Kabul to cities where warlords held sway or were fighting for power. The U.S. refused, either for fear of taking casualties or because of lack of interest in a poor country once its anti-western regime was toppled.

In Iraq, where there are no warlords and people feel they have the expertise to run the country themselves, the U.S. insists on moving in and staying.[12]

The U.S. military is an instrument of last resort. The fact that it is being used at all is generally an indicator that the U.S. has gotten itself economically and politically cornered. Somalia was a sideshow that came center-stage for a few weeks, then receded again. The U.S. felt relatively secure politically and economically, and Somalia was an anomaly. But the U.S. is now in the throes of a political crisis (masked for a time by a waning chauvinist fervor), a national economic contraction that is synchronized with a global recession, the collapse of Argentina foreshadowing a generalized Latin American crisis, the slow implosion of Japan, intensifying inter-imperialist rivalry with Europe (now perhaps partnering with Russia), the stealth war with China, and a rising tide of anti-American sentiment around the world. Latent in these turbulent and sullen winds is the potential for that perfect storm.

We cannot know from where. The situation is nonlinear, dynamic.

This neo-cons bit off more than they can chew. By the same token, circumstances probably do not give the Bush administration any very palatable options. This is an important point. This is not an exercise in immorality. It is an exercise in desperation, from a certain perspective, necessity.

Militarily, they quite simply can not conduct successful military operations simultaneously in Afghanistan, Iraq, the Balkans, Colombia, Syria, Iran, North Korea, etc.

If there is any real resistance, they will break the bank at home. Deflation is now the invisible enemy waiting in ambush, and infinite war is a kind of crazed firing into the Bushes in anticipation of it.

Argentina, Ecuador, Venezuela, Bolivia, and Brazil. These modern semi-urbanized societies that are about to be forced onto an independent course are no longer subjectable by U.S. military force. Even a small, poor country like Haiti could probably sustain a successful (if protracted) insurgency against a U.S. occupation, so long as it employs the right combination of strategies, campaigns, and tactics.

This is why the U.S. is resurrecting the old covert operations crowd from the Cold War. But this too will fail. If ever there were a propitious time for people around the world to rebel against the diktat of the U.S., it is right now. Because the foundering and desperate neocons would not be able to handle one, two . . . a hundred Somalias.

FULL-SPECTRUM FUCKUP

> *The mathematical intuition so developed ill equips the student to confront the bizarre behaviour exhibited by the simplest of discrete nonlinear systems.*

—Robert May

"Full-spectrum dominance" (FSD) is the key term in "Joint Vision 2020," the Department of Defense "blueprint" issued under Henry Shelton, the chairman of the Joint Chiefs of Staff during the Clinton administration. Full-spectrum dominance means "the ability of U.S. forces, operating alone or with allies, to defeat any adversary and control any situation across the range of military operations." They did use the word "any" twice, making it perhaps the most grandiose hallucination in U.S. military history, in contrast to the semi-conscious caution inherent in the Powell Doctrine. "Full spectrum" refers to three things: geographic scope, level of conflict, and technology. This is a doctrine that implicitly aims at world military domination, taking on everything from street riots to thermonuclear war, accomplished with a blank check to weapons developers for an array of highly sophisticated gadgets. This is the doctrine from which Rumsfeld evolved his "revolution in military affairs" (RMA) and the corresponding doctrine of "network-centric warfare." Rumsfeld is a narcissist who has convinced himself he is a military genius. His boss is a preppy pretending to be a cowboy, and he is a techno-geek pretending he is the new Clausewitz.

This explains his selection of the singularly undistinguished air force general Richard Myers, of Space Command (SPACECOM), who shares Rumsfeld's radical technological optimism, as the Bush chairman of the Joint Chiefs of Staff.

It is important to make a distinction between full spectrum dominance (FSD) and network-centric warfare (NCW). Rumsfeld has always seen technology as the dominant feature of FSD, and so he transformed FSD to make it his own. Goal: world domination by arms. Method: technological dominance. But Rumsfeld's new doctrine actually begins to substitute formulaic digital "thought" for human leadership, using computerized battlefield systems that go well beyond the mere extension of senses. This dramatically increasing an ever more exclusive reliance on technology in fact carries with it a corresponding increase of latent disorder that can happen abruptly in a kind of tectonic shift. Bakara was a whiff of how this will look.

Reality is nonlinear and dynamic, and it will never conform to a formula. James Gleick explains: "The equations governing a pencil standing on its point have a good mathematical solution with the center of gravity directly above the point—but you cannot stand a pencil on its point because the solution is unstable. The slightest perturbation draws the system away from that solution."

In November 2001, a man at Atlanta's Hartsfield International Airport, the biggest air travel hub in the southeastern United States, left his camera bag in the terminal just before boarding his flight. He rushed back to the terminal to retrieve his bag. When he ran back to catch his plane, fearing he would miss the flight and seeing long lines at the security checkpoint, he impulsively ran up the down escalator to bypass those checkpoints. It was stupid. And it was illegal. But it was, on its own, trivial. Individuals forget things. Individuals take shortcuts. Individuals can be impulsive. Impulsive actions typically lack good judgement. This impulsive act, however, at untold cost, shut down air traffic into and out of the major air traffic hub for over four hours, forced the evacuation of around ten thousand people, and had immeasurable and cascading consequences for each and all of those people. It forced the rerouting of aircraft, and rescheduling, cancellations, and reticketing for days afterward. It was the weekend before Thanksgiving. AirTran alone evacuated eighteen flights awaiting takeoff on the ground at Atlanta. This is the actualization of entropic potential based directly on system complexity. That disorder can be released by an up-the-down-staircase shortcut, or by flying an airplane into a building.

It might be argued that this was an example of system resilience since Hartsfield returned to operation, but this is not simply a matter of whether the glass is half-empty or half-full. Redundancy adds strength to complex systems, but it also increases the disorder any system creates within its material base—which is invisible, fetishized out of sight.

This points directly to the finite limits on material inputs into the system and the system's underlying unsustainability. As a whole, the capital accumulation regime as it currently exists, with its huge dependency on complex technology, steadily increasing its own entropic potential, is quite simply overshooting its financial and ecological, and therefore social, basis. Hartsfield is presented here as an example of a small-scale entropic cascade. Larger ones are imminent.

A highly technologically dependent military upon which American power now ultimately rests, operating in a far more chaotic environment than an airport, will eventually see this same law of unintended consequences with far more momentous outcomes.

Colin Powell, whose own doctrine could accommodate and even welcome a broader range of tactical options, is still a trained military officer who at least understands the Principles of War, which, taken together, emphasize leadership above all other priorities. Powell is enough of a realist to recognize the delusion of *any* adversary.

Rumsfeld and company seem to believe that technical superiority is some guarantee of military success, and that military force can somehow always resolve underlying economic and political contradictions. Powell, for all his inadequacies, knows better.[1]

Mike Davis, author of *City of Quartz*, *Ecology of Fear*, and *Dead Cities*, describes Rumsfeld's peculiar techno-religious vision in his article "Slouching Toward Baghdad" (*ZNet*, February 2003):

> Although the news media will undoubtedly focus on the sci-fi gadgetry involved—thermobaric bombs, microwave weapons, unmanned aerial vehicles (UAVs), PackBot robots, Stryker fighting vehicles, and so on—the truly radical innovations (or so the war wonks claim) will be in the organization and, indeed, the very concept of the war.
>
> In the bizarre argot of the Pentagon's Office of Force Transformation (the nerve center of the revolution), a

new kind of "warfighting ecosystem" known as "network centric warfare" (or NCW) is slouching toward Baghdad to be born. Promoted by military futurists as a "minimalist" form of warfare that spares lives by replacing attrition with precision, NCW may in fact be the inevitable road to nuclear war.

Which well it may, because it doesn't work. Along a continuum of conflict, the U.S. is burning its bridges along that continuum by standing down its capacity for comparatively low-tech, limited conventional conflict. If their current doctrine fails, they will be faced with the choice to quit or to escalate. And that escalation is nuclear.

I've been relating some stories about war, but now I want to tell a story about war games.

In 1985, I beat the shit out of Delta Force in a military exercise in Panama, and in 1989, I captured the key aircraft in an exercise against 2nd Ranger Battalion in Florida.

Okay, there were some mitigating circumstances from their points of view. In both cases, I knew the modus operandi—because I was a member of Delta and a Ranger, respectively. I did, however, defeat Delta's B-Squadron with two light infantry squads of young Rangers playing the part of Colombian guerrillas under my command, and I captured the key aircraft with my own platoon against two companies (eight platoons).

The common denominator in each case was *simplicity*.

In the former case, we simply waited until after dark, built a big fire to white out the night vision equipment of any observers, then unobtrusively faded into the night two-by-two to rejoin at a rendezvous point less than two kilometers away. The sun came up, and we were gone. Game over.

In the second instance, again at night, we attacked a small strongpoint that we could easily overwhelm. Instead of seeking cover afterward to hide from the swarm of "killer eggs," AH-6J helicopter gun ships that were buzzing overhead to provide cover for their Rangers, we stripped the infrared "I'm-an-American" glint tape from the helmets of those we had "killed," and fixed it on our own heads. We strolled straight down the middle of the airfield, blending into the beehive of activity on the "secure" airfield, and climbed right up on the aircraft. "Hi, guys. You have just been captured." Dead simple.

In the latter case, we were told to leave and everyone pretended that we hadn't done it at all. A lot of really important people were watching this exercise, and it had to succeed.

So I was entertained to read in September 2002, about retired Marine general Paul Van Riper. Van Riper is another simple guy, who was selected to play the Opposing Forces (OPFOR) commander named Saddam Hussein for a three-week-long, computer-simulated invasion of Iraq called Operation Millennium Challenge. Van Riper had the same experience I had back in 1989. He won. Then his victory was overruled.

He defeated the entire gazillion-dollar U.S. electronic warfare intelligence apparatus by sending messages via motorcycle-mounted couriers to organize the preemptive destruction of sixteen U.S. ships using pleasure vessels.

At that point, the exercise controllers repeatedly intervened and told him what to do. Move these defenders off the beach. Stop giving out commands from the mosque minarets. Turn on your radar so our planes can see you . . . Every time Van Riper was left to his own devices, he kicked their asses.

While all this is surely amusing, what does it really mean? Would the Iraqis defeat the U.S. during an invasion?

Certainly not.

Not even if, as some then reported, Yugoslavs were giving Iraqis advice on how to "passively track" U.S. warplanes in order to tease them in close enough to shoot, as the Yugoslavs did in 1999 against an F117 Stealth Fighter. Cost: $2.1 billion a copy, and that's not including maintenance. The decoys the Yugoslavs used on the ground were microwave ovens, at $150 a pop. The differences between Iraqis, Yugoslavs, and Afghan-based al-Qaeda would be instructive in assessing the so-called "doctrinal" shift of the U.S. military that played out so badly against retired General Van Riper, but that would be a digression.

The Iraqi military didn't prevail because they couldn't, though I would be one of many who grossly underestimated them.

I said before the 2003 invasion began, "They [the Iraqis] are weak, under-resourced, poorly led, and demoralized. They will come apart like a two-dollar shirt. I could be wrong about that, but I doubt it. So do Bush and Rumsfeld. If they thought the Iraqis could really resist, they wouldn't be cooking up this invasion."

I was wrong about their level of resistance. I was right about Bush and Rumsfeld's prognostications of a "cakewalk," with some boosters predicting the war would last two days.[2]

This was Donald Rumsfeld's second tour of duty as secretary of defense. His first was under Gerald Ford, where he was already demonstrating his deep affinity for big-ticket, high-technology military acquisitions. He had wrangled his Ivy League background into a job as a Navy flight instructor for three years in the mid-fifties—a ticket any really ambitious politician will punch in peacetime. A close identification with expensive war toys stayed with him.

Even in 1977, his priorities as secretary of defense were that "U.S. strategic forces retain a substantial credible capability to deter an all-out nuclear attack," and he indicated three key areas of concern: (1) U.S. submarine and bomber forces, (2) preventing the *appearance* that the Soviet Union had a greater strategic capability then the U.S., and (3) increasing and upgrading America's nuclear arsenal.

This fascination with and faith in military high-technology as a strategic panacea has been a Rumsfeld constant. He was protected in that faith by those who would not allow Van Riper to beat the U.S. military in their computer game.

But there was another constant at work here. Bullying. That's why the appearance thing was a priority. Bullies depend on appearances.

Most of us know what bullying is. It's the cheap gangsterism encountered on shop floors and in schoolyards, marriages, and offices, where a party who has the literal or figurative size to get away with it beats down the smallest among us in order to intimidate everyone into compliance with its wishes.

Let's revisit Yugoslavia for a moment.

NATO claimed they had killed three hundred or so tanks in the massive bombing attacks that followed the Kosovo provocation, but the number was actually fourteen.

The war was won by bullying, not combat. By bombing unarmed

civilians and civilian infrastructure mercilessly, in violation of the Geneva Convention, the Hague Convention, the U.N. Charter, the Nuremberg Charter, and the Laws of Armed Conflict.

(These are the same laws, by the way, that ostensibly protect American soldiers should they be captured in combat. Those soldiers should pay attention. The people, like Bush and Rumsfeld, who are ordering these serial violations of international law, will never face capture. They will make belligerent manly noises from comfortable rooms while U.S. prisoners are having the electrodes attached to their testicles. Hey, what goes around, comes around. They're not my bosses any more, troops. They're yours.)

The Department of Defense claims that Apache helicopters were never used in Kosovo because of a deployment glitch. Bullshit. They were not sent into combat because they fly close to the ground where some very competent and motivated soldiers equipped with shoulder-fired anti-aircraft missiles were hiding with a decided willingness to fire.

Look at where the U.S. has engaged in combat since the U.S. defeat in Vietnam, then look at the type of combat and the opposition. Massive bombing, including of civilian targets, characterized the wars in Iraq and Afghanistan. Iraq had been bled white by a decade of trench warfare with Iran before the 1991 invasion and twelve years of deadly sanctions and bombing before 2003. Afghanistan was a backward, starving nation, shattered by internecine rivalry.

The only substantial ground combat in the 1991 invasion of Iraq was the surprise attack ordered by General Barry McCaffrey (again in violation of every international law and convention) to slaughter tens of thousands of demoralized Iraqi military and civilians two days after the cease fire, when the Iraqis were conducting an orderly retreat. Iraqi soldiers were actually sunbathing on the Baghdad-bound tanks—tanks whose main guns were reversed and locked into non-combat positions—when McCaffrey's lethal "turkey-shoot" began.

Ground operations in Afghanistan have been a series of military blunders that are the stuff of sick humor, including the vaunted Operation Anaconda that turned into Operation Blind Garter Snake, a wedding that was converted into a mass funeral, and the cover-up of

U.S.–supervised war crimes at Mazar-i-Sharif.

Other battlefield glories include the illegal *coup de main* against the superpower of Panama, in which thousands of civilians were killed in the process of defeating the "formidable" Panamanian Defense Forces; the invasion of Grenada (population 90,000) to secure the world's strategic supply of nutmeg; and Reagan's other adventure in Lebanon— where engagement on the ground with credible opponents resulted in another disaster. For anyone interested, *Hideous Dream* bathes the U.S. military in glory for the Haiti invasion of 1994.

The point is, of course, that the U.S. military is restricted to attacking defenseless opponents, what commentator Pepe Escobar referred to in March 2003 as "theatrical militarism"—bullying.

Beat up weak people to show what a tough guy you are.

Note that the U.S. didn't pounce on the Democratic People's Republic of Korea (DPRK) when it was claimed to have announced it had bomb grade plutonium. Wasn't this one of the Axis of Evil, admitting it had weapons of mass destruction? (An admission which it turns out wasn't true.) But . . . DPRK has a very tough and disciplined military that is close enough to Seoul to throw rocks at it, and a lot of American GIs are concentrated between the demilitarized zone (DMZ) and the capital, and in the capital, which may be why Rumsfeld has since announced they will all be pulled back from the DMZ.

I'll tell you a story about that later on.

The U.S. seems disinclined to commit conventional ground troops to Colombia. That's because the FARC-EP and the ELN fight. I'll go out on a limb and say they won't send troops to Venezuela either. I've seen the Venezuelan army, most of who are still loyal to populist President Hugo Chavez, and they didn't strike me as pushovers.

Bullies avoid people who won't put up with them. Were it not for the waning U.S. capacity to bully economically, our foreign policy establishment would be honored with a lot of middle-finger salutes.

There's a new term popular in military circles, even being repeated by Wolf Blitzer-types, self-appointed military experts that have become an artesian spring of impressively arcane military jargon in the televised news.

Asymmetric warfare.

It applies to suicide bombers and guys who hijack airplanes with box cutters. Get it? It's kind of a double entendre. Asymmetrical force. Asymmetrical bang for the buck. It's also asymmetry of technology, but Donald Rumsfeld hasn't grasped that implication yet.

It's funny that we never heard of the "asymmetry" of Barry McCaffrey's slaughter of the Iraqis, or the "asymmetry" of the United States invading Grenada, an island nation with the population of Cary, North Carolina. But that's a moral digression.

The principle behind "asymmetry" is simplicity. When they retreat, pursue. When they attack, retreat. Match your strengths to their weaknesses.

Simplicity, as any officer who paid attention in Military Science 101 can tell you, is a Principle of War. "All other factors being equal, the simplest plan is preferable." That's what Van Riper understood. That's how I beat the U.S. army's supreme commandos. That's what happened to the World Trade Center. (I am in no way endorsing the attack of September 11. I'm talking about cold, calculating, military success.)

The reason Van Riper's victory had to be overruled is that it tears the scary mask off the bully and lets the whole world see the fundamental weakness of the vastly complex and expensive U.S. military monstrosity—the one that will invite not less but more "asymmetric warfare," the very monstrosity that is already mortgaging our children's future.

Then whose victories will be overruled?

Well, the answer is not pretty.

There are huge tactical voids in Rumsfeld's technocentric vision, and I will pick up the thread in a moment that shows where Special Operations will be used to plug the holes.

But the most discomfiting conclusion, which Mike Davis outlines lucidly, is:

> If the American war-fighting networks begin to unravel (as partially occurred in February 1991), the new paradigm—with its "just in time" logistics and its small "battlefield footprint"—leaves little backup in terms of traditional military reserves. This is one reason why the Rumsfeld Pentagon

takes every opportunity to rattle its nuclear saber.

Just as precision munitions have resurrected all the mad omnipotent visions of yesterday's strategic bombers, RNA/NCW is giving new life to monstrous fantasies of functionally integrating tactical nukes into the electronic battlespace. The United States, it should never be forgotten, fought the Cold War with the permanent threat of "first use" of nuclear weapons against a Soviet conventional attack. Now the threshold has been lowered to Iraqi gas attacks, North Korean missile launches, or, even, retaliation for future terrorist attacks on American city.

For all the geekspeak about networks and ecosystems, and millenarian boasting about minimal, robotic warfare, the United States is becoming a terror state pure and simple: a 21st-century Assyria with laptops and modems.

Bush might listen to Wolfowitz, the Dr. Strangelove of American politics, and consider the use of tactical nuclear weapons in the quest to restructure the planet's political geography. Rumsfeld has already begun calling for research into low-yield, atomic bunker-buster munitions.

But as the Haitian proverb goes, "If you don't say good morning to the devil, he will eat you. If you do say good morning to the devil . . . he will eat you." There is no option for most of the world but to fight imperialism. And it can be fought militarily. Just not conventionally.

Shout out to all of you in the periphery. Don't underestimate this beast from whose belly I write. But don't buy its invincibility mystique either. It can be beaten. You just have to think out of the box.

IRAQ: WOLVES AND SHEEP

(apologies to Canis lupus)

Therefore, when that regime is removed we will find one of the most talented populations in the Arab world, perhaps complaining that it took us so long to get there. Perhaps a little unfriendly to the French for making it take so long. But basically welcoming us as liberators. Then it's up to us to behave as liberators, and I'm sure we will.
—Paul Wolfowitz,
February 21, 2003

Now, I think things have gotten so bad inside Iraq, from the standpoint of the Iraqi people, my belief is we will, in fact, be greeted as liberators
—Dick Cheney,
March 16, 2003

Admiral Kelly, Captain Card, officers and sailors of the U.S.S. Abraham Lincoln, my fellow Americans, major combat operations in Iraq have ended.
—George W. Bush,
May 1, 2003

The World Bank, under the direction of James Wolfensohn, is posing a problem for neocon Wolfowitz. The World Bank, though dominated by the U.S. which has 16.2% of voting shares, has an institutional loyalty to multilateralism. As U.S. unilateralism advocated by U.S. neocons gives the back of its hand to the very foundation of the U.N., which is the institutional manifestation of multilateralism, there is predictable conflict between the two Wolfs. The World Bank Wolf is a neo-liberal, while the Defense Department Wolf is a neocon.
—Henry C. K. Liu,
April 2003

Henry C. K. Liu, who runs an investment company and has written extensively on "dollar hegemony," has hit another nail on the head. I would add entertainment media cheerleader Wolf Blitzer, CNN's Pentagon sycophant in Kuwait City, as representative of the neon press, neon being that colorless, inert gas that lights up on command.

The self-congratulation of the Bush regime after the fall of Baghdad was matched only by the despair of those who, in the first days of unexpected Iraqi resistance, thirsted for an American tactical defeat in Iraq.

My late friend Mark Jones insisted on grasping things firmly, especially those most consequential things that we might sidestep because of an emotional paradox—like the fact that we are now certainly entering a very dark period of human history within which there are, with equal certainty, historic opportunities for human emancipation. They are times that will require our deepest compassion and our most dispassionate—and sometimes ruthless—cunning.

In that spirit, let's review the adventure in Iraq.

Fade In

By March 17, 2003, I dropped my stubborn belief that the full-scale invasion of Iraq might be averted. I held out longer than most, fully understanding that for the Bush administration, (1) the invasion of Iraq would end up being a total political disaster and (2) the failure to invade Iraq would be a total political disaster. I had finally accepted that the boat had tipped past the point of no return and the invasion would happen. The full-scale, unilateral U.S. invasion of Iraq appeared imminent. The spoiled preppy frat-fuck from Texas gave Saddam Hussein a seventy-two-hour cowboy ultimatum to leave the country or else the bombs would start falling.

The Bush regime seemed to have a clear understanding of what desperate straits they were in well before 9/11. The empire was in decline, and this meant that Americans would someday soon have to reconcile themselves to a new world order alright, one in which their profligate lifestyle would become a thing of the past.

Americans do not understand that this is an irremediable situation. That is why we are witnessing the beginning of what is possibly the most dangerous period in human history. American culture is a sheep culture—long on talk about individualism, but even longer on absolute conformity. Most still believe that individuality is based on which model car you like best—commodity identity, a selection of personalities on a shelf full of products approved by the Federal Identity Administration. I'm a Taurus aspiring to be a Lexus.

If the administration had decided miraculously in the last days not to invade, the most unthinkable risks would have receded significantly. But the Bush and his coterie had repeatedly displayed a reckless adventurist streak that alarmed even their own political allies, and it appeared that the hotter heads would prevail.

The actual tactical situation, never terribly auspicious because of the Kurdish regional wild card that continues to receive far too little attention, had deteriorated for the U.S. The denial of a ground front from both Saudi Arabia and Turkey had completely reshuffled the tactical deck and caused many a sleepless night for harried commanders from Task Force Headquarters all the way down to lonely infantry platoon leaders.

The ground attack would now go though Kuwait, a single front across which an unbelievable series of heavy, expensive, high-maintenance convoys would pass, many originally bound on long journeys for eighteen provincial capitals, nineteen military bases, eight major oil fields, over a thousand miles of pipeline, and key terrain along minority Shia and Kurdish regions as well as Baghdad. But attacking forces were not the only mechanized ground combat forces.

The huge logistical trains that were to consolidate objectives, set up long-term lines of communication, and deliver daily support would also be held up until airheads were seized within Iraq to augment ground transportation with airlifts of people and equipment. This shifted a higher emphasis onto airhead seizures and would force the security of the airheads themselves before they can become fully functional.

Baghdad began to look like it would require a siege, which had already been planned, but now that siege wouldn't begin without a much lengthier invasion timeline that depended much more heavily on airborne and airmobile forces that could be dropped onto key facilities to hold them until mechanized reinforcement arrived. The 101st Airborne (which is actually a helicopter division) had not even completed its deployment into the region. Sections of the 82nd Airborne (a genuine paratroop division) were still occupying Afghanistan.

The increased dependence on airlift was further complicated by weather. While extreme summer heat doesn't reach Iraq until May, the pre-summer sand storms had already begun. U.S. commanders pooh-poohed the effect of these storms, but they were simply putting on a brave face for the public. Sand can be a terrible enemy. It clogs engine intakes, just as it clogs eyes and noses, gathers in the folds of skin, falls in food, works its way into every conceivable piece of equipment, and takes a miserable toll on material, machinery, and troops. When air operations become more critical to overall mission accomplishment, and when light forces (like airmobile and airborne divisions) are operating independent of heavier mechanized logistics, weather like sand storms matter—a lot. (By June, U.S. forces would feel the brunt of 120 degree midday heat.)

Even with all those debilities and setbacks, the results of the invasion were certain. Iraq would be militarily defeated and occupied. I myself didn't believe there would be any sustained Iraqi guerrilla resistance, nor a Stalingrad in Baghdad. I've never bought into the U.S. bluster about their invincibility, but neither did I buy into Iraqi bluster.

It was clear to any who wanted to see, however, that this invasion would ignite the fires of Arab and Muslim humiliation and anger throughout the region.

And there were, and are, the Kurds.

That Kurdish issue had already come out into the open in the Turkish parliament, delivering a shocking setback to the U.S. with the denial of a northern front. To this day, the vast area that is Kurdistan, with its insurgent armed bodies, overlaying Iraq, Iran, Turkey, and even parts of Syria, will realign the politics and military of the entire region in yet unpredictable ways.

As part of the effort to generate an Iraqi opposition, the U.S. had permitted northern Iraqi Kurdistan to exercise a strong element of national political autonomy for the first time since the 1991 war. This was a double-edged sword for the U.S. in its current war preparations, particularly given the administration's predisposition for pissing all over its closest allies. Iraq's northern border is with Turkey, who has for years favored the interests of its own Turkmen in southern Turkish

Kurdistan at the expense of the Kurds, who have in turn waged a guerrilla war for self-determination against the Turks since the 1970s.

The *Partiya Karkeren Kurdistan* (Kurdish Worker's Party) or PKK , Turkish Kurds fighting for an independent Kurdish state in southeast Turkey, were singled out on the U.S. international terrorist organization list several years ago in deference to fellow NATO member, Turkey. Captured PKK leader Abdullah Ocalan is so popular with the Kurds that Turkey was forced to commute his death sentence to life imprisonment for fear that his execution would spark an uprising.

Other non-leftist Kurdish independence organizations developed and alternatively allied with and split from the PKK and each other. Turkey now claims that PKK bases are being constructed in Iran, with Iranian complicity, from which to launch strikes against Southern Turkey. Groups more acceptable to the U.S. than the PKK, including the Kurdistan Democratic Party (KDP) and the Kurdistan Patriotic Union (PUK) had been administering northern Iraqi Kurdistan as an autonomous zone under the protective umbrella of the U.S. no-fly zone.

The Turkish government feared (and still fears) the influence of this section of Kurdistan in the wake of the U.S. invasion because Kurds have in the recent past stated their intention of declaring an independent Kurdish state there. The Turks find this absolutely unacceptable, and issued their own forthright declaration that they would invade to prevent this happening. They have also threatened to attack Kurds in Iran, but this was a far less credible threat.

Kurdish nationalists have a long experience with betrayals and alliances of convenience, and know American perfidy very well. They declared at the outset that in the event of an invasion, they will defend themselves from Turkish incursions. They are unlikely to give up the autonomy they gained during their eleven years under U.S. air cover in northern Iraq. This not only put them at odds with U.S. ally Turkey, but it still potentially puts them at odds with the U.S., even after they participated in indigenous actions against Iraqi forces under U.S. Special Forces leadership. The U.S. did not want that region destabilized in the postinvasion period because Kirkuk, in the east of Iraqi Kurdistan, is a huge oil producing zone.

The big complication of postinvasion Iraq may still be the demand that U.S. commanders disarm the Kurds. In the interim, the problem became that of the Kurds attacking Arabs in Iraqi Kurdistan and laying claim to farms thereabouts on the basis that they were taken from them and awarded to Arabs by the Ba'athists.

Northern Iraq could easily become contested terrain involving partisan warfare between the Turks, three factions of the Kurds, the Iraqi Arabs, the Iranians, and the U.S., with the Syrians in a position to play the silent interloper. This would amount to the devolution of a key strategic region into another Afghanistan or Somalia. It has already severely strained relationships between Turkey and the United States, NATO allies, even as the NATO alliance itself remains under severe strain, with a Euro-American trade war as a backdrop.

And the Kurds have the motivation, tenacity, and fighting spirit to do those kinds of things that General Van Riper did to defeat the Rumsfeld "robo-military" in Operation Millennium Challenge.

Three days before the war began, it was clear that the Bush junta was the equivalent of a mad beekeeper, who no longer leaves the hive stable and merely smokes it into a stupor to harvest the honey. It now proposed to simply start swatting all the bees and taking the honey by brute force.

Perhaps most remarkable, given all the variables at play, was that Donald Rumsfeld and the whole neocon clique still believed the war would be decisively won within a couple of days.

Supporting the Troops

On March 20, 2003, the rich coke-snortin' frat-fuck from Texas declared the initiation of the U.S. aggression against Iraq, now framed by the ministry of propaganda (aka CNN) as the *U.S. War against Saddam.*

The military situation was entirely unpredictable, since every operations order becomes obsolete the minute of its own execution. The Brits and the U.S. administration were spinning away on television and claiming operational security, which was only partly true. There was a look of worry about them. I began to suspect that the flurry of last-minute plan changes since Turkey's dastardly betrayal had produced some awful goat-screw on the ground, exposing yet again the vast incompetence of the U.S. military's narcissistic officer corps that lurks just below the surface of their incredible technological power.

Back in the States, we saw a preemptive attack from the Republican Party toward Tom Daschle, the Democratic Senate minority leader. Daschle made some anemic criticisms of the Bush cabinet's diplomatic prowess, whereupon the Republicans unleashed a torrent of accusations that Daschle was somehow failing to support the troops. It was a preemptive attack directed at Daschle, almost as a ritual, but ultimately this censure was directed against all of us.

This hasn't been an easy time for Bush and his cabinet. It hadn't been an easy time for a lot of so-called liberals either. An antiwar movement had come onto the scene, and not just any antiwar movement. It was now the fastest and broadest international movement of its type in history. It involved anarcho-kids, olde tyme lefties, and pacifists, to be sure, but it also involved soccer moms, Black preachers, Italian dock workers, women who write books, nerds, doctors, Indian garment workers, Nigerian intellectuals, Brazilian coffee pickers, Japanese students, Haitian peasants, Filipino street cleaners: every-damn-body!

And that wasn't all. Many of them were picking up bad language. When I heard a sixty-year-old middle school teacher using words like "imperialism," I knew something was going on, and those who wanted every one of the rest of us to just go along with the program, including weak-kneed red-baiting liberals like Hitchens and Gitlin and Cooper and all their ilk, had become alarmed. There was a very dangerous consciousness that was emerging in the face of our would-be fascists, and many "liberals" were developing a McCarthy itch.

Out came the last trick in the bag, the one that was supposed to silence us for good, goddamnit! We had to support the troops. This is the mother of all social-policing strategies to stifle the criticism of naked emperors: patriotism, the last refuge of scoundrels.

It goes, we must close ranks and support our president, who is after all the commander in chief of the armed forces (our sons and daughters, our sisters and brothers, our spouses and sweethearts), because without that support, [enter name of your loved one in the military] and his or her comrades will not be adequately filled with our spirit of support to effectively defend him or herself, whereupon lack of said spirit will result in American casualties, which makes all of us who withhold said spirit complicit in killing and wounding American troops, and therefore traitors.

Let me explain something, by way of another war story.

In 1983, I took part in the invasion of Grenada. Aside from being an incompetent operation, it was also one that no one in the United States even knew about until it was pretty much over. Hey, it doesn't take long to conquer a nation that is a ten-mile-wide island with fewer than ninety thousand people . . . even if it *was* planned by idiots.

When America was informed that its treasure and youth were being risked to secure the global nutmeg supply, over ninety-nine percent of the country couldn't tell you where Grenada was. We who conducted the operation had committed it to memory less than forty hours earlier.

The invasion was ordered in part to take advantage of internal turmoil in Grenada to install a new pro-U.S. government. Mainly, however, its aim was to flex a little American muscle after 258 Marines were killed by a car bomb only days earlier in Beirut, whereupon the U.S. expeditionary force in Lebanon was unceremoniously withdrawn.

Like a bully that gets his tail kicked, Reagan & Co. had to beat down someone smaller to save face.

The whole thing suddenly became a "rescue mission" when someone stumbled over a low-rent offshore medical-diploma mill full of American students and Reagan's staff cranked up the propaganda machine. *Let me explain this carefully.* None of us involved in Operation Urgent Fury (not joking; it was called that) had heard anything about medical students. I was with Delta Force, the highest priority unit in the United States Army, and the designated drivers for "rescue" operations, and we had never heard of a medical school. Bonzo lied, just like his simian cousin Dubya would lie two decades later.

The first hour of the operation was an old-fashioned country ass-whuppin', with us on the receiving end.

We were forced to defend ourselves, or rather, face a determined initial defense against our little invasion. But we didn't have the "support" spirit of the American people, because as far as they knew, we were all still home, cheating on our spouses in Fayetteville, North Carolina. America woke up scratching its head, trying to figure out why Ronald

Reagan had just invaded a Spanish city named after a Ford compact.

When the helicopter I was riding on with sixteen other people reached the island, we were greeted with small-arms fire before we even crossed over the first mangrove swamp, and it got worse fast. By the time we reached out "target," Richmond Hill Prison, where we were gong to "liberate" prisoners that weren't there, we already had four people shot. As we hovered over the prison, deciding whether or not to slide down ropes into Grenada's drunk tank, machine-gun fire poured through both doors and stitched up the belly of the fuselage from below. By the time we left, having decided not to put up with this any longer, seven members of our group were shot, and most of the rest of us were having our clothes shot off.

In all this mayhem and confusion, while we (the army's most elite, whitest forces) were being spanked by skinny Black folk from Grenada and equally dark Cuban construction workers, I can honestly say that I didn't give a flying fuck about what anyone in the United States might be thinking, or how much supportive spirit they might be psychically channeling my way to cuddle up against.

I didn't stop to consider that many of my countrymen and country-women made jokes about our commander in chief once co-starring with a chimpanzee, or how that might seem . . . unsupportive.

I was extremely busy using a K-bar knife to cut the jammed harness off a wounded door gunner to lay his pale, shocky ass on the helicopter floor while I commandeered his portside machine gun to suppress some of our most persistent assailants across the valley.

Nothing I did would have changed one iota, even had the entire population of the United States gathered naked at Stonehenge to chant supportive mantras out across the bounding seas to our precise geographic coordinates.

I can say now that we were wrong, but once engaged the goal is to keep breathing. For that, no one needs invisible cheerleaders.

During Bush's invasion of Iraq, nothing we did or didn't do here had any impact on how the troops comported themselves in Iraq either. The support-the-troops thing is a mystifying old red herring. What our new fascists really wanted us to do was shut the fuck up. And shutting up was exactly what we refused to do.

That doesn't mean protests didn't have an impact on the war. They very much did, and should have. But it didn't change the ability of a single troop to fight. Only the neocons' mad overreaching and Rumsfeld's simple-minded reorganization of the military have been able to destroy the morale of U.S. troops.

The False Start

Rumsfeld's war plan was initiated on the March 20, with expectations that the high-tech advance northward from Kuwait would resolve all major tactical difficulties within two days. Simultaneously, another rumsfeld scheme, "decapitation" strikes, was launched to target Saddam Hussein. The whole venture was designed to come off like Bill Gates meets Caesar. Instead it came off like George Orwell meets Al Capone.

The Orwellian aspect, of course, was the American press and its near complete merger with the Department of Defense, specifically Central Command (CENTCOM).

Beginning almost immediately after the first tanks crossed their lines of departure into southern Iraq, we were witness to the surreal recurring spectacle of the CENTCOM-Lie-of-the-Day—a parade of spin doctors from the military, including the actual commander, Tommy Franks, who would make erroneous and often ridiculous claims about the progress of their aggression—even as the entire Rumsfeld lunacy unraveled before the eyes of the world in the face of sparse, but extremely courageous and totally unexpected, Iraqi resistance.

Umm Qasr had fallen. Well, not yet. Basra was taken. Well, not yet. A brigade of Iraqis surrendered. Oops. Fudged casualty statistics. Phantom Republican Guard columns advancing south. Saddam-is-dead rumors circulated daily. Chemical weapons sites were discovered then undiscovered. The victims of American bombs were *really* caused by falling antiaircraft debris from the Iraqis.

The wild stories, outright lies, and subsequent rationalizations were reiterated uncritically by CNN, MSNBC, and Fox, among all the others, to an ovine American public (the most notable exception being Black Americans, who remained largely skeptical of the whole enterprise). Embedded reporters, who had been completely immersed in U.S. military units—self-censoring, based on deep identification with and absolute dependence upon those units—sent back prescreened images almost minute by minute, and the world saw its first truly stage-managed war.

Then cracks developed in the stories. The internet allowed legitimate journalism to end-run the CENTCOM news network. And the generals, chafing under the arrogant presumptuousness of Donald Rumsfeld and smarting from setbacks in the field, began to leak.

As a veteran of operations gone bad, by March 25, I was experiencing a powerful sense of vicarious deja vu.

Four days earlier, I couldn't watch CNN for more than ten minutes at a time or I was risking my own mental health. By the twenty-fifth, I watched it with the perverse fascination one experiences when seeing a fifteen-car pileup on the freeway.

Obviously, the parade of aging white generals—even including my old B-Squadron Delta commander, Dave Grange—who simultaneously knew that the U.S. would prevail militarily through sheer force and that this entire operation was going to shit, did not understand the wider political implications of what they were witnessing.

My Delta team had put Dave Grange through the Delta training course in 1983. After we'd trained him, he became my commander when we did that god-awful operation in Grenada. I remembered him when he was a fire-breathing tri-athlete and when he was my regimental commander during the Somalia fiasco (though he wasn't there for that one). For all his foolishness, he had some dignity because he was doing a hard job. Now he was bumbling through his commentary, self-conscious and silly, trading on all that experience for whatever CNN was paying these days. It was actually sad, and I wanted to ask him, *What in the fuck are you doing?*

The retired generals seemed discomfited. They had been converted into cheap propagandists, and for me it was a lot like seeing a formerly tyrannical but respected sergeant major who's retired and become an oily insurance salesman, reduced to haunting the barracks, kissing up to his own former troops to earn his way in the real world by selling them policies. There but for the grace of whatever . . .

How the mighty can fall from great heights! Perhaps that's too majestic. The Haitians say, the higher the monkey climbs the tree, the more you see nothing but his ass.

I watched Wesley Clark, the CNN military star, whose reputation in the army had been that of an inveterate ass-kisser. He harbors presidential pretensions, and he was smooth as a baby's butt. And his worry lines were coming right through the pancake makeup.

Donald Rumsfeld had become positively humble—a first in his lifetime—during his Pentagon briefs for about twelve hours.

George W. Bush was nearly absent. Once he looked drunk on television. Had his klavern determined not to risk his extemporaneous gaffes? Might he have been medicated? His two-line appearances were hoarse and fatigued.

What was happening?

What was happening was that the superpower came face to face with its new counterpart: an international popular movement, focused against this war, but increasingly targeting U.S. global hegemony itself. A worldwide movement had become a material force on the battlefield and was positioned to midwife a deep crisis of legitimacy for the U.S. military-political junta.

In this sense, we must be honest, we were not supporting the home team, and we *did* contribute to the battlefield difficulties experienced by American forces, and we should not apologize for it, because we defended Iraqi sovereignty against imperial aggression.

The whole adventure was rooted in systemic crisis, a reality that so far only the left wing of the movement itself understood. How had the antiwar movement become a material force on the Iraqi battleground?

A snapshot of the tactical situation, as least what could be gleaned from different accounts, revealed that the original battle plan was scrapped. The complexity of planning a military operation of that scope is simply indescribable, and it takes months to do it right. But the unexpected loss of ground fronts, in Turkey in the north and Saudi Arabia in the south, forced a complete reconstruction of the plans in a matter of days. The operation could be put off no longer. The aggressor's back was against the weather wall. The pre-summer sandstorms had already begun, and by late April the heat index inside a soldier's chemical protective gear could be 140 degrees Fahrenheit.

The international antiwar movement had firmed up political opposition around the world and forced the delays that culminated in the

U.N. Security Council becoming a key arena of struggle. For all the ossified left who couldn't see beyond their own simplistic shibboleths and who dismissed the U.N. on ideological—and therefore idealist—grounds, there was an example of how politics translates dialectically into military reality.

The antiwar movement had pushed back Bush's war calendar. That delay had a material effect on the conduct and outcomes of the war. There is an effect to this day. Never doubt it.

The entire 4th Infantry Division was still sitting in the barracks waiting for their equipment to steam around the Arabian Peninsula in cargo ships because the Turkish parliament denied them their battle-front. Medium and short-range tactical aircraft that could have struck dozens of key targets were sidelined because they were forbidden to take off from Saudi Arabia to deliver their payloads.

Inside the Department of Defense there was another war raging between the generals of the army and Marine Corps and the clique of doctrinal "revolutionaries" pushing Rumsfeld's crackpot theory, cyber-war combined with commandos.

The new "doctrine" was creating a military debacle in Iraq. Rumsfeld was refusing to learn what was in front of him, that in war, which is an extreme form of politics, success is not measured on a point system like a golf tournament. It is not measured in body counts or inventories of destroyed war materiel. In fact, it is not perfectly measurable at all. Success has to be gauged against the expectations of the military operation and its final objectives—which are always political. The U.S. inflicted a terrible empirical toll on Southeast Asia and ultimately lost the Vietnam War. The U.S. never grasped the political character of that war.

Complex technology had displaced decision-making from human commanders to computerized hardware/software. Each strength carries with it a corresponding weakness, and once military leaders perceive the strengths and weaknesses of their opposition, they can avoid the strengths and exploit the weaknesses.

The Iraqis did just that.

Accusations by the United States that the Russians were providing material assistance were likely true. The Russians had now thrown in their lot with "old Europe" and China, and they were aiming to undermine U.S. power at every opportunity. I suspected they had not only provided equipment and training on that equipment, but advisory assistance on the reorganization of the Iraqi military.

Someone surely did.

The Iraqi military had abandoned its former Soviet-style doctrine, predicated on armor, mass, and centralized command. It had seemingly now adopted tactics more suited to Special Operations: agile and decentralized. Such a switch requires a very intentional and systematic reorientation from top to bottom. This is an "asymmetrical" response to the high-tech doctrine the U.S. developed to overcome the doctrine of its own predecessor. This Iraqi doctrinal reorientation proved stunningly effective, even though it was often tragically amateurish in its execution, with Iraqis simply stepping into the street to fire RPGs and being cut down by a tsunami of fire and lead.

Rumsfeld's notion that he might "decapitate" the Iraqi military led to an incessant and inane press speculation about whether on not Saddam Hussein was dead or alive. As the reports rolled in of one setback after another, he was asked by the press whether there was any evidence to show that Saddam Hussein is dead. His response: "The word evidence is a hard word."

Less ridiculous and more telling was the statement by a Pentagon official, now dissing his boss Rumsfeld: "This is the ground war that was not going to happen in his plan."

Rumsfeld's computers told him that the Iraqis would be shocked and awed into capitulation within two days. Instead we had the (suppressed in the U.S.) spectacle of ground troops in disarray as they attempted to cross their initial lines of departure, columns being stopped by urban resistance, ambushes of logistics tails, advances halted by blinding sandstorms, and captive American youngsters on television.

These first American prisoners of war were not Navy Seals or Delta Force, but military maintenance people and cooks, kids who signed up for an enlistment bonus, some college money, and a saleable skill. Now they stared hauntingly back at us all, with their fear almost an aura in their photographs.

The earlier uncomplicated advances, however, were remarkable. In set-piece war, Rumsfeld's impressive display of new battle software worked perfectly. Tank commanders could keep their lines perfectly dressed by simply referring to a digital display, and no one was pulling ahead into an adjacent unit's gunsights.

It all worked, right up until the first Iraqis fought back.

The generals were preoccupied now with retrieving their tactical victory from the chaos, a retrieval that could cost treasure, lives, and careers. And they were almost certainly also sharpening their knives and fantasizing about the spaces between Donald Rumsfeld's ribs.

The first images of the war were supposed to see were the "liberation" of Basra, where jubilant crowds of Shia Muslims would welcome the conquering American heroes. Instead, Basra fought back with a spectacular ferocity.

Now U.S. ground forces were attempting to bypass every urban center on the road to Baghdad, but they were in the restricted terrain of the east, where bypass is not always an option. In Al Nasiriya, victory toasts turned to vinegar in their mouths.

City by city, sieges had now become a real possibility, and the longer this war went, Bush and his lieutenants began to see, the sharper would be the reaction throughout the region.

Aside from stalling, antiwar forces and the naked self-interest of the U.S. regime had given those who opposed the war another multifaceted victory. The U.S., fearing further erosion of its wounded legitimacy, had set out to genuinely limit civilian casualties. We have to be honest and clear about this. It happened. There were certainly civilian casualties, but not nearly the mass slaughter many predicted.

One factor at play was the need to avoid great damage to the infrastructure of the new prize. The other was the heat from the flames of an erupting international rebellion that the administration could ill afford to fan any higher.

Sixty miles outside of Baghdad, the whole advance screeched to a halt. CENTCOM explained the "operational pause" as an exercise in flexibility, "all part of the plan."

On March 27, Bush and his errand-boy Tony Blair had an emergency meeting.

The bombing of Baghdad, circumspect until then, was intensified—almost a gratuitous act of frustrated rage. Independent journalists reported the same targets being hit from the air as many as six nights in a row.

The generals went back to the drawing board. The 4th Infantry, whose equipment was stranded on the ocean when the Turkish government denied the Americans their northern front, prepared to deploy as reinforcement. Supply lines were shored up by diverting combat power to convoy security in order to resupply the points of the advance, Army along the Euphrates Valley and Marines along the Tigris. Some troops were low on water and down to one MRE (Meal, Ready to Eat—a military field ration) a day. Sandstorms had eaten into the engines of the Abrams, Bradleys, and helicopters, and fuel was low.

On March 27, the 173rd Airborne Brigade parachuted onto northern Iraq's Harrir Airfield with Kurdish security waiting on the ground. CENTCOM referred to this operation as "opening a Northern Front."

The Bush government's diplomatic vandalism had systematically alienated the masses around the world, a force they underestimated wholly, and the underlying intent of the Bush cabal—a military solution for economic war—was understood clearly by the northern capitalist powers, and by Russia and China. The Latin American supercolony, already in a process of break-up and rebellion, had inaugurated a renewed wave of anticolonial struggle, as others from the global South watched. The hegemon was breaking up, and war was seen by the Bush faction as its best, last chance. Even America's former multilateralist partners—stung by disrespect and alarmed by the bright-eyed bellicosity of Bush's advisors—had begun to thirst for U.S. humiliation.

Now all thought their thirst would be slaked.

The depth of U.S. cultural decay had been on display for months, as impunity and falsehood characterized political discourse and the last crumbs of American journalism were lapped up into the maw of the media-military nexus, leaving only Ken & Barbie media personalities breathlessly pandering to a public whose heads have been softened by a diet of info-kibble and *Survivor*.

Half the U.S. population had evidently accepted one central and demonstrably idiotic assertion, that Iraqi leadership played some facilitative role in the September 11th attacks. Now enough of American-society-in-denial—especially white society—had its rationalization. The international legal framework that took six decades to assemble, starting with the Charter of the United Nations, was ripped apart and shipped to the same landfill as the detritus of U.S. bourgeois democracy—similarly cast off in 2000, when most of white America had talked about hanging chads for a day or two, then went shopping. We had placidly accepted the imposition of a putsch, that used the 9/11 attacks as the pretext to transform itself into a junta.

The entire adventure was conceived from a really existing condition of weakness. I have said that for some time. Even progressive forces were intimidated by the raw power and outlandish price tag of the U.S. military machine and the demonstrated willingness to use it. There was the sense that it was a juggernaut. That's how bullies operate—through intimidation.

We had underestimated the quality of Iraqi resistance, and I had overestimated the scope of the initial air campaign. In April, I had stated, "The Iraqi military won't prevail because they can't. They are weak, under-resourced, poorly led, and demoralized. What the delays mean is that the U.S. will depend on sustaining the initiative and momentum through brutal, incessant bombing designed to destroy every soldier, every installation, every vehicle, every field kitchen in the Iraqi military."

While Donald Rumsfeld was imposing his vaunted "revolution in military affairs," the Iraqi military was reorganizing from the ground up for an agile, decentralized, urban-based warfighting capability that abandoned Soviet-style, conventional, armor-centric doctrine for something more akin to doctrine that was taught but seldom practiced by Special Operations forces in the U.S. during the Cold War, particularly "stay-behind" disruption of enemy lines of communications, once the primary mission of 10th Special Forces in the event of a general conflict with the Warsaw

I was reminded now of T. S. Eliot's poem, "The Love Song of J. Alfred Prufrock," where Prufrock's neurotic internal voice tells him there will be "time yet for a hundred indecisions, / And for a hundred visions and revisions / . . . In a minute there is time, / For decisions and revisions which a minute will reverse."

If we had sent a copy of "Prufrock" to the Bush cabinet, they might have wept with recognition.

Everything that could have gone wrong with the American invasion was going wrong, and the longer it went, the wronger it got. And with these reversals, the danger to everyone increased by orders of magnitude. Especially the danger to Iraqis.

The efficacy of Iraqi tactics was being met with revisions of the rules of engagement (ROE). These were the rules related to when soldiers can and cannot "engage" (that means attempt to kill) enemy soldiers and civilians. As the invasion began, the ROE was comparatively strict. Embedded reporters were pretty close to the action, after all, and there was the underlying assumption that there would be no significant resistance. On Tuesday, March 25, CENTCOM began openly saying they would change the ROE to reflect the "new reality."

With the end of the sandstorms, the U.S. Air Force and Navy resumed their air assault, this time testing 4,700-pound bunker busters on Baghdad. Army Apache helicopters and Air Force A-10s (the flying 30-mm electronic chain-guns that fire depleted uranium rounds) were hitting forward of the Army and Marine axis of advance, using the "new" ROE, and reports were already filtering out of Iraq of nightmarish scenes of scorched and shattered vehicles and bodies that include passenger cars, buses, and plenty of civilians.

It became apparent, given the continued furious resistance of the Iraqis, including audacious attacks on both U.S. supply lines and combat units, that Baghdad might not be a cakewalk. Bush and his generals were at a fork in the road, where they had to choose either to wreck Baghdad or to lay siege to it. House-to-house fighting in Baghdad would begin a televised file of military caskets returning to America. That would quickly become intolerable, and the administration would collapse. The other unthinkable option was that Bush had would quit.

But they couldn't. They were now caught in the same deadly trap they had built for Iraq.

The sad truth seemed to be, we were witnessing the certain political self-destruction of Bush & Co., but it would come at a cost paid with many Iraqi and American lives. I expected a renewed American assault before the weekend was past, and this one with a shattering display of air power.

During a CENTCOM briefing on Thursday the twenty-seventh, the charming and affable Brigadier General Vincent Brooks became short with reporters and flatly stated that CENTCOM would not release U.S. casualty figures any longer. He reversed that statement in less than two days, but it was an indicator of the stress level at CENTCOM, likely besieged now with lunatic tirades from Donald Rumsfeld.

The night prior, an embedded CNN reporter had broadcast in real-time that Marines near Nasiriyah were engaged in a firefight with Iraqis that wounded twenty-one Marines within one hour. Eleven from Camp Lejuene, North Carolina, near where I live, were dead.

Things were going very badly for troops on the long northbound column. Vehicles were deadlined from the sand. Soldiers were frightened, they were short of sleep, and they stank. The tempo that had exhilarated them three days earlier was now turning to deep muscular and psychological fatigue. Many were now wondering what they had gotten into. Thoughts of dying in a state of discomfort and images of being maimed for life, were appearing uninvited. Tempers were flaring. The food was all starting to taste the same. The mosquitoes and sand flies were thick at night. Supply disruptions had created a tobacco shortage. Home was unreachable. People were crying silently in the dark. A goodly number of these people hadn't yet reached their twentieth birthdays.

These were the lads who would be driven forward soon in the next assault. An image on the television: a Marine Amtrack rolled over, upended in a swamp—literally, a quagmire.

Donald Rumsfeld had taken to threatening Iranians and Syrians and excoriating the press for their "mood swings." Rumsfeld was living to regret his Orwellian propaganda ploy of "embedding" the press. Now many stood to become witnesses.

His revolution in military affairs had become a revolution in rationalizations.

The conventional generals, steeped in their own orthodoxies, were saying Rumsfeld's mistake was trying to "do it on the cheap," that he didn't put enough forces on the ground. He stretched them thin along their primary avenue of approach to Baghdad and exposed their supply lines. This was all true, but it's very incomplete.

My outgoing battalion commander when I first reported in the 2nd Ranger Battalion in 1979 was then-colonel Wayne Downing. Downing is a retired general now, and was another pundit working for MSNBC. He had a different take. "These are people who love their country," he said, "and apparently they're willing to fight to defend it from an invader." I didn't see him again after that.

When Downing and I were assigned to the 1970s Rangers, we trained incessantly on the same kinds of tactics that were being employed by the Iraqis. Reconnaissance, ambush, and raid.

Rumsfeld's error was not only the size of his forces. What the media had failed to recognize was the role that technology played not only in projecting violence onto the battlefield, but in replacing the intuition of field commanders with digital calculations to make decisions.

The administration had impressed the whole chain of command into the service of lies. The U.S. killed civilians in a marketplace: "The Iraqis did it." The Iraqis were "forcing their own people to wage suicide attacks." What began with an insipid conversation about whether or not Saddam was dead had progressed through a chemical factory that wasn't operational, a Basra uprising that didn't exist, thousands of phantom Iraqi prisoners of war, the miraculous rediscovery of the Geneva Convention, to this lurid tale retold by *Washington Post* reporter Thomas Lippman on March 28:

> As U.S. warplanes pounded Iraqi defenders with bombs and missiles, several Army and Marine units engaged in close combat with Iraqi paramilitary forces and regular army units. Brooks said they "conducted active security operations to eliminate identified terrorist death squads," a reference to Iraqi cadres who U.S. and British officials say are threatening Iraqi civilians to compel the men in their families to fight.
>
> Rumsfeld said these "death squads" take orders directly from Hussein's family, and he denounced them in some of the strongest language he has used since the war began.
>
> "Their ranks are populated with criminals released from Iraqi prisons," he said. "They dress in civilian clothes and operate from private homes confiscated from innocent peo-

ple and try to blend in with the civilian population. They conduct sadistic executions on sidewalks and public squares, cutting the tongues out of those accused of disloyalty and beheading people with swords. They put on American and British uniforms to try to fool regular Iraqi soldiers into surrendering to them, and then execute them as an example for others who might contemplate defection or capitulation."

Cutting out tongues. Other rumors suggested "the Fedayeen also run after dogs in the capitol, capture them, tear their limbs one by one, and sink their teeth into them. They had finally outdone the 1990 Kuwaiti incubator story, where Iraqi soldiers allegedly dumped Kuwaiti infants on the floor of the hospital to die, an outright fabrication by the PR outfit Hill & Knowlton—under contract with the Kuwaiti royal family—to whip up support for the first U.S. invasion of Iraq. The outrageous story was publicized through Congressional hearings stage-managed by California Congressman Tom Lantos, complete with phony witnesses who turned out themselves to be members of the Kuwaiti ruling family.

On March 28, Lt. Gen. William S. Wallace of the U.S. Army had a moment of clarity when he spoke the real truth: "The enemy that we're fighting is different from the one we'd war-gamed." Van Riper must have had a grim chuckle.

Saddam Hussein had become the embodiment of a resurgent Arab pride. Bush had been reduced to one of those dolls with a string on its back that you pull to hear "Iraq will be free, Iraq will be free, Iraq will be free."

It might have been funny if had it not been for the gloomy truth that the price of admission to this farce was a river of blood.

On March 29, a suicide bomber in Najaf killed four GIs and the rules of engagement (ROE). Now the war would begin to take on a Vietnam-like character for American soldiers and Marines, who were pushed one step closer to seeing the entire Iraqi people as the enemy. It was after this that the non-in-bed press from outside the U.S. would begin to send out photos of dead Iraqi soldiers, heads blown off next to the white flags that the U.S. soldiers didn't think to remove from the scene. And civilians would be more routinely shot dead at U.S. checkpoints.

Generals grew nervous as the "operational pause" began to stretch out and U.S. positions became almost semi-permanent installations, bait for hit-and-run guerrilla attacks. CENTCOM said on March 31 that the U.S. might wait weeks to begin its assault on Baghdad, which was probably a ruse to lure defenders at Baghdad into the open to strengthen positions so they might be attacked more effectively by air. The same day, Robin Cook, the House of Commons leader and Blair cabinet member who resigned on March 17 to protest the war, launched a blistering criticism of Tony Blair.

Euphoria began to infect the Arab world. People began to identify with the tenacity of these Iraqi defenders of their homeland against the juggernaut of U.S. militarism. Many anti-imperialists outside the Arab world caught the same bug. No head for numbers.

Perhaps the most brilliant aspect of the U.S. strategy was the "embedded journalists" program. This is a masterpiece of Powell Doctrine: controlling public perceptions.

The criticism of the military "pool" system from the first Gulf War was checkmated. Reporters were put directly on the battlefield and integrated into the actual military units. Those reporters are then dependent on the troops around them for their daily human contact, and grow quickly to identify directly with the people in those units.

Overt censorship was no longer needed.

But as the campaign went further and further awry, there was a chance the embedded journalists would see some of their new friends wounded and killed, and then Powell's anxiety would be realized, with a messy war in our living rooms again, just like Vietnam. This fear of graphic audio-visual images of war was why there was such outrage at al-Jazeera showing dead GIs.

In the north, far from the most visible action, the Turkish military had already begun its incursions. The Kurds, in response, were already signing onto yet another Faustian deal with the Americans, now mostly Special Operations—Rangers to seize airheads and Special Forces to establish relationships with the Kurdish fighters. Without its northern front, the U.S. was more dependent than ever on using Kurdish combatants to fight the Iraqis around the rich oilfields near Kirkuk.

Fragile Turkey was beset by a severe economic crisis. Its majority-Muslim population had just elected a moderate Islamic Party and the popular opposition to the war was overwhelming.

The Turkish ruling class could not afford another insurrection from Kurdish nationalists, and the Turkish military had no intention of watching a Kurdish state take form to their south. As a result of the U.S. invasion of Iraq, Turkey was becoming a powder keg behind its stable exterior, and Kurdistan was a furnace.

The political implications reach deep into Europe, where less than two years ago the U.S. pushed behind the scenes for the admission of Turkey into the EU as a stalking horse. Germany has a substantial population of Turks and Kurds, and the German government still has a real and justifiable fear that open warfare in Iraqi Kurdistan will spill over into the streets of Germany.

To mollify the Kurds, the U.S. had to menace back the Turkish military, and the Kurds softened their language about an independent Kurdistan.

That diplomatic minefield was fobbed off on Colin Powell. If he didn't feel a trickle of sweat between his shoulder blades, he wasn't paying attention. If the invasion had encountered much more resistance, heads would have rolled, and the visceral enmity between Powell and Richard Perle was well-known. It's Powell, the Kissinger-style realist and brilliant bureaucrat, versus Perle, the racist, right-wing visionary. There were already whispers that Powell would be scapegoated after the war, and other rumors that Cheney, Rumsfeld, Wolfowitz, and Perle would be handed walking papers, and Powell would run in 2004 as Cheney's replacement for vice president.

Perle—called the "Prince of Darkness" by friends and critics for his legendary ruthlessness—resigned under a cloud on April 2003. Seymour Hersch had written an article about Perle's recent meeting with arms-dealer Adnan Khashoggi of Iran-Contra fame. Perle was considering a business deal with Saudi financiers. Perle had earlier excoriated Saudis as supporters of terrorism. And Khashoggi was already being investigated by freelancers for his role in the 2000 election on behalf of George W. Bush. Keeping Khashoggi below the public radar apparently outweighed Perle's contribution to the administration.

Uranium Rain

Bombs began to rain on Baghdad again. Colin Powell was trying to placate the Turks. Rumsfeld—stung with deep humiliation—began to make threatening noises at the Iranians and Syrians as the firestorm of recriminations in Washington raged and the damaged umbilical supply line from Kuwait was repaired.

By April 1, U.S. ground forces on point had refueled and refit, and they were ready to resume the offensive. The cautious advance north began on the second, with the 3rd (Mechanized) Infantry Division backed by paratroops from the 82nd, Apache helicopters from the 101st advancing on the Karbala Gap, and the 1st Marine Expeditionary Force moving on Al Kut in the Tigris Valley. Special Forces in the north were organizing with the Kurds, as supplies now flowed in by air, for an attack on Mosul and Kirkuk, where some of the richest oilfields in the world lie.

The Iraqis fought a delaying action in the Karbala Gap, but multiple engagements had given U.S. commanders the experience necessary to develop countermeasures to the Iraqis' new (Russian-designed?) asymmetric tactics. The Iraqis now began to suffer from a loss of command and control as well as a genuine lack of fresh tactical adaptation. U.S. commanders had adapted, however, and regained their technological advantage, their logistical tail, and above all, their air superiority.

Iraqi combat losses were horrific, and in short order, the Nebuchadnezzar and Medina divisions of the Republican Guard melted back into Baghdad, leaving small ambushes along the route to delay the Americans.

Firing precious anti-aircraft weapons became a death warrant, so the Iraqi triple-A was retired northward, probably beyond Baghdad. And U.S. commanders had forged a seamless integration of A-10 Warthogs with ground units to open up defenses in advance of ground attacks.

The A-10 is a 30-mm Gatling gun with an airframe built around it—firing up to 4,200 rounds a minute of depleted uranium alloy bullets. It is comparatively slow, so it can only be put to good use when there is total air superiority. But it is one of the most agile fixed-wing aircraft in history. In one second, the A-10 can reduce a tank to a scorched shell or shatter a fighting position. Working in pairs, the A-10s can rubble multi-story building in five minutes, or—as General Barry McCaffrey demonstrated in 1991—they can transform a retreating column of thousands of men and hundreds of tanks into a meandering file of smoldering wreckage and dismembered corpses.

Corpses have now become a familiar phenomenon for a new generation of U.S. soldiers. Many will return now with their heads filled with corpses and their bodies filled with depleted uranium. They will have their moment of intoxicating adulation in public. The corpses will sneak up on them in private. Then the uranium will begin to take its toll.

Some people learn to live with corpses. Some learn to relish the freedom of killing and develop a taste for it. Perfect masculinity is sociopathic. A young Marine who had just killed a woman at a checkpoint matter-of-factly stated, "The chick was in the way."[1] Gangster. Badass.

Others, as the transitory adulation fades, will sense the barrenness of their wounded psyches backlit by the barrenness of a decaying consumer culture, and their alienation will flower into addiction, psychosis, suicide . . . and then we will be taught to see *them* as pathological.

We didn't see that pathology on April 3, not in the troops, not in ourselves, not on CNN. Like the air, we breathe alienation until we take it for granted. *Community* is what is abnormal. On April 3, we watched the seizure of Saddam Hussein Airport on the outskirts of Baghdad, and CENTCOM led the cheer.

Rumsfeld's pet drones began buzzing like Tigris River mosquitoes over Baghdad, trying to vindicate themselves at $37 million apiece for Global Hawks, $40 million for Predators (not factoring in years of R&D money). They shot pictures of Iraqis pointing skyward at them, as combatants took the complex countermeasure of stepping under a doorway to evade their digital gaze. Then the real planes came.

A-10s again, like lethal storms tearing into Baghdad's suburbs, shattering the homes and histories of the ancient city in advance of the next ground assault.

This was the new strategy: incremental mass murder. And it began to gain traction.

Saddam Hussein Airport was renamed by its occupiers. Ali Hassan al-Majid—"Chemical Ali" was the name given to him by the press in their frenzy to find new caricatures for their melodrama—was allegedly bombed (now he's alive again, yet another miraculous resurrection), and this story was fanned for days—the latest smokescreen to preoccupy the American herd so it wouldn't be awakened to the uncaricatured corpses.

War of Symbols

The 3rd Infantry made its little foray—a reconnaissance in force—into Baghdad on April 5, met with sporadic but furious resistance from those who lurked in doorways as the drones flew helplessly over the day before. The hospitals in Baghdad were now overwhelmed, corpses lying sloppily under blankets in the corners of rooms, the most critical left to die while doctors and nurses worked around the clock to salvage the salvageable with meager resources. Reports filtered out past the compliant media that the floors were swimming in human blood, the flies drawn to it in buzzing pestilential clouds.

The Iraqi fighters—now a symbol to a hopeful and humiliated Arab world—found reality singularly unsymbolic. Their new Russianized tactics were being met with the cancellation of Rumsfeld's cyberwar and the U.S. adaptation of sending blood, rubble, and dust down the streets with the A-10s. Their decentralization—at first an advantage, even when applied in an often amateurish and tragically costly way— now became simple disarray in the face of the lethal rain of uranium.

The U.S. was demonstrating its resolve to conquer Baghdad by converting it to rubble if necessary, and civilians were paying an appalling price. Then some "leftists," safely ensconced in Europe and the U.S., began publicly dressing down the Iraqi combatants for not paying the ultimate price to turn Baghdad into an Armageddon.

The lights went out in Baghdad, and the U.S. forces tore a path to the banks of the Tigris. On April 7, the U.S. tested its bunker buster munitions on a house where they claim they thought Saddam was hiding. The U.S. press made scant mention of the civilian deaths, including children, as CNN et al. went into yet another three-day speculation frenzy about the visceral status of one man.

Killing civilians was routine by now. This harrowing description from Laurent van der Stockt, a Gamma Agency photographer with the *New York Times Magazine*:

> On the morning of April 7, the Marines decided to cross the bridge. A shell fell onto an armored personnel carrier. Two marines were killed. The crossing took on a tragic aspect. The soldiers were stressed, febrile. They were shouting. The risk didn't appear to be that great, so I followed their advance. They were howling, shouting orders and positions to each other. It sounded like something in-between a phantasm, mythology and conditioning. The operation was transformed into crossing the bridge over the River Kwai.
>
> Later, there was some open terrain. The Marines were advancing and taking up position, hiding behind mounds of earth. They were still really tense. A small blue van was moving towards the convoy. Three not-very-accurate warning shots were fired. The shots were supposed to make the van stop. The van kept on driving, made a U-turn, took shelter and then returned slowly. The Marines opened fire. All hell broke loose. They were firing all over the place. You could hear "Stop firing" being shouted. The silence that set in was overwhelming. Two men and a woman had just been riddled with bullets. So this was the enemy, the threat.
>
> A second vehicle drove up. The same scenario was repeated. Its passengers were killed on the spot. A grandfather was walking slowly with a cane on the sidewalk. They killed him too. As with the old man, the Marines fired on a SUV driving along the river bank that was getting too close to them. Riddled with bullets, the vehicle rolled over. Two women and a child got out, miraculously still alive. They sought refuge in the wreckage. A few seconds later, it flew into bits as a tank lobbed a terse shot into it . . .
>
> With my own eyes I saw about fifteen civilians killed in two days. I've gone through enough wars to know that it's always dirty, that civilians are always the first victims. But the way it was happening here, it was insane.

Resistance shrank into pockets, some still doggedly determined while the bulk of the resistors melted away behind the screen. Tens of thousands of Iraqi combatants are missing to this day, and speculation that they might eventually use Syria as a jumping-off point to stage operations back into their nation has led the U.S. administration to rattle its saber, even as U.S. capacity to wage war effectively anywhere else in the world right now is next to zero.

If ever there were a time to thumb one's nose at the U.S., it is now. It is a big dog at the end of a thick chain.

The imperial crowing about this lopsided attack is tempered behind the scenes by the knowledge that—contrary to all the bullshit about destruction of Iraqi units—the boldest sacrifices by Iraqi fighters were made not in conventional confrontations but in delaying tactics. Those tactics worked. The Iraqis took good advantage of the U.S. aversion to high "friendly" casualties and their obsession with "force protection." The fact is, the lion's share of Iraqi forces had managed an orderly retreat . . . somewhere, and the U.S. suspected Syria.

There were still thousands of tanks and armored personnel carriers unaccounted for in Iraq, and they didn't drive themselves away. Hundreds of thousands of small arms. Up to three thousand wire-guided anti-armor missiles. Over fifteen hundred artillery pieces, possibly a half dozen SCUD launchers, more than a thousand MOWAG light anti-aircraft weapons as well as a decent supply of unfired surface-to-air Missiles, a dozen Hind attack helicopters, several dozen smaller choppers, and up to two dozen PC-7 and PC-9 fixed-wing aircraft.

These numbers haunt U.S. military commanders, as they should. They didn't faze Rumsfeld, who was already becoming self-congratulatory over his great victory.

On April 8, the U.S. tested the new limits of its impunity by deliberately attacking a convoy with the Russian ambassador, then claimed it was a "crossfire." Only days before, Rumsfeld in one of his more frequent fits of pique, had made threatening noises at the Russians.

Al-Jazeera had been publicly chastised days earlier in a CENTCOM briefing for daring to show American dead (and thereby eroding domestic support for the adventure). They should have paid attention. When al-Jazeera engaged in journalism in Afghanistan, the Americans had unapologetically bombed their offices.

On April 8, the American forces destroyed the al-Jazeera offices in

Baghdad and simultaneously attacked independent journalists in the Palestine Hotel. The symbolism of the name was not lost on the Arab world, as the U.S. tested the feasibility of eliminating witnesses.

Countersymbolism was deployed the following day. As the U.S. continued the slaughter, thrusting from three directions into Baghdad and initiating its attack to take Kirkuk, the American military gathered together a sparse crowd around a Saddam Hussein statue, then pulled it down while the fake crowd cheered. The embedded press, in a shameless and slavish display, kept their lenses tight to make the paltry mob appear larger. That image plays still today—long after it has been repeatedly exposed as a tawdry scam. They even refused to show the American flag that one overenthusiastic young Marine had used to cover the statue's face. A little too much symbolism there.

Rumsfeld cracked on television once, when the word "occupation" was uttered, saying over and over, "It's a liberation, it's a liberation, it's a liberation."

Then the looting began, and the U.S. stood by. I saw it in Haiti. Let the chaos rein for a bit and they will beg for order, even if it comes from unwelcome quarters. Certain facilities were protected, like the oil ministry building. Then there was the most symbolic event of the war, in my opinion.

Iraq is the geographic and cultural cradle of Western civilization. The U.S. military was sent to attack this cradle of civilization, and the U.S. military initiated the looting of the Museum of Archeology, where seven thousand years worth of priceless artifacts were kept for posterity. Eyewitnesses report that before the looting began, Americans had been keeping the streets clear with gunfire. Then they pulled up in front of the museum and started firing into it. I saw a tank round's hole in the front on a CNN report, far too high for a looter to have made it. They murdered the two Sudanese guards in front of the administrative building, then directed the looters, *through the U.S. military's Arabic translators*, to enter the building and gut it.[2] By April 15, the National Archives as well, where millions of pages of historical documents, some centuries old, were stored, was looted, some of the precious records burned by a street mob while U.S. military looked complacently on.

The Nondenouement & More Moral Imperialism

The rest of the story could sound like a denouement. Kirkuk fell. Mosul fell.

On May 1, 2003, George W. Bush engaged in a bit of political theater that should have embarrassed even his supporters. Flown onto the deck of the carrier U.S.S. *Abraham Lincoln* in a fighter jet, stepping out in his flight coveralls to give a thumbs-up to dutifully cheering crew members, Bush declared that the war in Iraq was over. Banner in the background, placed strategically by his handlers for the camera frame: Mission Accomplished. (In a late October news conference, he had the temerity to claim that his people didn't hang the banner.)

The further up the tree the monkey climbs, the more all you can see is his ass.

Now politics would began, the war was anything but over, and the Bush junta would begin to see just what kind of tar baby it had here.

"Intelligence leaks" began to trickle out and circulate on the most uncontrollable communications medium in the world, email lists. Saddam was alive and well, and reorganizing with forty thousand fighters. Rense.com, a shoot-from-the-hip anti-imperialist/conspiracy-affinity web site, published this report on May Day, and it spread like a drought fire.

Many considered the source and chalked it up to a combination of sloppy journalism, polemical frustration, and Ba'athist bravado. Included in the report was the repetition of the claim that the abrupt fall of Baghdad was a case of bribery and betrayal by key Iraqi commanders, in particular Jamal Mustafa al-Umar, Saddam's son-in-law. Many others, crestfallen at the inevitable military victory of the U.S., bought this story, never appreciating the reality of uranium rain.

But there was resistance planning afoot. That much was inevitable.

If there was any validity at all in this "betrayal thesis," it has to be taken into account that in war, bribery counts too. The more important thing to understand, however, is that the Americans were determined to take Baghdad, and they had the means to do it. Wasting more Iraqi combatants in a high-attrition toe-to-toe confrontation with them would severely deplete any future capacity for "asymmetrical" resistance.

> "A people who want to win independence
> cannot confine themselves to ordinary
> methods of warfare. Mass insurrections,
> revolutionary warfare, guerilla detachments
> everywhere—such is the only way."
> —Frederick Engels

The more the U.S. was allowed to consolidate militarily, the more quickly could resistance forces take their measure of them and begin to craft an anti-occupation struggle. The Americans were now in a position where there were no trusted agents—only competing agendas—leaving the U.S. military isolated, continually deluded by their own cultural myopia. U.S. military commanders would come to rely on the distorted and self-serving reports of opportunists, filtered again through their own ground forces, to construct a strategic picture for themselves.

This was precisely the situation in Haiti, where without any armed struggle at all, the U.S. would finally withdraw its military occupation. Ignorance, too, can be a remarkable weapon. The liberation fighters of the future will learn to make allies of chaos and their enemy's ignorance, which feed each other.

Perhaps even more importantly, Halliburton was already surveying the oil refineries, where they were met with sullen hostility by the "liberated" Iraqi oil workers.[3] Within a month, the principle of simplicity—long understood by the Colombian ELN—would lead Iraqi resisters to an unprotectable target, the network of oil pipelines.

In Turkey, meanwhile, Nicholas Birch of the *Irish Times* reported, "Trying to understand the idiosyncracies of Turkish politics? Start by looking at the images on Turkish television yesterday and today, of the monthly National Security Council meeting . . . On the left, some smiling, some slouched in their chairs, the country's senior cabinet ministers. On the right, straight-backed and stern, generals."

One is reminded of the lesson the Chinese learned regarding flies. During the Cultural Revolution, the whole nation was mobilized to eradicate houseflies. And it was a nearly complete success. But then a species of eagle nearly went extinct, and salmon fisheries began to die off. This was the lesson of unintended consequences; Murphy's law meets chaos theory. They allowed the flies to reflourish, and the eagles and salmon came back.

The American occupation began to reverberate thus into Turkish parliament. Where will the ripples go internationally? In Baghdad, retired General Jay Garner, a devout Zionist and an *intifada* magnet, held a meeting with Iraqis and excluded nearly every organization with a genuine popular base. By mid-May, Garner was cast out in a stunning reversal that the American media pretended was meaningless—but which represented a brick wall into which the junta had run face first, blinded yet again by its own hubris.

Soon, a new town would gain recognition in American popular discourse: Fallujah. In Afghanistan, the U.S. refused to send stabilization forces into the hinterlands. There is no oil there. In Fallujah (and every other key city), U.S. soldiers were sent there whether anyone wanted it or not.

Once Iraqi combatants displaced from Fallujah, local imams stepped in. They stopped the looting and vengeance attacks, re-opened public services, and established an interim constabulary. Normalcy was beginning to take hold there, then the Bradley fighting vehicles rolled into town in late April, and the Americans took over a recently re-opened school for their headquarters, arrested the imams, installed their own mayor, and roadblocked the whole city. These actions were their orders, orders from people who knew nothing of Iraqi society, and this ignorance was delivered into the hands of the Iraqi resistance like a priceless gift.

Popular outrage was swift. The Americans—still tightly strung from recent combat—were besieged by angry demonstrators, who they then began to shoot. Between April 28 and April 30, twenty Iraqis were killed and scores wounded.[4] Lies about weapons in the crowds were concocted, and eyewitnesses were effectively excluded from the American media. CENTCOM could say anything, no matter the number of witnesses, and it would be given equal weight against all claims to the contrary.

But lies are only misrepresentations of reality. They do not erase reality. In Fallujah, the masses were now served a helping of occupation reality, and they were galvanized by it. Resistance is fertilized by blood, and the American guns in Fallujah nourished the greening fields of Iraqi opposition. The popular basis for a guerrilla struggle had been established by the American military's hand, and it wouldn't be long in coming. A whole population was now prepared to take a supportive role in an armed resistance. This was a signpost, but it was written in a foreign tongue for the Americans.

On May 8, Patrick Healy of the *Boston Globe* reported from Fallujah:

> Abraham Ghanan's body is stunted by malnutrition—a 16-year-old whose sallow frame is fit for a boy of 10—but he keeps his arms strong, he says, in hopes of throwing grenades with perfect aim someday.
>
> "I eat in the morning, a little in the day, not at night," Ghanan said, standing outside a U.S. Army outpost in this city's center. "But I have strength to kill. We want to put bombs on our body, to make a suicide operation to show we are not down."
>
> "These soldiers, they are the sons of George Bush," adds Omar Nizar, a reed-thin, barefoot 14-year-old. "We will fight them."
>
> Stunning poverty and youthful bravado are a dangerous, common combination on the streets of Fallujah, known for its proud Bedouin families whose hot-headed streaks are legendary.

Perhaps so. But on the day of this report, the armed resistance had already begun in earnest, and it was anything but hot-headed. It was systematic, well planned, and effective. In Baghdad and Fallujah, attacks combining assault rifles and rocket propelled grenades had begun. In a week, thirteen U.S. servicemen were killed, even as Paul Wolfowitz, the neocon heavy with the Defense Department, grew impatient with his own cover stories and openly conceded that Iraq would never have been targeted were it not for the oil. This was after a mid-May strike by suicide bombers in Riyadh, Saudi Arabia, killed thirty-four people, including eight Americans.

In the last week of May, the U.S. occupation authority announced that half a million Iraqis, including the army, would be terminated without pay. The resistance recruitment ground had expanded. In May alone, there had been at least eighty-five attacks against American soldiers, but now they were achieving new levels of sophistication.[5]

The number of American wounded during this first week and a half of June was unknown, but they were likely to be far higher than fatalities. The employment of full-truncal body armor and Kevlar helmets have dramatically reduced the fatalities among U.S. casualties. Heart and lungs are covered fore and aft, as well as half the head.

The attacks were triangulated, engaging U.S. forces from two or more points, and coordinating the use of Soviet-era RPGs and Kalashnikov assault rifles. Striking in this way, with both bullets and explosives, from more than one direction, removes the element of cover from targeted forces. When they get behind one side of the vehicle to take cover from fire, they are exposed to fire from another direction. When they use the vehicle's light armor to block rifle ammunition, the RPGs can be used against that same armor for concussion, secondary missile hazard, and flame.

If the Iraqi resistance acquires precision, long-range rifles—real sniper weapons—and learns to integrate them with these omnidirectional ambushes, they will become a formidable and terrifying force. Precision shooters do not target people. They target body parts like surgeons. And they have standoff.

When I was a sniper, we would bet cases of beer on which eye of an FBI "cartoon" target we could hit at two hundred yards. We shot poker chips at a hundred yards. At four hundred yards, we could hit within a four-inch circle with machine-like regularity. Snipers shoot *around* body armor and Kevlar helmets. Iliac and femoral arteries. Under an armpit where there is no armor and a bullet can find lungs, heart, aorta. Through the nose and out the brain stem. Or through an elbow or a knee, wounding and disabling an enemy combatant for good, forcing four of his comrades to carry him, and shifting the mission from combat to medical evacuation.

The reason many militaries don't employ snipers or sniper training is centralization of command. Sniper teams consist of two to three people, with spotter and shooter working in tandem, and maybe one security person to protect the spotter-shooter position. These small independent teams are anathema to centralized command structures like the former Iraqi military. But now, there is space for innovation.

Innovation had already happened by June 8, and the methods of a Van Riper had begun to emerge. Horn honks, camouflaged among traffic, were used to pass signals. Some honks were employed to relay the size and direction of approaching forces. Noncombatant foot messengers relayed information to fighting positions about the positions of American troops.[6]

This kind of multiple pinprick strategy has two objectives: one, to stretch your enemy's capacity thin in force protection, and two, to drive a permanent wedge between the occupier and the population.

Lieutenant Harry Heinz, a twenty-five year-old white boy from Georgia running a Bradley platoon deployed to Fallujah, cracked in front of reporters. Punctuating his speech by pounding a table, he spat at them, "If they kill one of our guys, it's going to be tenfold. If you shoot one round, I'll shoot a thousand. You have to make an example . . . We're like a pit bull on a chain. You cut the chain and you're going to have problems."[7]

Lieutenant Heinz was taking the bait. He said this before the coordinated attacks had even begun.

Fallujah would have more significance than being the emblem of resistance. It can also be counted among the emblems of the loss of credibility for Bush and Blair.

Chlorine is routinely used around the world for all the things we know so well, not the least of which is water purification. There is a chlorine plant in Fallujah. In May, Colin Powell, ever the loyal sycophant, declared that the Fallujah chlorine plant was a mustard gas facility. This was one declaration in a growing list of claims about weapons of mass destruction that failed again and again to materialize, and that were the beginning of the end of Bush/Blair legitimacy. Along with the failure of the war to be over, as Bush had claimed on the USS *Abraham Lincoln*, the mainstream press had finally picked up the story that the rest of us had been telling since Scott Ritter dropped a dime on the CIA-controlled weapons inspections teams in 1998. There were no "weapons of mass destruction" (WMD).

John Pilger quipped that Tony Blair would have WMD etched into his political headstone. George W. Bush is already eligible for impeachment, and all that's missing is the public outcry and a Democratic major in Congress. The evidence is abundantly clear.

The U.S., now under siege by the press for the WMD issue and the reluctance of Iraqis to observe George Bush's declaration of peace, decided to re-amplify the war by blaming all attacks against Americans on "terrorists" from Saddam's old government. All attacks, henceforth, would be conducted, according to CENTCOM and their U.S. press corps, by "Saddam loyalists" or "Saddam holdouts." It was to be Saddam again, the one evil man.

But collective punishment was in order, and the U.S. was now to be converted into an Israeli-like occupation force. Operation Peninsula Strike commenced on June 11, followed immediately by Operation Desert Scorpion, with over four thousand armor, mechanized infantry, and light infantry troops, accompanied by massive air support, in a zone that would be called the Sunni Triangle, from Baghdad to Fallujah to Balad. In Fallujah proper, an equal number of troops were employed in an assault designed to become a sustained and direct occupation.[8] In the one decisive ground engagement, an American F-15 and an Apache helicopter were downed, but for these prizes, the Iraqi fighters paid dearly. Air power was concentrated on them at a "camp" around ninety miles West of Baghdad, and over one hundred Iraqis lost their lives under a lethal downpour of U.S. ordnance. Elsewhere, U.S. troops simply went house-to-house terrorizing residents, handcuffing toddlers, beating down people with rifle butts, and trashing their homes.[9] Hundreds of Iraqi civilians were killed.

Part of the Bush plan to divert the U.S. public and to attempt to soften Arab/Muslim rage around the world was the implementation—in the midst of the growing Iraqi guerrilla resistance—of the so-called "roadmap to peace," another formulaic imposition from the neocons and the "Quartet" (U.S., U.N., Russia, EU), to interrupt the Israeli aggression against Palestine and the corresponding Palestinian resistance. During the Bush regime's aggression on Iraq, Ariel Sharon had intensified Israeli savagery against the whole Palestinian population with the tacit approval of the neocons, who are, generally speaking, Zionists themselves.

The whole roadmap scheme was given a red carpet by the press, while close observers from the region said there didn't seem to be much that had changed. The demand that a Palestinian rump, hand-picked by the U.S. and Israel, would stop all Palestinians from engaging in armed struggle was at the top of the list, and this alone was a non-starter. But the Bush plan was to switch emphasis.

Bush & Co. attempted to use their newfound position in the region to lay the law down to Israel . . . we don't need you as our forward-deployed imperial surrogate any longer, so you'd better go along with the program. But, like everything, they overestimated themselves and the value of a merely military disposition. In Israel, Sharon's willingness to bow to U.S. pressure provoked a deep political crisis for the Likud and almost fractured it.

Just as the U.S. press was on the verge of giving George W. Bush a slow hand job for his success with the "roadmap," a suicide bomber in Jerusalem killed sixteen people, and Sharon countered by launching two savage air attacks against Palestinians in Gaza. George Bush moved to reinforce his authority with Sharon by publicly criticizing the Israelis, and then Bush felt the sting of Israel's true strength in the U.S.: political strength based in Jewish Zionist blocs in key electoral zones and in the substantial minority of the Republican Party base that is Evangelical Christian and Zionist. One tiny censure of Sharon by Bush, and Zionism bared its teeth through Democratic Party electoral threats. There is no possibility—politically—in the current situation in the U.S., of any viable presidential contender defying Israel.

Attack followed counterattack, and Bush found himself standing amidst a swirl of violence over which he could exercise no control—he, the master of the hegemon nation, commander of the most expensive military in history, surrounded by his mad courtiers. And all I found myself thinking as I watched through daily news updates was, *Welcome to Palestine, motherfucker!*

By June 14, the press was openly ridiculing the roadmap; the questions about WMDs were a daily feature; the U.S. military headquarters in Ramadi, Iraq came under an intense mortar attack; and insurgents fired rockets at a U.S. installation in eastern Afghanistan—where by now battalion-sized elements of the supposedly defeated Taliban were roaming parts of the country with impunity.[10]

The military occupation was a fact on the ground. The Washington gangsters had occupied their new turf. Now we'll see if they can keep it. There will certainly be no new military adventures for a while, at least not if the Bush junta has an ounce of rational capacity left to them. Again, those who fear this have not done the arithmetic, political or military. The United States has extended its military reach almost to its conventional limit, number one, and two, the objective was Europe and China, with Iraq's petroleum the strategic key.

The antiwar movement needs to quit letting these gangsters and their sycophant press spook them, and quit confusing ruling class blather with ruling class motivations.

Bush's apocalyptic-sounding soundbytes about evil was a sop to the Christian right in the United States who believe this period is the fulfillment of Biblical prophecy. They are a key part of the Bush regime's popular base in the United States. But the neocons' blueprint, laid out some years ago, for leaping over this period of an impending severe crisis of U.S. hegemony, is hard-eyed secularism. Their true weaknesses are ruling class myopia and astonishing hubris. They are constitutionally incapable of understanding history as a process that involves the masses.

Neoliberalism—the form of U.S. imperialism—was falling into disarray before September 11. It was a transformation of U.S. imperialism that dated back to the Nixon administration, wherein the industrialized North collaborated in the harvest of the dependent global South. The character of that transformation has been written on at length—but dollar hegemony was its linchpin, and the basis of dollar hegemony, at the end of the day, is military might.

The story was told of journalists who traveled in Laos in the final days of the Vietnam War. They went to a Chinese roadside boutique to buy cigarettes. A Pathet Lao guerrilla was buying a few necessities, and he paid for them in Pathet Lao currency. When a journalist stepped up and offered the Chinese mini-merchant Pathet Lao currency for his cigarettes, he was refused. Objecting that the guerrilla had just paid with that currency, the Chinese merchant told the journalist, "He had the gun."

The most fundamental former characteristic of neoliberalism was that this "benign" leadership of the U.S. was accepted by lesser imperial powers because the U.S. served as an essential umpire for a multilateral system of exploitation and accumulation.

The difference between the neoliberals (think of the Democrats) in the U.S. and the neocons (think crypto-fascists among the Republicans) is not on the question of exploitation and accumulation. They are equally devoted to preserving the status and privileges of the U.S. ruling class, of which both are a part.

The difference revolves around two opposing delusions; the neoliberal delusion that there is a way to return to the multilateral gluttony of the recent past—with the U.S. reassuming its public role of benevolent father (while discreetly destroying economic rivals with finance capital as a weapon of statecraft)—and the neocon delusion that the U.S. can have its economic cake and eat it too, escaping the law of value by playing the part of a global protection racket on energy markets.

The neoliberals cannot solve the problem of rebellion in the periphery and the organic composition of capital—ever increaasing masses of productive hardware run by ever fewer workers and ever smaller aggregates of profit. The neocons cannot solve the problem of military costs, economic and political.

Meanwhile, back in the U.S.A., the initiation of wholesale hostilities on March 20 erased the broadest basis of its unity for the antiwar movement.

The strength of the broad antiwar movement prior to H-hour was the convergence of different political tendencies, including many sections of the managerial and ruling classes, around a single demand: No War!

Anti-imperialists were standing exposed again, no longer folded unobtrusively into the larger mass. Liberals (including neoliberals) immediately began their retreat down familiar paths.

Not least among them was the denunciation of Ba'ath Party leadership, especially of Saddam Hussein. This was a world-class red herring. Ba'athism was a movement that could not be judged through the rosy lenses of Western morality. It's akin to measuring Black prejudice with the same yardstick used to measure white prejudice. The reality of relations of power make these points of view irreconcilably and qualitatively different.

Moral imperialism (again) is such a very slippery slope.

Ritual denunciation of Saddam Hussein before, during, and after the 2003 invasion did not prevent the antiwar movement from being mercilessly red-baited and patriot-baited. What it did do was set the stage for a huge fraction of the pre-H-hour antiwar movement to have its legs knocked out from under it when tanks rolled north. The failure to grasp the nature of U.S. imperialism and how it was responsible long before the war—as a global system—for every single aspect of the situation in Southwest Asia, left so-called progressives grappling in the dark after ahistorical moral comparisons. These judgments were based on a thirteen-year campaign of demonization, and then after military operations were predictably successful, calling for the U.N. to take up the task of occupation. Not an end to occupation, but a kinder, gentler, legitimizing occupation.

Michael Keaney, an economist living in Finland, put it well when he noted that

> various people in the metropolitan left are, in the midst of all that is going on at present, spending valuable time and resources telling others on the left "I told you so" or lecturing them on the finer points of "democracy" when the real task at hand is to work against imperialism. Under current circumstances, the effective result of getting even slightly bogged down by this "sugar-coating" is to legitimate imperialism. We surrender valuable ground when we give any credence whatsoever to the propaganda claims of cruise missile liberals and neo-cons alike concerning other regimes whose development has been twisted, tortured, stunted, manipulated, thwarted, squashed, halted . . . by the constant interference of the metropolis which has, to use Edward Said's very appropriate phrase, "driven them crazy after decades." And right now I don't really need to hear about the venality of "Saddam". [A] proper class analysis of pre-invasion Iraq would be in order so that we might understand better how things will develop in the future. But quite honestly, for the time being and until it is proved otherwise, Saddam Hussein and his cohort are a part of the anti-imperialist movement.

This recognition has become more important now that there is a real struggle against the American occupiers. That struggle cannot be held to account by the standards of western progressives, even of western leftists. It will require a form of unity and struggle appropriate for those who engage in the resistance, and it will not be pretty enough for BMW Bolsheviks sipping lattes while they plan the resistance for places they've never lived, in circumstances they can never appreciate.

Resistance began in May with the ubiquitous mini-rebellions against American occupation, street mobilizations that forced the U.S. military to withdraw or overreact. The rejections of U.S.–installed colonial surrogate leadership has certainly queered the U.S. pitch. To sustain the disruption will require blinding the U.S. to plans and intents. That will mean merciless ferreting out of collaborators with the U.S. It might even mean suicide bombing. Some might disappear, leaving the country to sharpen their skills: precision marksmanship, non-technical communications, mechanical ambushes, and small-unit planning. Organizing units and staffs, some blending back into the population to monitor the mood of the street. Let the situation ripen. The fault lines are already appearing in Iraqi society, and resistance to the Americans had begun even before the guns fell silent, and now they will not fall silent. Now there is a guerrilla war.

My first guess was that they would wait and plan for one or two totally unexpected and devastating blows delivered when the occupiers guard is down, one to one-and-a-half years from now, maybe more, patiently organizing the insurgency in the meantime, setting up safe houses and rat lines, developing intelligence networks, establishing tactical caches and supply lines. But the resistance has apparently opted to never give a perfect day's rest to the occupiers. And it's their resistance.

We don't know where this will go. Neither does the Bush-Cheney crime family.

Exercising my prerogative as the author, I will editorialize a bit here and say that so-called progressives need to learn how to stand with *whatever is necessary* to expel the invader. People don't choose suicide bombs because the bomber is less ethical than someone in an American suburb. They choose them because it's the only weapon and method left to them in the face of an uncontestable conventional military power. This is the essence of what is now called asymmetric warfare. We cannot put an abstract morality above the people.

LOW-CASUALTY WAR

Cannibalism is blessed.
—Gloria Anzaldua

Morale at home is also a factor as the de facto American rulers continue to reconstruct the world by dint of arms. The economic, then the social costs, will rekindle the political crisis that was temporarily quenched by the 9/11 outburst of national chauvinism.

The official story is becoming more difficult to sustain each day. It persists now only because of the grandest of American appetites: denial. Even that can't last forever. And when it goes too, this administration can add a legitimacy crisis to their lengthening list of woes. It may be this crisis, at the end of the road, that will be their undoing.

Legitimacy may be the key to power in the approaching conjuncture, as the material benefits of imperialism to the First World working class are liquidated in a domestic structural adjustment program. There is a legal facet of legitimacy, as well. George W. Bush committed impeachable offenses in waging war in Iraq. But then there is a Republican majority in Congress, so we shall see.

Along with these other forms of growing delegitimation, there is the shell-game of the low-casualty war.

I was still serviceable when I ran two miles in 11:26 at forty-two years old. I went to the mess hall afterwards and had two pancakes with plenty of butter, patty sausage, bacon, an omelet with cheddar cheese and jalapeno peppers, a boat paddle full of cottage cheese, four glazed doughnuts, and a quart of orange juice.

Once I had a little something on my stomach, I had my first of three 800-mg ibuprofens for that day. The joke used to be that I didn't need the Motrin in pills any more, I needed a Motrin lick outside my door. At this point, my C-7 vertebra was already a half-tick out to the left, where it occasionally and abruptly impinges on a nerve and turns my entire neck into a throbbing, inflexible post.

Stateside, we had deer tick alerts. So I kept plenty of DEET on my skin. While deployed abroad, there was malaria and dengue to think about, so along with DEET, we swallowed chloroquine or mefloquine once a week, and sometimes doxycycline to protect against protozoa and spirochetes like leptospirosis. We started impregnating our uniforms with Permethrin around 1990, which didn't merely repel bugs. It killed them. We were told, no problem, it's okay to have it against your skin—even when you sweat like a quarter horse.

It was around that same time I started taking hydroxizine hydrochloride, a mild antihistamine, every night to control the hives I got from "cholinergic urticaria," which is Latin for "the doc doesn't know what it is." Talking with other vets, I discovered that some of us who sat on the ground and ate their C-rations in "defoliated areas" in Vietnam—as I had—woke up every night with hives.

In Vietnam, they killed foliage with a Dow product called dioxin, Agent Orange, so they could expose logistical shipments by the North Vietnamese Army.

In Panama, they sprayed our street every Thursday with Malathion which is used generously in almost all military camps.

I've had more diagnostic x-rays than I can count.

I have an alphabet soup of inoculations circulating around in me to this day.

Let's see, what else? Oh yeah, my knees are shot, my lower back acts up, I don't hear very well, and I have problems sleeping. But that's life, right? I'm getting older.

The point of this physio-pharmacological review is that most folks would think, wow, forty-two and he ran two miles in eleven minutes and twenty-six seconds. What a stud! But it was a deceptive performance, like a poorly cared-for automobile with two hundred thousand miles on it that a crazed driver takes out for a last lark.

I'm fifty-one now, and it has become ever more apparent that I bought my disabilities on a balloon-payment plan. The interest is paid and now the principal is very due.

And I was one of the lucky ones. There were broken ribs and some falls, but I went to eight conflict areas, and the only place I ever got shot was on Central Avenue in Hot Springs, Arkansas. Yeah, I also developed a problem with alcohol—a mainstay of GI culture.

Then we had another "low-casualty war" in Iraq in 2003. By casualties, we mean wounded-in-action (WIA) and killed-in-action (KIA). If the ramp on a track vehicle free-falls and squashes you, that doesn't count. If your helicopter goes down with mechanical problems during an administrative ferry, that doesn't count. If your helicopter gets shot down, and the public affairs office (PAO) says it went down for mechanical difficulties, well, that's technically true. But you're not WIA. You had an accident.

If your life is stripped away from you one piece at a time by debilitating illness related to toxics exposure, the Department of Defense will spend decades and millions of dollars trying harder than they did to conceal the fact that a helicopter was shot down to conceal the causative agents of your debilitating disease.

In the late 80s, the Department of Defense contracted for acquisition of a 30-mm tank-killer bullet to be fired from the A-10 tank-buster aircraft. The bullet penetrates armor because it is tipped with an alloy of titanium and depleted uranium (DU). DU used to be a form of atomic waste, the slag left over from the production of fissionable uranium. But it's twice as dense as lead, so when it's hardened with a dab of titanium, it can go through metal armor like a hot knife through butter. It has other qualities as well. Smart people call it "pyrophoric." That means high-energy impact makes it burn.

Oh, yeah. It's also radioactive. Not super-radioactive, like the cesium-137 (that will shoot gamma rays into us when the inevitable U.S. nuclear power plant Mother-of-All-Accidents finally happens). DU emits alpha radiation, which nuke proponents will minimize by telling you, "Alpha bounces off a mere sheet of paper."

Yes, that's true.

Alpha radiation is emitted from tiny particles of dust that don't aim themselves at people in nice straight lines. They float on the air. When a tiny particle of this stuff goes down your neck and into your lung, there's no microscopic person in there to hold a piece of paper between the DU particle and your alveolar tissue, and the alpha radiation can cause cancer better than thirty-five pack-years of Marlboro.

Ah, and one other thing. DU is a heavy metal. That means it's just plain poison.

All over Iraq, right now, mixed into the dust and disseminated by everything in motion from wind to flatbed trucks to tired children who drag their feet when they walk, is an unknown quantity of DU. Before the Bush II attack, there was around 387 tons of this crap. Every soldier who went to Iraq, even the majority who are not in combat specialties, will have the opportunity to share an experience with the people of Iraq: the experience of breathing air that is generally contaminated with DU.

Maybe DU is not the causative agent for (initially non-existent, according to the Department of Defense) Gulf War Syndrome (GWS) . . . by itself. More likely, GWS is a form of synergy between several causative agents.

Burning oil fields filled troops' lungs with toxins for days on end in 1991. Iraq's chemical weapons bunkers (stocked with the assistance of the U.S. Department of Defense just a few years earlier) were bombed to hell and back in 1991, and when troops chemical alarms went off, commanders—seeing troop performance degrade inside the protective gear—declared the alarms defective and had troops remove the batteries. Troops were given thousands of gallons of diet soda, soda that sat on pallets in the Arabian sun, whose heat converts the aspartame into high concentrations of formaldehyde. And Brit doctors have established synergistic pathology when immunizations against cholera, anthrax, and plague are given at once, then combined with insecticide exposure.

Yum.

A quick look at U.S. military history shows that the Department of Defense doesn't give a rat's ass about a soldier once they are done with him or her. In fact, sometimes we're expendable even before our tour of duty is complete. Not expendable in combat. We expect that. But to experiment on us with atomic weapons, administer hallucinogens, or just plain ignore the danger of that stuff we walked through in Vietnam that killed every leaf, every ant, every cricket, and turned a cacophonous mountain rain forest into a rolling corridor of dead brown silence.

WIAs and KIAs were comparatively low during the 1991 invasion of Iraq. And they are still comparatively low during this occupation. But U.S. *casualties* will again be in the thousands.

Count on it.

SPECIAL OPERATIONS IN A SPECIAL PERIOD

> *The gradual conquest of true freedom leads to the creation of a new humankind and a qualitatively different society. This vision provides, therefore, a better understanding of what in fact is at stake in our times.*
> —Gustavo Gutierrez

I said earlier that Special Operations fill in the gaps in the Rumsfeld Doctrine.

Let's take a closer look at what Special Operations are, and how they fit into the current military paradigm. In particular, let's look at Special Forces, the subset of the Special Operations that is the centerpiece of ground operations in Afghanistan, and that is taking on a larger and larger role in postinvasion Iraq. Special Forces is also heavily involved in Africa, Latin America, and Pacific Asia as advisors.

Special Forces (commonly referred to, since Barry Sadler's chauvinist ballad, as the "Green Berets") traces its lineage—as does the CIA, incidentally—to the Office of Strategic Services (OSS), an Allied covert operations group organized during World War II. They still fuss about this, and they are probably both right. In actual fact, this Army organization in its current form more or less was midwifed by President John F. Kennedy to intervene in Vietnam.

The French defeat at Dien Bien Phu in 1954 heralded the end of French colonialism in Asia and the beginning of American intervention in the region. By 1961, this included direct military intervention by these Special Forces "advisors," specialists in the new doctrine of counter-insurgency.

The U.S. had become the guarantor of the corrupt South Vietnamese government, assuming that role from the French in 1956 and initiating military advisory missions through an ad hoc organization called the U.S. Military Assistance Advisor Group (MAAG). The MAAG identified the need for specially trained advisors, and organized a unit in Fort

Bragg, North Carolina, building on an experimental unit that had been around since 1952, called 10th Special Forces Group. It was commanded by former OSS officer Aaron Banks, who would later become a sharp critic of the Vietnam War.

The story of Banks, which I won't detail here, points to the dilemma of Special Forces. In summary, the very strength of Special Forces—their ability to work autonomously immersed in other cultures, and called upon constantly to exercise extreme resourcefulness and creativity—is the greatest contradiction they carry into an imperialist military. They are asked to conduct operations in the world's most "politically sensitive environments," often on missions of profound strategic significance, but to do so, they must think independently, observe carefully, and exercise a great deal of personal and cultural sensitivity. This exposes them to subversive influences, like international reality.

During the Cold War, the vast majority of military officers mistrusted Special Forces and widely resisted their doctrine, which rejected top-down battlefield decisionmaking and often emphasized concepts developed by the OSS, the Yugoslav partisans, the Chinese communists, and even Che Guevara, in his writings on guerrilla warfare. These all stressed tactical agility and organizational flexibility—an anathema to the commanders of the heavy mechanized units facing down the Soviet Union's likewise heavy conventional forces in Europe. Special Forces was regarded at best as a doctrinal sideshow and at worst as a dangerously disruptive element inside the army.

Special Forces, over the years, actually took a perverse pride in their stepchild status, their perennial shortage of funds, and their reputation as soldiers who forgot drill and ceremony, took too long between haircuts, wore rumpled and non-standard uniforms, and often addressed their officers by their first names. Their individual level of technical skill in weapons, communications, medicine, explosives, construction, and small unit tactics, however, were unparalleled in the rest of the U.S. military, and they were required to study foreign languages. In a military that was ever becoming more standardized, with each soldier almost an interchangeable part, the Special Forces rank-and-file ferociously defended its status as a kind of artisan class in the ever-more-Taylorized military.

Special Forces specializes—and has specialized from the beginning—in working directly with foreign forces, and even in foreign civilian communities.

This differentiates them from 1st Special Forces Operational Detachment-Delta (Delta Force), a direct action unit within the Joint Special Operations Command (JSOC), an interservice command designed to correct the "counterterrorism" deficiencies identified after the failed raid in Iran in 1980, in which the then-infant Delta, along with a company of Rangers, was the ground unit. It also differentiates them from Rangers, who are organized as shock-infantry battalions and who are specially trained to conduct airfield seizures and adjunct security for Delta operations. The inclusion of Special Forces, Delta, Rangers, 160th Special Operations Aviation Regiment, 1st Special Operations Wing, Air Force Combat Control Teams, and special ops paramedics, under one command is problematic, as we shall see.

One of the key skills emphasized throughout Special Forces training is the development of rapport with the *indij*, as the indigenous population is called. Consequently, one of the most common problems within Special Forces has been the danger of Special Forces operators "going native." This is so common that the term is widely used and understood throughout Special Forces. "So-and-so was kicked off his team and transferred to SWC (Special Warfare Center). Went native in the Dominican Republic." It's spoken of like it's a virus.

Paradoxically, Special Forces has been characterized for some years, especially since its rapid expansion in the last decade and a half, when it began recruiting heavily out of the notoriously white supremacist Ranger battalions, for its culture of increasing anti-Black racism.

The mix of individuals in Special Forces detachments has reflected this institutional contradiction. Klan sympathizers are teamed with white men married to Black, Latina, and Asian women. Strict chauvinists limit their contact with foreigners to professional relations on missions, while other teammates happily spend every free minute away from the garrison, eating local food, enjoying local culture, and flirting with local women. Violent homophobes on teams are sometimes baited by other team members who stir one another's drinks in the bars with their dicks.

The launch of Operation Rice Bowl, the (failed) 1980 raid in Iran, signaled a new emphasis on large-scale direct-action operations (as opposed to counterinsurgency) by Special Forces, and the abject failure of the actual mission signaled to some the need to better coordinate interservice operations. (Ground commander Charlie Beckwith opposed the use of Air Force rotor-wing pilots from the beginning, preferring combat-experienced army helicopter pilots, but was overruled to quell interservice rivalry.) This inaugurated a series of new administrative and operational structures within the military called Special Operations, which would eventually subsume Special Forces, Rangers, Seal teams, Special Operations Aviation, Air Force Combat Control teams and paramedics, civil affairs, and psychological operations. This reorganization failed to take into account a key difference between Special Forces (who formerly had "civil affairs" and "psychological operations" as part of their mission) as a unit that had to establish rapport and work directly with indigenous communities, and direct-action outfits like Delta and the Rangers. Forcing these two antithetical methodologies together under the same administrative apparatus would magnify several contradictions.

With the Reagan administration, Special Operations took on increased importance in U.S. foreign policy. Money flowed into Special Operations. Fort Bragg became a growth industry. Then the destruction of the Eastern Bloc drastically reshuffled the geopolitical and military decks. Special Operations, once the stepchild of the military, now became the centerpiece of the urgently developing post–Cold War doctrine. Eventually, Henry Shelton, an ex-Special Forces officer, would become the chairman of the Joint Chiefs of Staff. Less than two decades before, a Special Forces officer could never expect to pass the rank of colonel. Shelton had breached the "Special Forces ceiling" by homesteading in conventional paratroop assignments until Special Operations became a privileged empire within the military, whereupon he re-emerged as one of the few general officers with any Special Forces experience at all.

But major contradictions began to emerge. The strength of Special Forces had been its idiosyncratic resourcefulness and agility. A new Special Operations administrative bureaucracy that extended, layer upon new layer, all the way up to the Joint Chiefs was now imposed on Special Forces. And there was a mandate to massively expand troop numbers, thereby lowering the overall "quality" of the individual operator. Many far younger troops, who were more impetuous and less adept at practical problem-solving, entered Special Forces. The very elements of flexibility and agility that had defined the peculiar value of Special Forces were undermined by the administrative necessities—and corresponding bureaucratic friction and standardization—of a much larger command. Special Forces, in the teeth of ferocious resistance from its own operators, was being conventionalized. Henry Shelton was part of this process and his ambiguous background, which hovered between special ops and conventional army, specially suited him to it.

The expansion of Special Forces brought in a flood of young Special Forces soldiers. They were too young to have been the direct or indirect "beneficiaries" of the rigors of Vietnam. These white middle-class children of the late seventies and early eighties, unaccustomed to long, austere, and harsh stays in the field, often extremely self-indulgent when they entered the service, were entering Special Forces for the prestige and the attraction to a kind of macho, laid-back, rebellious lifestyle. They wanted the long hair, the "debauchery deployments" and the sexy missions, but they didn't want to suffer hardship. Special Forces was becoming a prima donna force with more than its share of incompetents and loudmouths.

During my tenure in Delta (1982–1986), I served with a five-and-a-half-foot Napoleon-complex named Danny Hobson. His claim to fame was killing a fourteen-year-old intruder in his home with a pistol—and who was widely regarded in the unit as a little odd (one has to consider the composition of Delta to appreciate the import of this assessment). An ex-Delta operator promoted to sergeant major and working at the Special Warfare Center (SWC) in Fort Bragg in 1988, he sold himself as the man with a solution for the "softie conundrum" in Special Forces.

He implemented a new Special Forces assessment and selection course (SFAS) for all Special Forces applicants, a brutally physical thirty-day "torture course" based on the model employed by the Australian Special Air Service (SAS). It worked, kind of. The softies were weeded out, and the rest of us were "purified" by running as fast as we could, rucksacking as fast as we could, dragging wheel-less vehicles, and carrying huge loads of sand along the fire trails and abandoned ranges of Fort Bragg and Camp Mackall for a month. The biggest single pool of soldiers interested in and capable of surviving SFAS were Rangers—again, the whitest units in the army.[1]

By the late eighties, before Danny Hobson's sadistic male purification ritual was implemented, Special Forces had expanded massively. With the expansion of Special Forces came money, and with money came equipment. Lots of equipment, especially gadgets. Special Forces, whose commo sergeants had tapped out Morse code on antiquated radios and used barbed-wire fences as straight-wire antennae to boost their range, received state-of-the-art everything. Satellite communication radios with digital encryption and frequency-hopping. Special Forces got Zodiac boats with 150-hp motors, nine-cell parachutes that could be opened at altitude and flown ("offset") forty kilometers onto a target, laser range finders, seven-thousand-dollar sniper guns, a smorgasbord of night vision equipment, and on and on. Over time, as has happened in the ever more technocentric military, technological advantage became technological dependency, and a Special Forces doctrine that had centered on equipping men became recentered on manning equipment. Special Forces was now taking on all of the characteristics of the conventional U.S. military, and all of its weaknesses with it. They were also becoming spoiled, and they began to lose their resourcefulness. Morale in Special Forces had weakened in direct proportion to the increasing strength of this conventionalizing tendency. Corruption, racism, and the prima donna syndrome had all become endemic by the time the Eastern Bloc fell. The reaction was more top-down discipline, which again stifled initiative.

In June 2003, in the face of a massively overstretched Special Forces, Donald Rumsfeld seized yet another opportunity to announce a demonstration of his ignorance. The public was informed that Special Forces was going to expand its thinned-out ranks by recruiting directly from the civilian population. In a crash course that went directly from basic training through the entire Q-Course—two years for every specialty except Special Forces medics, who would be in training for an additional eighteen weeks. Rumsfeld simply didn't understand what this would do to the average maturity level of the operators, to the depth of collective military experience, or to the resourcefulness of the units. The language skills and specialized training were only half the strength of Special Forces. The other half were these intangibles related to age and experience. Rumsfeld dragged former Delta commander Pete Schoomaker out of retirement to become the Army's new chief of staff, after Enron's Thomas White quit rather than put up with Rumsfeld's bullshit any longer. But this will not blunt the resistance or resentment of the seasoned Special Forces operators—whatever their flaws—at the imposition of these shake-and-bake Green Berets or the inevitable slide in collective ability. Rumsfeld had already pissed off the conventional military commanders. Now he was aiming for the unconventionals. And this decision will drive a nail in the coffin of Special Forces morale.

The military as a whole underwent a concurrent development in the eighties and nineties, which in some ways coincided with the trends in Special Forces, and in some ways contradicted it. It is important to understand that military doctrine is not developed in a vacuum, but is variously influenced by biases from past doctrine, competing theories of military science, interservice rivalry, bureaucratic protectionism, weapons contractors and their elected representatives, the politics of promotion to the highest levels of command, and the peculiar biases, opinions, illusions, and delusions of the members of the National Command Authority (the president, the secretary of defense, and the national security advisor).

Out of that mix emerged two dominant tendencies within the military: the Powell Doctrine, and full-spectrum dominance (FSD).

As described earlier, the Powell Doctrine lists among its priorities public relations. With the emphasis on public relations, there is an emphasis on the appearance of the soldiers. This is an issue for Special Forces. From "Smarten-up rule could put lives at risk, claim soldiers," an article in the Glasgow *Herald* by Ian Bruce (June 5, 2002):

> Lieutenant General Dan K McNeill, a combat veteran of Vietnam, the Gulf and Panama, arrived at his Bagram airbase headquarters late last week and has already ordered his 12,000 soldiers to smarten up, wear standard uniforms and equipment, and to salute officers when they meet them.

Every army in the world abandons obvious badges of rank and saluting in a combat zone because it identifies commanders for enemy spotters and marks them as targets for snipers.

Some officers are now refusing to return salutes, but the reinstatement of the military protocol has been extended even to the special forces' "hooches"—a relatively anarchic tented encampment on the edge of the base which until now has been a law unto itself.

Many of the Delta and Green Berets troopers at the cutting edge of the war sport long hair, go unshaven and have been allowed to wear combinations of GI issue kit and practical and comfortable local garb for their dangerous behind-the-lines missions.

Even there, a sign which until Saturday read: "This is a no-saluting zone," has been removed and standardisation of appearance is to be enforced while the men known to their conventional colleagues as "snake-eaters" are on base and to some extent in the public eye. General McNeill, who has made 300 parachute jumps [This statistic, of course, is meaningless, since all those jumps were on secure drop zones like those at Fort Bragg. —SG] , yesterday dismissed the protests as he settled in for what is likely to be the toughest phase of the war, rooting out and destroying small pockets of al Qaeda and Taliban fighters in remote mountain strongholds.

This bone-headedness about uniformity and conformity has a real impact on morale in Special Operations. It's partly an impediment to operations, partly an affront to their perennial craving for autonomy, and partly antithetical to the plain vanity of many Special Operators, who enjoy this outward manifestation of their mystique.

There is an unspoken reason for the employment of Special Forces in the first publicly acknowledged Special Forces operations since Vietnam, in which military planners accept the probability of ground combat: the racial composition of Special Forces.

Grenada and Somalia both surprised planners, who underestimated opposing forces and employed foolishly arrogant tactics. In both cases, the heaviest fighting was with Special Operations troops but *not* Special

Forces. Panama and Iraq were the ultimate expressions of Powell Doctrine, with crushing force, heavy media spin, little anticipated likelihood of intense ground combat, and even then, the riskiest missions reserved for Delta, the Rangers, and SEAL Team Six—units with very few Black operators.[2]

This is a factor in the composite doctrine emerging from the fevered mind of Donald Rumsfeld.

Special Forces is being asked to fill many of the tactical voids, voids in the "full spectrum" in Afghanistan, Iraq, and elsewhere—asked to do those things that no one else can do because they are reputed to be flexible, agile, and language-capable. Special reconnaissance. Training of Afghan militias. Providing command structures for Kurds.[3] Security for civil affairs and psychological operations. Direct action. Gendarmes. Spies. Bullies. Bodyguards. WMD hunters.

The reality is that few if any speak the local dialects in Afghanistan and damn few speak passable Arabic or Farsi, relying on translators who are vetted on almost the sole criterion of their ability to speak English.

The tasks for which Special Forces soldiers are being held accountable are now listed in a Special Forces Soldier's Manual like instructions to a McDonalds employee. They are too numerous and often irrelevant, in a situation that is culturally impenetrable and changing by the moment.

There is little doubt at this point that they are being manipulated by various factions. Let's look a little more closely at the attack on hundreds of civilians in Kakarak, Afghanistan, where the U.S. military is conducting the investigation to determine if the U.S. military did anything wrong.[4]

The Afghan civilians at Kakarak were not "bombed." It's an important distinction. It's already been confirmed that Special Forces was conducting a mission there, and they use AC-130 gunships in close air support, not bombers. The AC-130 is a computer-enhanced turboprop, a converted cargo ship that fires a variety of weapons from a computer-controlled, five thousand–foot circular orbit with a thirty-degree bank that aims the door-mounted armaments *directly* at the target on the ground. Imagine a funnel with the point on the target, and a plane circling overhead along the rim.

The gunship carries direct-fire ordnance, not bombs. It is a precision weapons system. It does not fire "errant" anything. I have worked with these birds, and they can be called in on a motorcycle fifty yards away from one's own position. They are not being fired by a bomber pilot who is "bowling" into a largely unseen target. They are being fired by a flying tank commander, who knows exactly what he is firing at, with adjustments and confirmation on "target effect" from the Special Forces forward observer on the ground.

Kakarak was attacked deliberately. As was Khorum in October—more than one hundred killed; Moshkhil in December—sixteen killed. A civilian convoy in Paktia Province in December—sixty-five dead; Qalaye Niaze in December—fifty-two dead, including twenty-five children. The May 12 Special Forces raid on "the wrong village" in Kandahar, where five were killed outright, including a thirteen-year-old and a fifteen-year-old, and thirty-two people "captured;" the May 24 raid in Bandi Temur—two dead and fifty-nine abducted, including a one-hundred-year-old who died from a rifle blow to the head and a thirteen-year-old girl who fell in a well and drowned when she tried to run away.

Either factions were using U.S. forces to settle their issues or the CIA has aligned with a certain faction and was "paying some bills."

Welcome back to Mogadishu.

Powell Doctrine and full-spectrum dominance/network-centric warfare were both employed, to one extent or another, in Afghanistan and Iraq. Media control and indiscriminate high-altitude bombing are Powell Doctrine stand-bys. The trick is to coordinate the aerial shock tactics of the Powell Doctrine with Special Operations troops employed in various styles of low-intensity conflict on the ground. They are all myopic doctrines on their own accounts and absolutely incompatible when employed together, when a significant part of that "full spectrum" is Special Forces work.

The attempt to combine massive destruction of lives and property, through high altitude carpet bombing and terror-raids on villages with rapport building and military cooperation among the population was tried once before by the U.S., in Vietnam. And the attempt to coexist as a (foreign) military force in an essentially stateless combat milieu (Afghanistan), with ethnic and clan-based warlords making and breaking alliances with each change of the political wind, was also tried once before by the U.S., in Somalia. In Iraq, they are trying to impose a hated occupation, as they expect Special Forces to play a key role in "nation building."

While Special Operations was developed using models from successful unconventional and guerrilla movements, its own record has been pretty horrific. The highlights of Special Operations—the Son Tay Raid into North Vietnam, Operation Rice Bowl (the Iran raid), the Grenada invasion, Task Force Ranger—*were all failures*. The latter were attempts to use the organizations, tactics, techniques, and mindsets developed for insurgent forces *that are suited to an insurgent political task* and employ them with high-technology warfighting systems that gave them the worst of three worlds—they were too light to fight, too heavy for basic agility, and too dependent on high technology.

To date, Afghanistan has been an unmitigated military bust. Every independent source available confirms it. Osama bin Laden has not been captured or killed. The Taliban simply went to ground around Afghanistan and Pakistan to wait for the U.S. to become more deeply submerged in the growing quagmire. By March 2003, the AP reported that Afghanistan was the number-one opium producer in the world. Pakistan has become destabilized to the point of risking nuclear war with its neighbor, India. The potential fossil fuel pipeline easements still can not be secured. The collateral damage inflicted by bombing and bad intelligence, combined with support for the corrupt and inept Karzai regime, turns ever-larger segments of the population against the Americans each day.

The quagmire in Iraq is still in a more formative stage as this is written, but the outlines of an Israeli-like occupation and a Palestinian-like *intifada* are already clear.

Who is caught in the middle? Special Forces. Caught between bombing and rapport building. Caught between the expectations for unconventional fighters and the spit-and-polish command structure.

Caught between the official pronouncements about the war and their own intimate contact with the realities of Afghanistan and Iraq. And caught between the imperative to show the public some action and the utter incomprehensibility of the missions that are being crafted, like the dangerous and ultimately pointless Operation Anaconda.

In early March 2002, the American public began to hear about Operation Anaconda in the usual breathless idiom of the U.S. press—awestruck and triumphal. But what really happened there?

On March 8, the U.S. military publicly congratulated itself for having killed off "hundreds" of "al Qaeda fighters" hidden in icy caves along the rarified slopes sixty miles south of Gardez.

What apparently happened in the real world was that the American military in its well-known culturally clueless way received "intelligence" from Badsha Khan, the nom de guerre of a Khost warlord, Zadran. The Americans apparently failed to factor Zadran's record as a perpetually scheming liar who had provoked them into killing civilians in the past and took him again at his word. Zadran gave the U.S. the "tip" that led them to slaughter a civilian convoy of Paktia elders in December 2001.

On the mighty Khan's word, the U.S. launched what was supposed to be an overwhelming assault against "150 al Qaeda." Waiting for them, however, was not al Qaeda, but the Taliban—seasoned fighters led by Saifur Rahman, a young, energetic, and talented commander, thoroughly familiar with the local people and terrain, who proceeded to organize a successful ambush of one hundred Special Forces and Afghan troops. Only one American was killed, but U.S. fatalities have been consistently low since the introduction of heavy body armor and the Kevlar helmet (which also makes them slow as cattle). The ambush blunted the American attack and disrupted the entire U.S. plan.

For all its lip service to tactical agility, the U.S. military displays a distinct inability to respond to surprise contingencies with anything except overwhelming force, largely due to the Powell Doctrine preoccupation with "force protection," which has rendered the U.S. officer corps toothless. We would see this paralysis again in the Iraq invasion of 2003.

The U.S. piled on attack helicopters to overcome its impasse, whereupon the Taliban veterans dropped one helicopter and disabled five of them, not with shoulder-fired surface-to-air missiles, but with assault rifles and grenade launchers, exactly the same armaments used to dispatch the well-known "blackhawk(s) down" in Mogadishu. This level of marksmanship and plain audacity should have alerted the U.S. about the character of the force they had encountered, but they blundered ahead.

Another ambush killed six Americans. The U.S. military then reinforced their ground force with over a thousand additional troops (the core U.S. force being Army Rangers) and militiamen of—oh yes, they did—Zadran. The U.S. and its "allies" continued to suffer heavy losses in the snowy, labyrinthine mountains, so U.S. commanders fell back on what they knew. The air force.

After tearing apart the pristine mountains with heavy bombing, U.S. ground forces advanced cautiously to find a few corpses. Local Pashtuns, united again with the Taliban in their common desire to expel the Americans, assisted the bulk of the Taliban force to diffuse themselves back throughout Paktia.[5]

The centrality of Special Forces in the current doctrine and the apparently unquenchable thirst for war by the Bush coterie will soon outstrip the capacity of Special Operations forces. This is not only a logistical issue; it is a morale issue.

When military planners evaluate the "enemy situation," they take six categories into account: size, location, composition, disposition, and strength. The sixth category is morale.

Morale, unlike the others, is something difficult to quantify and operationalize. And it doesn't correlate well with material well-being. I've seen a highly provisioned, well cared-for Special Forces A-Detachment turn into moping adolescents, and I've seen troops in protracted and gruelingly austere conditions imbued with a wild fighting spirit. Consider the conditions of the NLA/NVA in Vietnam or the Cuban revolutionaries, whose morale seldom flagged.

Troops exposed to actual combat react in a variety of ways. Some develop post-traumatic stress disorder (PTSD). Some seem to adapt pretty well, then readapt to noncombat situations. Some become addicted to the pure, visceral, adrenaline-fired sensuality of it. Some become homicidal sadists, drunk with the power of life and death over others. Some surrender to the meaninglessness and become suicidal. (The spate of spousal murders and murder-suicides by Special Forces operators returning from Afghanistan should have told us something.)

Some become critical.

Special Forces troops generally begin their military careers in pursuit of some vague, culturally constructed, masculinist ideal. They are often apolitical. Few go public with their doubts or their feelings regarding what they do for a living. It is, after all, a very prestigious job. So many are capable of just saying, "It was a goat fuck," and they move on with their lives. But many are also intelligent, even sensitive people, who bear the scars of cognitive dissonance. Afghanistan and Iraq will be a lifelong burden for some of them and it will not be surprising when the first stories of dissent and disgust that come directly out of the military in these occupied territories. Some will certainly come from Special Forces operators.

HANGUL:
KOREA

When I first saw America,
it was like a huge giant,
and I was like pygmy woman.
I made a desperate struggle with this giant
Not to fall. He whistled merrily, waving his
hands.
He was a huge man, but a man like a snake.
—Sook Lyol Ryu

"Oon jeeki jee mah! Chun chunee, moo ree ay son oonjah!" What this means is "Everyone freeze! Now slowly put your hands on your heads!" This, along with hello, thanks, and you're welcome, is what I remember of Hangul, the language spoken in Korea.

The 1988 Olympics were scheduled to take place in Seoul. In 1985, my old unit, Delta, was tasked with training the Republic of Korea (ROK) 707 Special Forces in counterterrorism.

We bonded with our students in the day by practicing shooting and assaults on captive airplanes. At night, we bonded with alcohol and local women along the amerikanized strip in the Yitaewon shopping-and-saloon district. We stayed in the Seoul Garden Hotel, where you get a foot massage with your haircuts. One of my associates went to the barbershop every other day, until he had hardly a hair left on his head.

ROK saves a lot of money by having its paratroops practice out of a cable-tethered balloon instead of airplanes. As part of our bonding with the ROK Special Forces, we spent a day jumping out of these balloons with them, doing standard static-line jumps from one thousand feet. Very strange, because there was no noise. Just a breeze going over the gondola, which carried six people. The jumpmaster simply unhooked a little chain that separated the occupants from all that vertical space and quietly said, "Go."

We each stepped off the gondola and could even hear the static line popping out of the pack bands as we dropped like potato sacks through space. It took a good six seconds to feel the tug of the canopy opening.

One of the ROK paratroop sergeants wanted to make a video of our jump, so he hopped onto the gondola. The diesel spool operator paid out cable, and the balloon began another ascent. At around two hundred feet, a red-faced lieutenant stormed onto the scene, raging in words we couldn't understand, and the cable operator revved up the diesel motor and reeled the balloon back down.

Everyone was ordered off the gondola, and as the lieutenant ranted and spat, all the Korean NCOs were put at the position of attention in a single rank. We were afraid the lieutenant would blow a gasket with all his screaming. He stirred the air with his bellicose noise, stalking back and forth and pulling on a set of white gloves. Suddenly, he went down the line and delivered brutal right hooks to the heads of two NCOs. They rocked under the punches then stood back at attention, tears welling in their eyes, their bruised cheekbones instantly beginning to swell. The lieutenant then punctuated his authority with a front kick to the chest of one of the castigated.

We Americans stood with our mouths open.

The interpreter, wide-eyed and wary now, came over and told us, "Only six on the balloon. Seven is a safety violation."

Got it, buddy.

That night, one of our teams went to Yitaewon with ROK Special Forces escorts. When they boarded a bus that was full, our guys offered to wait for another bus. The two ROK soldiers with them shook their heads no, then shouted orders to the passengers on the bus, whereupon they ejected six passengers irrespective of age or sex. ROK Special Forces are accustomed to this kind of despotism, and apparently so were the passengers.

I have to wonder how many of the people recently demonstrating against the U.S. in South Korea had ever been thrown off a bus by ROK soldiers with American companions.

Koreans know the imperial arrogance of U.S. soldiers in military vehicles, who speed across Korean thoroughfares with a get-out-of-my-way recklessness. This is the attitude of occupying troops everywhere.

That's why the whole country is in an uproar about the exoneration of U.S. army sergeants Fernando Nino and Mark Walker, whose armored vehicle ran over and killed Korean fourteen-year-olds Misun and Hyosun, two schoolgirls on their way to a birthday party.[1]

What's rankled Koreans and brought decades of anti-American resentment boiling to the surface is not just an apparent negligent homicide, in which the company commander is also implicated. ROK courts have long abdicated their jurisdiction over U.S. occupying forces through a Status-of-Forces Agreement (SOFA), which turns the vast majority of GIs who commit crimes in Korea back over to U.S. military authorities for adjudication. SOFA is more than a symbol. It's the legal embodiment of U.S. imperial domination of the ROK since the Korean War.

American soldiers commit around six hundred crimes a year in the ROK. Less than four percent are tried inside a ROK court.[2]

The recent ROK presidential election of populist-nationalist Roh (pronounce it "no") Moo-hyun came in the wake of a campaign where the defining issue became who could demonstrate the brawniest anti-Americanism.

Korean grievances against the U.S., however, date back to well before the killing of the two schoolgirls.

They begin with the U.S. occupation of Korea in 1945, after the defeat of Japan.

Korea had lived under the merciless jackboot of the Japanese since Japan's 1905 annexation of the Korean peninsula.

Korea was a distinct culture in the region, one that had leapt ahead of other East Asians in literacy when an enlightened despot, King Sejong of the Choson Dynasty, phonetically alphabetized the Korean language in 1446, making literacy the province of the whole population. The alphabet, called Hangul, eventually gave its name to the language itself, and Koreans even refer to themselves by this term—a form of powerful national identification.

Annexation and occupation by the Japanese was a terrible humiliation and the genesis of Korean popular resistance.

When the Americans occupied southern Korea in the wake of World War II (with Soviet occupation of the North), Koreans in both regions looked forward to a quick transition to reunification and self-determination. But a racist U.S. general, John R. Hodge, was installed as the virtual viceroy of the ROK. The U.S. quickly moved to re-establish relations with its recent enemies in Germany and Japan as part of a containment strategy against the Russians and Chinese. Hodge summarily put the most despised and venal Japan-collaborators and quislings in charge of the nation's government, under his direction.[3]

Nationalist insurrection broke out with various nationalist and communist groups joining forces, and civil war ensued. This is not the space for a recounting of the whole Korean War. But Korea simultaneously became an international battleground involving the Americans, Soviets, and Chinese—eventually with American pressure dragging in the United Nations, a situation which should be familiar by now.[4]

In 1950, forces based in the Democratic People's Republic of Korea (DPRK) of the North launched a blindingly successful offensive ground action against ROK forces, pushing ROK forces off the peninsula and almost wholly onto Taegu Island. An American expeditionary force that was sent to help the ROK—fully expecting the DPRK forces to break and run at the sight of white U.S. troops—was instead delivered a swift and humiliating defeat at the hands of a highly disciplined and seemingly fearless DPRK military. U.S. ground forces had been allowed to deteriorate in number and quality since the Second World War, and their performance was miserable.

As U.S. reinforcements poured onto the peninsula to engage the Korean War in earnest, Hodge declared that fully thirty percent of the Koreans in the south were sympathetic to communist forces, a claim that was only partially true since the issue was not ideological, but national. A secret policy in the U.S. Armed Forces was adopted, one that is just beginning to see the light of day: episodic massacres of Korean civilians.

Revelations of the massacre at No Gun Ri, where upwards of three hundred Korean civilians were systematically murdered by the American 1st Cavalry Division and the U.S. Air Force, led to further investigations of American conduct during the Korean War. It is becoming ever clearer that hundreds of thousands of Korean civilians were murdered with the complicity and participation of U.S. troops by the ROK's hated Syngman Rhee regime.[5]

The U.S. media enthusiastically collaborated in the cover-up of No Gun Ri and the whole U.S. conduct of the war, which is why it is still not generally understood.

After the lightning advance of the DPRK against the ROK and American troops in 1950, General Douglas MacArthur ordered the wholesale destruction of Korea. His orders were to destroy "every means of communication, every installation, factory, *city and village* from the front line to the Yalu River." (Emphasis mine.) This was the world's introduction to a new weapon, napalm. Within two years, nearly every human settlement in the north had been subjected to firebombing, and the vast majority of targets were civilian. Electricity production was destroyed. Dams were ruptured, flooding the precious rice plains that had been carefully developed between the rugged mountains. American pilots machine-gunned the peasants in the north for sport. Tibor Meray, a Hungarian correspondent returned from a tour of the North in a state of utter shock. There were, he reported, "no more cities in North Korea." In the south, American-led massacres were combined with wholesale executions by the ROK quisling government of anyone remotely suspected of being "subversive." In the end, according to General Curtis LeMay, "we burned down just about every city in North and South Korea both, and . . . we killed off over a million civilian Koreans and drove several million more from their homes." (Four million people died in the Korean War).[6]

When the war was fought to a standstill at the demilitarized zone (DMZ), with Chinese and DPRK troops having mounted a blood drenched war of attrition to push the U.N./U.S. back, the DPRK consolidated itself against future attacks by placing itself on a permanent war footing and by adopting an internal policy of isolation and self-reliance, called *juche sasang*. This official ideology is what the U.S. now portrays as deranged.

The authoritarian U.S.–client government of the ROK continued harsh repression of its population for decades afterward, as U.S. troops occupied bases across the country, generating hundreds of GI border towns whose primary industry is vice and whose activities offended the sensibilities of the majority of Koreans.

A popular rebellion against the Chun Doo Hwan regime and the U.S. broke out in Kwangju in 1980, and the ROK army, with assistance from the U.S. armed forces, massacred over two thousand resisters.

Presiding over the U.S. during this atrocity was none other than Nobel Peace Prize–winner Jimmy Carter.[7]

In 1993, Private Ken Marcel, U.S. Army, was drunk. He attempted to coerce sex from Yun Kum Yi, a young Korean woman, who rebuffed him. So Marcel beat her to death, tore off her clothes, pushed an umbrella into her anus, a bottle into her vagina, then shook a box of laundry detergent onto her bloody, desecrated corpse. Anti-American demonstrations flared again, and a lot of organizing.[8]

The next year Jimmy Carter would be back, this time as a spoiler of imperial ambitions. Because in 1993, at the same time Private Marcel was desecrating the body of Yun Kum Yi, the government of Bill Clinton was planning to start a war on the Korean peninsula.

The ROK's emergence as one of the Asian industrial-economic tigers brought with it the big cat of a militant trade union movement that has shown the willingness to go toe-to-toe with the army and police in the streets. This militancy has been more than matched by the long-standing student-led struggles for self-determination and an end to U.S. occupation. Now that student-labor resistance is being mainstreamed to the general population of Korea, which is demographically ever younger. The recent election of a president who wants the American presence curtailed and a rapprochement with the DPRK appear as harbingers of potential renewed militancy. The popular resistance to Korean participation in the 1991 aggression against Iraq had been ferocious. This combination of independent development, popular street politics, and a growing movement to reintegrate the two Koreas was simply too much to bear, and the U.S. fell on a plan to start a war there to stop it.

The Clinton administration would eventually find a new, equally risky method for attacking the Asian economic challenge when Robert Rubin opened up hedge fund attacks on the region that almost toppled capitalism in 1998. But in 1993, the Clinton administration was hell bent on an old–fashioned military action.

Early in 1993, the U.S. redirected some of its intercontinental ballistic missiles in Alaska from targets in the former Soviet Union to targets in the DPRK. This was in conjunction with the announcement of a massive war game off the coast of Korea. The U.S. press then portrayed the DPRK as unstable when it responded by threatening to withdraw from the Nonproliferation Treaty (NPT). The deranged North Koreans—in their irrational paranoia—believed that pointing multi-warhead thermonuclear weapons at them was a hostile act.[9]

Once the press did its job of convincing the public that the DPRK was in the hands of schizophrenic leadership, the U.S. pressured the International Atomic Energy Agency (IAEA) to demand that the DPRK submit to inspection of "undeclared" nuclear sites. The IAEA had never made that demand of any nation before. Pyongyang—in its infinite paranoia—regarded this as a hostile act too, and one that was intended to expand intelligence gathering by U.S. delegates with the inspection teams. This, of course, turned out to be true.

With not a whit of evidence—à la Iraq—the Clinton administration then leveled the claim that the DPRK was developing nuclear weapons with plutonium from its Yongbyon reactor. Even though scientists pointed out that the DPRK didn't have the technical wherewithal to use this reactor for weapons-grade plutonium or to convert it into a deliverable weapons, the story was amplified and repeated as gospel by the U.S. chihuahua press, then echoed worldwide on newswires.[10]

Once the fictional atomic bomb program was developed by the Clintonites, the fiction's authors demanded that the DPRK put an end to it. The whole plan was put on hold after the Somalia debacle, but once Les Aspin was sacrificed for the sin of Somalia, his replacement, defense contractor William Perry, was appointed defense secretary, and took up the cause of attacking the DPRK again.

The central feature of their opening salvo was to be an attack on the Yongbyon reactor. Perry later admitted, "We readied a detailed plan to attack the Yongbyon facility with precision-guided bombs (manufactured, of course, by Perry's former employer, Martin-Marietta). We were highly confident that it could be destroyed without causing a meltdown that would release radioactivity into the air."[11]

Gregory Elich, who wrote an account of this whole sorry episode for the Center for Research on Globalization, understated, "It seems highly dubious that a release of radioactivity could have been avoided." In fact, my current day job involves researching nuclear plants and their dangers, and I won't understate it. Bombing attacks directed at active nuclear power plants certainly will cause Chernobyls, or worse. But

Perry and Clinton are now regarded as sane. They can charge out-landish speakers fees around the country. The DPRK's leaders, who were the target of this plot, are "insane."

Those of us who are amazed by the Strangelove-like quality of the Bushites should take caution before we posit Democrats as a saner alternative. The Clinton administration was preparing a war in which they freely admitted among themselves that the "intensity of combat would be greater than any the world has witnessed since the last Korean War." Given that it would initially center around the ROK capitol of Seoul, where over ten million people live, that may have been another understatement.

Kim Young-Sam, the ROK president, figured out what was hap-pening when troops started shifting into forward positions and U.S. warships formed a ring off the coast. He called Bill Clinton and basi-cally asked, "What the fuck are you doing, you fucking nimrod?" (Okay, I'm paraphrasing.) Clinton actually tried to convince Kim that this was a really good idea, and after half an hour, Kim told Clinton, "You can count on the military of the ROK not to lift a finger for you, you lunatic." (Another imperfect translation, I'm sure.)

This was when Jimmy Carter got involved, and probably redeemed himself from earlier sins by stopping a second Korean War. On June 15, 1994, Carter met with DPRK leader Kim Il-Sung and with no authori-zation whatsoever arranged a deal wherein the DPRK would agree to freeze their upgrades of aging reactors if they could gain assistance with developments of newer, safer ones. This was an offer by the DPRK for a diplomatic solution to a malignant crisis manufactured in the USA. Carter, knowing full well that the entire Clinton administration was off its medication, then invited CNN to broadcast his meeting with the North Koreans—an unprecedented breach of protocol—which forced the Clinton administration, described by alarmed State Department insiders as "crestfallen" at the loss of their war, to accept the publicly outstretched diplomatic hand of the DPRK.

We have to back up now for a moment to understand the real domestic crisis that was just beginning to sink in on the DPRK. Its prin-cipal trading partner, the Soviet Union had recently disintegrated, which resulted in a steep loss of critical oil and gas supplies. The DPRK has one peculiar resource on its own real estate that gave them a temporary fix: uranium. Quite a bit of it, actually. But their uranium doesn't work in the light water reactors the U.S. was pushing in its "diplomacy." The older, graphite-moderated reactors, like the one that crashed in Chernobyl, were what they knew how to use. By the time Clinton started his provocations, Russian oil supplies to the DPRK had dropped to 10 percent of their Soviet-era level. The DPRK would have been more than happy to stay out of the nuclear business altogether, were it not for outrageous economic sanctions pushed by the U.S. that simultaneously limited supply and severely constricted North Korean access to dollars—the currency in which world oil is denominated.

The post-Soviet energy contraction in the DPRK was a cautionary tale for all of us in the oil-dependent world. Fertilizer disappeared. Crops lost yields. Factories closed. Spare parts began to disappear, closing down mines. Lights went out. The heat went off. Then nature stepped in—if you still accept that climate change and its consequences are not androgenic—and kicked the people of the DPRK to the ground. Severe floods wrecked a significant portion of its hydroelectric capacity.

This was the situation that forced the proud North Koreans—who had literally cut off lights and heat across this frigid nation, in the rugged spirit of *juche sasang*—to offer to abandon its critically needed nuclear power program in the face of U.S. bullying. One of the least understood aspects of U.S. statecraft, to this day, is energy as a political weapon. China understands it.

This was the the DPRK was in when it agreed to the Agreed Framework, as it was called, to a U.S. offer to provide heavy oil to the DPRK, amounting to a whopping eight percent of its energy needs, in exchange for a North Korean promise to build new light water reactors.

But in the emerging new international division of labor, the DPRK had become the Apaches, untamable and therefore superfluous, and this "treaty" was broken before the ink was dry, with the U.S. demanding yet again invasive inspections, then accusing the Koreans of bad faith when they refused to eat the diplomatic equivalent of a plate of warm shit.

And the DPRK was now in a position of extreme energy vulnerability. The great sorrow deepened.

In 1995, tremendous floods swept away over four hundred thousand hectares of prime farmland just before harvest in a nation with a short growing season, and rendered five million people who lived on that agricultural land homeless. Records showed it to be the worst flood in a century. To this day, crop yields are affected by that deluge.

The coal mines filled with water. The turbines on the hydroelectric plants clogged and went silent.

In 1996, before recuperation efforts from the '95 floods could get under way, another series of floods ravaged the nation. In 1997, a severe drought followed that killed seventy percent of DPRK corn. On the west coast, that same year, a tidal wave struck. Then came the typhoons that destroyed an additional twenty-nine thousand homes. In 2000–2001, Korea saw the worst drought in its history. In addition to the loss of both crops and seed, there was a water shortage like nothing anyone had experienced in Korea for over a thousand years. This is when the stories began about people eating the bark off trees, when the catastrophic cascade that began as an energy crisis combined with economic warfare from the U.S. and washed over the DPRK like a biblical scourge. The fat, fed U.S. ruling class and their house-trained press said of this poor, proud nation . . . they wrecked their own economy.

The people of the ROK, however, still seeing their neighbors to the north as sisters and brothers, pushed their own government to move more quickly toward rapprochement. The arrogance of the Americans only served to awaken the profound latent resentment of the occupied ROK.

With the lie that the DPRK claimed it was developing nuclear weapons (as it turns out, no leader from that country ever said that), Bush and his cabinet put themselves in the hot seat. Reporters were asking them if the DPRK is part of the Axis of Evil and has weapons of mass destruction, why aren't we doing to them what we threaten to do to Iraq? Ahhh . . . er . . . well . . . we uh . . . we'll get back to ya on that one.

Bullies only attack the weak.

When I first heard the story of the North Korean vessel that was boarded for inspection by the Spanish, I thought the U.S. had been set up. My hypothesis was that they deliberately painted over the markings on a legal ship taking a legal shipment of weapons to Yemen, making it appear suspicious and precipitating a U.S. demand that a Spanish ship conduct an armed takeover of the DPRK ship for inspection. The U.S. news media got drawn into it. Then the eggs blew up all over people's faces. U.S. arrogance and imperialism on display! Press idiocy on display! This was a long-standing arrangement between two sovereign nations. Legal to the last letter. Gotcha!

But that wasn't what happened, as it turns out.

The DPRK was sending a legitimate shipment of weapons to U.S. ally-for-the-moment, Yemen. This was another ham-handed attempt to bully, engineered by the U.S., in which the Spanish ship actually fired on the Korean vessel with machine guns. The subsequent embarrassment for the U.S. was created by those who have embarrassed them most effectively in the past: themselves.

The most recent repositioning of Chinese troops along the border with the DPRK, as reportd in *Asia Times*, has led to yet another round of speculation in the press. In particular, there is concern related to the reported deployment of heavy mechanized Chinese forces inside the one hundred kilometer exclusion zone established trilaterally between China, the DPRK, and Russia.

In fact, the key to understanding the immense and shifting strategic complexity of Korea is recognition of the fact that the peninsula has something in common with Afghanistan—really bad geographic luck. It borders two historic rivals, who happen to be strategic rivals with the United States—China and Russia. And the key to understanding the apparent rivalry between the DPRK and the United States is recognition that U.S. provocation on the peninsula is aimed not at the DPRK but at Korea as a whole.

China will become the world's largest consumer of oil within the next decade if current trends hold (I will say they cannot, but that's also another story). China's domestic production of oil has passed its Hubbert peak and is in permanent decline, increasing China's dependence on imports, and throwing it into direct conflict with the U.S.—now the world's biggest energy hog—which will also vastly increase its demand for foreign oil if current trends continue. (Kenneth Boulding said, "Anyone who believes exponential growth can go on forever in a finite world is either a madman or an economist." Ain't capitalism grand?)

China is now systematically hollowing out the U.S. industrial base with its sea of landless labor. In preparation for this historic conflict and in spite of the financial and economic Gordian knots that now bind China and the United States, the U.S. has already begun the attempt to achieve military encirclement of China. Well before 9/11, military plans were already off the shelf to invade Afghanistan, a country that lies directly on the land route between China and the Gulf States, where overland pipelines might transport energy from the sweet crude fields of Iraq, Iran, and Saudi Arabia to the world's largest and fastest growing economy.

Again without digressing too much, it is important to point out that simple military encirclement is inadequate as both a U.S. strategy and as a lens for understanding the geopolitics of Asia and the United States.

What must be demystified is Korea itself and *its* relationship to the U.S., beginning with the U.S. occupation of Korea in 1945 after the defeat of Japan.

The Bush strategy of reasserting control over East Asia and the Pacific Rim with Korea as a target is having the paradoxical effect of elevating the importance, status, and prestige of the primary challenger in the region to U.S. dominance: China, with whom the DPRK shares its longest border and who will take credit when they succeed in defusing the tensions there and block the U.S. government's revised plans for war. Complicating these relationships is the ROK and China's fear that any kind of sudden mass economic migrations out of the DPRK could deliver a serious blow to their own economies, if and when these tensions abate. This combined threat of U.S. provocation and DPRK economic refuges probably underwrites troop movements along the Sino-Korean border along with, quite possibly, a Chinese desire to signal the U.S. that there are lines that cannot be crossed even for the infinitely pragmatic Chinese.

The tensions in the region have not been improved by Japanese acquiescence this year to the U.S. request to station theater missile defenses on Japanese soil.

U.S. saber rattling and alarm ringing about North Korean nuclear weapons becomes more than a little hypocritical when one notes, like *Covert Action Quarterly*'s Karen Talbot, writing in July 2003, that the U.S., which possesses by far the largest arsenal of nuclear armaments, has failed to abide by Article VI of the Nonproliferation Treaty (NPT), which stipulates that the nuclear weapons states, including the U.S., accomplish the total and unequivocal elimination of their nuclear weapons. The existence of the U.S. nuclear arsenal is bound to lead other nations to try to acquire such weapons. Washington is maintaining a double standard by requiring other nations to respect the NPT when the U.S. is planning to develop new nuclear weapons.

Nuclear weapons specifically designed with Korea in mind.

In 2003, Rumsfeld notified the military of his intent to redeploy forward-based U.S. troops along the DMZ back toward Taegu, not to retreat, but to convert the DMZ and Seoul with its ten millions into a potential impact area for a war of extermination against the DPRK. That's why the Bush administration is pushing research into low-yield, atomic, bunker-penetrating munitions (which will be the dirtiest nuclear weapons yet). The DPRK has organized its whole society for (literally underground) war and civil defense, and the nation is a vast catacomb of tunnels and underground bunkers.

The Chinese, sensing American military and political weakness with the quagmire in Iraq deepening and the domestic legitimacy of the Bush administration waning in the face of one revelation of perfidy on top of another, may be looking at an historic opportunity in the region, possibly a decisive move to displace Japan as the Asian center of gravity.

The Hu Jintao government—even as they move to militarily secure their borders against any Korean exodus north—is keenly aware the DPRK knows China is its last best hope in the confrontation with America. China is now in a position to arrange a settlement of the "North Korean nuclear crisis," turning the U.S.–grown lemon into diplomatic lemonade for Beijing.

Everyone, including the mad hatters in the Bush cabinet—with the possible exception of Donald Rumsfeld (who, I have convinced myself, has a neurological disorder)—knows that U.S. military ground capacity is now stretched to its absolute limit. It is slowly dawning even on the most obtuse that the historical military blip that was victory from the air in Iraq I and Kosovo was anomalous. Iraq will likely be the Bush Waterloo, and the inevitable attempt to recoup from this even after a political transition in the U.S. will be both fraught with difficulty and immensely complicated.

It will likely be China, and not the International Energy Agency, who oversees the "deproliferation" of the DPRK.

I have perhaps been overly glib in my denunciation of the Bush regime. I am chronically tempted to caricature (which with our ruling class is becoming easier and more tempting all the time). It is important to point out, by way of rebutting their claims to invincibility, that these are just a bunch of white men. They're not even that smart. I have friends I see every day who are far smarter than the president, the vice president, or the secretary of defense. History just hasn't handed my friends the privileges of wealth and the levers of political power. George W. Bush and Donald Rumsfeld bumble and cough and fart their way through each early morning just like all the rest of us. They have mental lapses and bad dreams and dysfunctional relationships. They are every bit as imperfect and often more dangerously ignorant than the rest of us, deluded by poor critical faculties and their fragile, masculine egos. Bill Clinton was smarter by orders of magnitude than George W. Bush, and he wanted to start the second Korean War. These are fallible people, and they have access to and ever more direct control over a frightening nuclear arsenal. So let me not seem overly glib. These are serious times.

When I was in Vietnam, we were taught to refer to the Vietnamese as gooks. This name calling is always part of any military aggression because soldiers have to be brought along in their dehumanization of those they are obliged by conditions and ignorance to abuse, dominate, and kill. Social psychologists tell us that we are overcoming "cognitive dissonance" when we do that.

"Bitch" serves the same purpose in gender relations. Nigger. Raghead. See what I'm saying?

The term "gook" was invented in Korea by Americans who were ordered to abuse, dominate, and kill Koreans. The goal, of course, in the upper reaches of U.S. power, was to prevent the self-determination of this proud people. What happens on the ground is nothing so esoteric.

Dehumanizing leads people to underestimate those they dehumanize. Like the underestimation that led to the rout of the American expeditionary force in 1950. The Bush administration thinks they are dealing with "gooks." We shall see who deserves scorn at the end of all this. They won't be Korean.

OVERREACH

> *Whether anyone likes it or not, at the end of the blind alley that is Europe . . . there is Hitler. At the end of capitalism, which is eager to outlive its day, there is Hitler. At the end of formal humanism and philosophic renunciation, there is Hitler.*
> —Aime Cesaire

Odoacer was the Germanic military leader that led the final defeat of the western Roman Empire. These Germanic peoples were the oppressed nationalities of their day, and they were the final instruments in the death of an empire. I would also point out that Dessalines, the rebel-slave general who defeated Napoleon's armed forces in Haiti, fought alongside the French until just months before their defeat. He was waiting for the wet season, when he knew yellow fever would serve as a kind of heavy artillery and he could turn on his "allies," which he did to devastating effect.

The point is that when one is dealing with a too-powerful-for-the-present force, pragmatism demands one bite one's lip, play the game, and become very alert. People who are under the same hegemonic-for-the-time-being power become furtive. They drop comments to test one another. They feel out levels of resentment. They sniff for willingness to take eventual action.

On the surface of our current world situation, American hegemony appears more powerful than ever. Everyone is doing the boss's bidding. There are even more smiles than usual.

The smart bosses will spot this dissembling, but the most delusional will convince themselves not only of their omnipotence, but also of their charm. Our "leaders" since September 11, 2001, appear to have become delusional.

The whole world was suddenly envisioned by the Bush regime as their imperial province.

Almost a quarter of the world lives in China, where the political rulers are engaged in a long-term economic war against the U.S., Europe and Japan. That's what global capitalism is. War. Japan is already falling unwillingly into the orbit of the still-backward leviathan which can use its oceanic abyss of cheap labor to drown the industrial bases of its competitors—a long-term strategy of destruction by deflation. This is a controversial thesis, and one has to back away a good deal to get the perspective of it.

In 1972, the story goes, Secretary of State Henry Kissinger asked Chinese Premiere Chou En Lai, "What do you think was the final result of the French Revolution?"

With only a second's hesitation, Chou replied, "It's too early to tell."

China and the United States are locked into a kind of economic embrace right now, both with the full knowledge that at some point they will confront one another as antagonists over control of the Asian-Pacific economy and their fundamental visions of the future. The U.S. state sees that world as a Pax Americana and the Chinese hold onto a vision of multipolarity, with several centers of politico-economic gravity in some kind of balance.

The United States strengthened its ties with China after 9/11, partly as an effort to outflank Europe in a developing economic conflict. American capitalists had very significant investments in China, where low labor costs afford the U.S. capitalists expanded profit margins, and a mighty river of export commodities kept China flush with U.S. dollars to build a speculation firewall around the Chinese currency, the renminbi, and to purchase the energy (oil is denominated in dollars around the world) necessary to maintain phenomenal economic growth rates of over eight percent for years. China also held tens of billions of dollars worth of U.S. debt, much in the form of Treasury bonds. (It must be remarked that if everyone in the world who currently holds U.S. bonds cashed them in, the U.S. would be completely unable to pay. Everyone knows this would create a catastrophic deflationary spiral that would wipe out their own holdings, so they are trapped with these immense IOUs.)

China seems to be on a long-term trajectory of industrial and technological development that is designed to overcome its still substantial economic and social backwardness. It is easy to forget, looking at pictures of modern Shanghai, that China emerged from feudalism less than fifty years ago. If the Chinese gamble is that "market socialism" can accelerate this development, the gamble within a gamble is that there will be enough research and development capacity generated in this historic sprint to shift from an economy that exports for dollars to one that directs this newfound industrial and technological capacity along an independent course to its internal social needs—a shift that would require something on the order of a second Chinese Revolution.

In this whole process, the renminbi is now a very undervalued currency, while as of this writing the dollar is overvalued by as much as 40 percent, protected as the international reserve currency by its own hegemony—a position not insignificantly related to the dollar denomination of oil—and just as significantly, U.S. military power.

Paradoxically, it is China's "backwardness" that also constitutes its strength relative to the U.S. and Europe. This gives China immense room for continued growth and a vast army of cheap labor with which it could very well continue to hollow out the manufacturing base of the Untied States.

The U.S. investment in China is not only the door through which China gains access to new technology and industrial infrastructure The U.S. is the consumer of last instance—a situation that has been intensified with the global economic contraction that began in the mid-nineties.

At a far deeper and more significant level, it must be remembered that China will have to attend to its own social needs to prevent internal instability (as this is written, China has alarmed financial pundits by expanding its deficit to address precisely these issues—in particular, unemployment). In the short term, China does that by guaranteeing continued employment for the millions who manufacture for export by holding vast quantities of dollars (to keep the dollar's value up against the undervalued renminbi).

With around 1.4 billion people, the material wherewithal to do so is embedded in a global marketplace of actual things, wherein the U.S. standard of living (upon which the maintenance of U.S. political stability shall depend) is based on the per-capita consumption of more resources, beginning with energy, water, and food, the latter two depending on energy, than anyone else in the world. This means that China and the U.S. are objectively at war, whether it is acknowledged or not, even as they are closed in the current economic embrace. When they release one another—and they both know it—one will have to kill the other.

But China and the U.S. are not sealed hermetically in this objective conflict. One of the things we must guard against in this Western male bourgeois culture is adapting *our* patterns of thinking to Western male bourgeois assumptions. China and the U.S. are not alone in approaching an historic showdown. There is Japan with its technologically educated population (albeit now trapped in a deflationary crisis), Europe with its new currency that some think will mount a challenge to dollar hegemony (It will not. At best, it can become a satellite of the dollar.); Southwest Asia with its vast petroleum seas; coy Russia with its swing production for oil and its nuclear arsenal; Africa with its intense social turmoil atop a global warehouse of strategic minerals and oil; Latin America, now entering a state of open rebellion against the North; the ongoing class struggle regarding the international division of labor; and perhaps most unappreciated for its revolutionary potential, *women* growing daily more restless at their combined economic and sexual subjugation—this is the stage upon which the whole conjuncture plays.

Then there is China's Achilles heel—its oil is declining but it needs ever-increasing quantities of oil to sustain its growth strategy.

Like Dessalines, the Chinese aligned with the U.S. after 9/11 because, to pursue their long-term strategy against the U.S., they need cheap oil, and their own native petroleum production is waning even as their demand increases exponentially. They would risk being militarily encircled, even turn their backs on Maoist rebels in neighboring Nepal, to gain temporary access to post-Iraq oil at $15 a barrel—which now can never materialize, and from the U.S. standpoint *must* never materialize.

Still, they could not go too far in appeasing the hegemon. It was a careful and dangerous game of positioning they played—just enough resistance in the Security Council here, just what they can get away with in trade protectionism there, a plethora of irresistible business deals to U.S. capitalists who want to feed on the postindustrial corpse of the U.S., and multiple trips to the Redneck Ranch in Texas to reassure their support for the Infinite War. Then, with the changing winds, China aligned quietly with the Russians and the French to remove the fig leaf from the Iraq invasion.

Position is everything.

Meanwhile, other imperial provinces grow restive. They sense the underlying weakness of the blustering buffoons in Washington, like a crowd of hostages watching their armed captor growing sleepy during a long siege.

And they are calculating.

Argentina collapsed, and merely uttering the letters *I-M-F* is a call to be tarred and feathered. Brazil will almost certainly default. Ecuador elected its own indigenous Chavez (Gutierrez), even as the too-African Venezuelan president continued to enrage the melanin-deficient Venezuelan and U.S. ruling classes by surviving. Cuba's international prestige has never been greater. Peru is melting down in the streets. Haiti is almost in flames again. Bolivia is in open rebellion. In Colombia, where Bush and Clinton before him drew their line in the sand, the FARC-EP continues to deliver the U.S.–funded Colombian military one tactical defeat after another, and the ELN blows up oil pipelines with near impunity.

This is Uncle Sam's backyard.

These restive provinces know how high are the economic stakes in this desperate play for Gulf States domination.

The stakes are no less than the continued domination of world markets by the U.S. dollar.

The old neoliberal guard is chafing across the Euro-American North. "Why can't we get control of the crazies, these Wolfowitzes, Rumsfelds, Perles, Cheneys, and their Idiot Prince? Their adventures are costing us the stability of the old Pax Americana."

But they confuse causes and effects, as bourgeoisies are prone to do. The "craziness" of Bushfeld is not the cause of these growing rebellions. It is a reaction to them. It was that same old order the bourgeoisies yearn for—multilateral exploitation of the global South—that brought them here. All their institutions were failing before September 11, 2001.

Dessalines was simply waiting for the wet season, and now it looks like rain.

Perhaps even more canny than the Chinese (who behind all their subtlety still harbor a naive and unquestioning faith in that unsustainable chimera of "development") were the Russians, smiling, smiling over their bitter, wounded nationalism, their vengeful revulsion at American culture, with the seeds of humiliation growing malignantly in their political soil.

The Russians want nothing less than the end of U.S. imperialism. And they yearn not just for the American boot to be off them; they yearn for American humiliation.

Neoliberals the world over want the new multilateralism to provide stability like the old multilateralism. But that, like development, is a chimera. Its social and material bases are gone, used up, transformed by capital from a fertile, exploitable soil into a seething, toxic sludge.

As Mark Jones wrote in December 2002:

> If they [the Russians] succeed, and the French and Chinese, British and Germans succeed (because they are all doing their damnedest to block Bush and thus to destroy Bush politically) then U.S. imperialism will be weakened, will it not?
>
> But behind the realism and Machiavellian clarity and cynicism of these manoeuvrings, are these players still not driven by a desire to revert to the longed-for golden age of U.S. rationalism and paternalism? Which of them has a game-plan to deal with open and uncontrolled crisis, with no hegemon capable of refereeing play?
>
> I suppose that every major player (France, Russia, China, the UK etc) is making the same calculation, i.e., how to spin things out so that Bush loses the moment to make war, and how to dump Bush and get back to a softer so-called multilateral U.S. foreign policy; but also like with the fall of Rome, these sorts of calculations are based on illusions, above all the illusion that there ever was a golden age of multilateralism to revert to. In reality there were temporary phases of apparent stability, of calm local areas of equilibrium, on the surface of processes which were anything but calm, but which were characterised by great flux, incipient crisis, and by long-run trends (demography, resource-depletion, et al).

There was only ever, since 1945, extraordinary U.S. global dominance, but always within the confines of what 1917 created. The weakness of U.S. hegemony inevitably invokes an era of turbulence chaos and unpredictability, and however much the players may want to go back to the golden age of quiet peaceful gluttony they hanker for, there is no road back and in practice all the players, including the U.S., are now doing all they can to bring the whole tottering structure down on their own heads. If Al Gore wins the next election, for example, how will that help overcome the inevitable dollar/debt crisis, U.S. slump, world market contraction etc? What can slay the wolves of deflation now howling around the campfires?

Overreach. There is simply no way to predict what the conjuncture will look like. Who could have known in 2002 what an impact SARS would have? The variables are both too numerous and too interdetermined to simply calculate.

It will be military overreach, because Bush has put all its eggs in that basket.

He really had no choice. The United States is no longer economically competitive. It dominates only through dollar hegemony, and that dollar hegemony (which is really a global credit scam) must be secured militarily. It is partly secured by the imperial tribute that is cheap oil—denominated in U.S. dollars.

As the United States is slowly drained of its industrial capacity, its trade deficit bloating, the entire productive edifice of the U.S. economy looted until only a frangible speculative superstructure remains, its occupants now weighing it down with enormous debt to feed privileged white America's profligate lifestyle of SUVs, electronics, fickle fashion, high protein diets, and generalized degeneracy . . . the whole world watches and waits.

Many on the left are making the demand—in response to the current situation—that the U.S. cut military spending to shift funds into social programs. While this is an understandable (and even polemically effective) demand, it is not based on the fuller reality.

The citizens of the United States are only indirectly paying for our military adventures. In fact, the source for funding U.S. wars is also the foutainhead of the U.S. standard of living. The true source of funding for American adventurism is to be found in the central banks of Europe, China, Japan, and elsewhere. They are paying for U.S. wars. Since the U.S. abandoned the gold standard in the wake of Vietnam (where U.S. gold reserves were depleted almost to their legal limit), these central banks—holding U.S. Treasury bonds, which are basically IOUs—have been tied to U.S. currency. They dollar is effectively shored up by oil state investments in dollar-denominated assets and slaked like a vampire by the external debts of ruined economies. No country can afford to wean itself without risking the collapse of the whole house of cards. The U.S. is in the unique position of being able to print as much money as it wants to cover current account deficits, which has indebted the U.S. to the point that they know, and their creditors know, that they will never pay it back.

In 1972, Saudi Arabia said it intended to buy up U.S. companies—productive capital instead of bonds. The U.S. showed its sword, telling the Saudis in no uncertain terms that this would be considered an act of war. The deal was subsequently sealed that the Saudis could invest as non-controlling stockholders and in Treasury bonds, in exchange for certain "security" arrangements. The Saudis helped establish the petrodollar, and the U.S. was safe in the catbird seat.[1]

Now Europe, for example, had to pay for its oil in dollars, loaning their own value, as it were, to the U.S. for dollar paybacks through Treasury bonds. Europe was being forced to maintain large reserves of dollars to defend themselves from currency speculators, after the U.S. also abandoned fixed currency exchange rates. But this meant that the U.S. could pay for oil in money that it could print, which it did—a practice that would normally devalue the currency in an open market, were it not for the fact that that same devaluation would now wipe out creditors like Europe. This catch-22 remains the basis of dollar hegemony, which is the basis of U.S. economic hegemony. And it means that the U.S. government's debt is now a kind of Mafia arrangement, where Europeans and all the rest are essentially being "taxed" by this practice. They know the U.S. will never pay back its debt, but if they try to sell off their Treasury bonds, the dollar will crash down around all of them, beginning with their own central banks. So they are making "loans" via Treasury bonds that they already know they'll never get paid for. This is what is financing U.S. militarism. Pathet Lao currency, accepted because America has the gun. And, of course, it is outright unsustainable.[2]

The destruction of social infrastructure inside the United States does not transfer funds out of the same pool, so to speak. The massive tax cuts by the Bush administration and the transfer of wealth from bottom to top has been at the behest of a Wall Street that has been liquidating everything in sight—including social infrastructure—to stay afloat on the whirlpool of speculation that brought us the dotcom collapse and the string of scandals that included Bush-benefactor Enron. This is also unsustainable.

There was already an ironclad guarantee of a domestic economic-then-political crisis when Bush captured the 2000 elections through a judicial fiat. Then 9/11 gave the Bush administration the pretext to launch a bold venture to restructure the entire global architecture by arms. The gamble was that the seizure of Iraqi (then Saudi if necessary) oil would create the conditions for a fresh upwave of imperial accumulation . . . and the leverage to eventually strangle China.

This center cannot hold and the profound weakness of the whole system doesn't seem the least bit obscure. I am still bowled over by the timidity of many so-called progressives, especially when that timidity is in the face of what is so obviously a system stealing pieces of its own foundation to fix its collapsing roof.

Afghanistan. Iraq. Palestine. The Philippines. Indonesia. Ecuador. Colombia. Nigeria. Haiti. These are the "black holes" of the social cosmos with their multiple event horizons that capture more and more of the American budget in their intensifying gravitational fields . . .

The U.S. military has become a high-tech weapon of mass destruction, following a trajectory of development that began before the end of the Cold War and leading into an era that is nothing like the Cold War. It is eroding its own ability to engage in military occupation except at phenomenal international cost, and undermining its own ability to maintain a coherent doctrine by destroying states and assuring the global expansion of Mogadishu.

And occupy it must, or it will fail.

The natives everywhere are restless. Dessalines will pop up, because he is a spirit latent in the people that will cross over fear, set the fields ablaze, and massacre the occupiers . . . after biding much time.

America quite simply cannot afford what the Bush clique proposes, and that proposal—as even the Joint Chiefs have repeatedly reminded the tinpot generals of Bush's cabinet—cannot be done at discount rates. Even the delusional leaders of Europe will eventually figure it out. This ship will sink, and they have been rearranging the deck chairs.

If the Asians, Latin Americans, and Africans who are being bled gray by external debt ever get together and say they will default, U.S. power will drop like it's been shot through the brain stem.

The current conjecture is not a lesson—as the European bourgeoisie would have it—in the buffoonery of Bush and Rumsfeld (though there is plenty of that—remember that Caligula was not a cause, he was an effect). Gore would be pursuing the same path, albeit with slightly different specifics. His defeat was symptomatic of the death throes of bourgeois democracy in the U.S., but he is associated with Occidental Petroleum (that snuggles up to the death squads in Colombia). He knows oil. He knows dollars. Democrats simply have a different popular base than Republicans. As at the turn of the last century for the Democrats, the Republicans are taking their turn at being the party of white supremacy—this time with a theocratic mask.

Approaching just over the horizon, too, are the tidal wave contradictions of energy and demographics that this accumulation regime cannot survive no matter what it does.

The military is all that is left.

We are now seeing the naked brutality that has been there all along, as scale after scale of superficial legitimacy falls. And the military is unequal to the task. America cannot occupy the whole world. That's why Rumsfeld wants to develop the capacity to launch weapons from space. Bush is reduced to holding the whole world hostage.

But these generals and wannabe generals are not outside this world. This is their Cartesian error.

They are in it.

American society is part of the world system, and its imperial privileges will go by the wayside. In that convulsive process—closer than people realize—we will see the naked face of internal colonial oppression as well, the overt subjugation of Black and Brown peoples inside the U.S.A., and not long after, the open attack on the entire U.S. working class—working class divided by white male privilege and susceptible to the siren call of a new American fascism.

And there is a war that will be intensified against the deepest foundation of capital accumulation—the one that even socialists are guilty of having rendered invisible: women. The entire system is materially based on the exploitation (and not by the narrow definition of orthodox Marxism) of women, especially the incredibly diverse array of Third World women, who carry society through its worst agonies day by day with their unwaged work—women whose sex is the marker for their various oppressors and whose circumstances constitute a multiplicity of frameworks for the agency and resistance of women. Women—in my opinion—may constitute the most significant revolutionary forces in the world in the coming conjuncture. If you want to see the economy within the economy, and what will be left to build upon when we inherit the toxic scrap heap that capitalism is bequeathing us, go to those places where the environment has been stripped bare and the people reduced to septic squalor—like Haiti—and you will see our deepest current foundations and our firmest hope for post-capitalist renewal being carried about on the heads of calloused women. And not just women as workers and mothers, but women as fighters.

My next book will examine, among other things, the male revolutionary disinclination to see women as armed combatants, or as merely tokens in this role, and how these male revolutionaries have displayed a corresponding inability to escape liberalism's economistic and oxymoronic—as Catherine McKinnon says—notion of sexual equality. Then I can be everyone's heretic.

BLACK OPS

AMERICA'S *military special forces and the CIA are to set up a joint team of covert counter-intelligence agents to be known as the "proactive pre-emptive operations group" ["black ops"] for secret missions targeting terrorist leaders.*

The group of about 100 is to include experts in behind-the-lines intelligence gathering, computer hacking, and other clandestine skills dating back to the days of the cold war.

The PPOG, funded from an increased special operations budget, would be under the direct control of the White House and would carry out missions coordinated either by the Pentagon or by CIA head-quarters at Langley, Virginia.

Donald Rumsfeld, the U.S. defence secretary, is also considering a request for extra cash which would almost double the current £3.5bn annual budget for conventional special forces . . .

—From "U.S. Anti-terror Force Planned," Ian Bruce, *Herald* (Glasgow), 15 November 2002

When I was in Vietnam, I never saw two Black soldiers greet each other without givin' up dap. White officers were clearly uncomfortable with it, and some Black NCOs were pressured to put a stop to these elaborate improvisational handshakes.

It never worked. Dap was as much a part of Black GI culture as Motown.

And make no mistake. It was oppositional culture. White officers were right to feel uncomfortable with it. It was an open display of Black solidarity by *Negroes with guns*. When African American GIs spoke with one another, they referred to one another as "Black" with the same frequency guys call each other "man" (another vestige of Black opposi- tional culture, as opposed to "black ops").

This new, super-elite, "black ops" unit's "operators" will have hard- ly a Black face to be seen. In the U.S., "black ops" is always done by white operators. No one is going to teach large numbers of African Americans these clandestine skills.

Every time in the history of the United States that Black soldiers have fought its wars, there has been an outbreak of Black resistance afterward. Surely this is no surprise.

I referred earlier to Odoacer, a mercenary in the service of Rome and leader of the Germanic soldiers in the Roman army who deposed the western Roman emperor, Romulus Augustus, in 476 A.D., and thereby terminated the western Roman empire.

There is a limit to how much an oppressed people within a state will take. Rumsfeld and his ilk know this. You can bank on it.

When the Bush regime made the claim that the U.S. was attacked by people who hate freedom and democracy, the irony was not likely lost on African Americans or any other oppressed nationality.

I stress African Americans here because Black people are the very embodiment of white ruling class fear, especially in the military. Three out of ten soldiers in the Army today are African-American, as is one out of ten officers. Until you look at Special Operations.

Negrophobia, and not generalized racism, is characteristic of special ops units, and the more rarified the unit, the whiter it gets—with a few honorary Aryans from Hispano-Latina and Pacific islander ranks. There are special places for Black soldiers in Special Operations: kitchens, supply rooms, personnel offices, and motor pools.

This lack of "minority" participation as "operators" in Special Operations began to leak some years ago. In 1999, the Rand Corporation released a report that attempted to describe *Barriers to Minority Participation in Special Operations Forces* (SOF), which attempts to put an empirical mask over SOF racial exclusion, even repeating many of the urban myths within SOF about why Black sol- diers are so vastly under-represented there. "They can't swim," and so forth.

Horse shit.

When we put two and two together, we will likely end up with four. I saw Special Operations–schools cadre use every available opportunity, particularly those numerous aspects of periodic evaluation that are subjective, to weed out Black soldiers. Not all of the cadre did it, but there were enough spread out over the process to ensure the "correct" result.

Conventional ground forces were to be held back for any but the most banal military tasks: mop-up and guard duty. The new emphasis on using Special Operations Forces for any decisive ground combat tasks is partly predicated on the Powell Doctrine fear of U.S. casualties. Interestingly enough, in an article for the spring 2003 issue of *Color Lines*, Glen Ford, a veteran of the Vietnam-era 82nd Airborne Division, showed how conventional combat arms units are now being systematically loaded up with southern whites and Latinos, and lowering Black participation. No reason to take any chances.

The secret fear is BPCSSD. Black postcombat social stress disorder. Not to be confused with PTSD, post-traumatic stress disorder.

Black troops who go to war, especially if they are required to fight, become restive and uncooperative when they get home. They ask embarrassing questions, like "Where's ours?" BPCSSD.

Let there be no doubt that the American white terror of Black rebellion still haunts the psyches of our pale ruling class. The U.S. Army has a disproportionate number of Black troops. Having too many of them crossing the psychological barrier against squeezing triggers on human targets can't strike the Man as a very good idea.

Vietnam taught the white U.S. ruling class a lot of lessons about the military. One was that it's not wise to simultaneously maintain a large military conscript force of many oppressed nationalities and expose them to combat for colonial objectives, when their lives at home mirror the conditions against which their ostensible enemy is fighting.

Open and violent rebellion in the form of armed confrontations and fraggings by Black soldiers were common in Vietnam.

By 1973, as U.S. forces were well along in a phased withdrawal from Vietnam, the U.S. Armed Forces were dumping the draft.

They didn't want citizen-soldiers any more. They wanted mercenaries. Do what you're told and collect your check.

And now, with the immense expense of the new higher-tech War Department, whose cost will tear the frayed carpet from under the U.S. working class with workers of oppressed nationalities hitting bottom first, they sure don't want a bunch of *Negroes with guns* coming home with role conflicts.

They don't need any BPCSSD. In Iraq today, against all Rumsfeld's calculations, there are thousands of Black folk doing Uncle Sam's wet work, even as Rumsfeld's military is attempting to minimize their numbers in combat arms. As they are obliged to occupy Iraq, many come from communities that are occupied by the police at home. BPCSSD will be returning from Iraq, soon, at a station near you.

THE LEFT AND THE ARMED FORCES

Mask no difficulties, tell no lies, claim no easy victories.
—Amilcar Cabral

Who's gonna listen to you if you just go around makin' stuff up?
—Sherry Long

When I wrote *Hideous Dream*, like every writer I think, I had a reader in mind. I have been justly accused of being arcane in that memoir. The reason is, my reader was the only person I really knew at the time: a soldier.

I went back, of course, at the behest of my editor, to insert explanations, but he let me keep the basic idiom intact. Soldier to soldier. I still hope soldiers read it. It is intended, at least to some degree, to validate their experience.

Since my retirement from the army on February 1, 1996, I have divested of all personal relations inside the military. My friends and associates are now almost exclusively political activists whom we might refer to as "the left."

In 2001, after a book signing in Chapel Hill, North Carolina, I had the pleasure of meeting Dr. Catherine Lutz, an anthropology professor at the University of North Carolina who was in the final stages of publishing her own book about the military, *Homefront*.[1] She let me have a copy of the draft going to the publisher. I was intellectually impressed by the scope and erudition of the book, but I was emotionally moved by Cathy's personal accounts of soldiers. A very visible and active faculty radical from the state's flagship university had actually talked to soldiers and ex-soldiers and presented them in all their complex humanity.

I had grown very impatient with leftist stereotyping of the military and the omnipresent factual misrepresentation of the military by both the corporate and leftist press.

I would later learn that Cathy grew up in a military household.

Hollywood's stereotypical mystique and the left's simplified demonization of the military are abstractions that don't hold up well when you've seen your father, a stern captain, rummaging around the bathroom, or paralyzed by a spouse's anger, or sick and vulnerable, playful, reflective, sad, silly . . . or once you've seen your mother wash his dirty drawers.

Here's my main point, though, because this book is both for the left and for soldiers. I'd like to help build that bridge. When the time comes for the deep transformation of this society—sooner than later, I believe—a significant portion of the armed forces will either support us or refuse to attack us. Otherwise it won't happen.

If the left accepts that, then it follows that they need to study the military. We study bourgeois economists, so we can study workers in uniform.

We need credibility when we pop off on military matters, and the left surrenders its credibility all the time when it masks complexities in the interest of some short-term polemical advantage.

In particular, if we are to reach out to the people inside the military, most of them working class and a disproportionate number of them oppressed nationalities, then we have to do two things. We have to get our facts straight. And we have to think about their experience critically.

Most soldiers are voracious readers. One reason I failed to read much from the left while I was in the military, or even from the mainstream press (which soldiers mistrust enormously . . . are we listening?), is that within two paragraphs I'd generally encounter some technical or factual error or some preposterous, archaic stereotype. Just the other day, someone asked me if there were still more black people than white people serving as "orderlies" in the army.

Sure. They bunk with the wheelwrights and stable boys.

Pam Parker, who is a dedicated socialist, and a tireless worker in the anti-fascist movement that is emerging in the U.S., wrote an article in November 2002 called "Media try not to embarrass Pentagon," in which she says the following:

> Are the 10 people killed in the Washington, D.C., area delayed "collateral damage" from the last Gulf War? . . . John Muhammad cleared land mines and qualified as an expert with the M-16 rifle while serving in the Gulf War before being honorably discharged in 1994 . . . Although there was endless speculation about the psychological make-up of the shooter(s), for weeks most "experts" stayed away from making the obvious connection between sniper training and the armed forces or the police . . . So how does the Pentagon turn young people into killers?

It's a real shame that such intelligence and dedication is wasted printing this perfect example of what I was talking about—people on the left engaged in physical improbabilities and self-destructive behavior, i.e., talking through their asses and shooting their own credibility in the foot.

John Muhammad's military training was as an engineer and his marksmanship training—and qualification—ended with basic training and an annual forty-round requalification. "Expert" is one of three qualifications (Marksman, Sharpshooter, Expert) based on a score out of those forty shots at pop-up silhouette targets. Any soldier in the military is likely to earn this qualification if she or he goes to the range and has a good day. Once a soldier earns "Expert" one time, she or he can wear the badge around for good.

Any "sniper" shit Muhammad came up with, he came up with without the assistance of the U.S. military.

No one with more than two weeks experience in the military will take the above piece seriously, and many will use it to dismiss everything they hear by socialists thereafter. As a socialist who used to be a soldier, I take issue with that.

I was a "sniper"—as my primary job description—for two years in Delta Force. I later developed, coordinated, supervised, and taught battalion consolidated sniper training for 2nd Battalion, 7th Special Forces.

It is a specific skill-set and role, and when the media, even leftist media, starts using the term interchangeably with anyone who shoots people without warning, it's the equivalent of calling everyone in an auto factory a millwright welder. It's just sloppy and imprecise, which would naturally bug the hell out of an ex-sniper, but it was Lenin who said that precision of terms is a revolutionary imperative.

Muhammad and Malvo used a civilian deer rifle, and they did not engage in precision shooting, one specialty of snipers (along with detailed planning, stalking, advanced overland navigation, camouflage, hide-site construction, communications, report writing, photography, and recognition of dozens of vehicles, weapons, and aircraft). All Muhammad's and Malvo's shots were within one hundred meters, which from a strictly technical standpoint, if readers will forgive me for being so clinical, is not particularly notable marksmanship. What they engaged in were ambushes, defined as "surprise attacks from concealed positions on moving or temporarily halted targets." They are not snipers. For whatever reasons, if they actually did what is alleged, they are sociopaths.

I don't know what motivated them, but as far as I can tell Malvo was too young to have been in the military unless whatever "disengagement" Muhammed had from being a combat engineer—whose major weapons include road graders, bulldozers, metal detectors, and backhoes—was contagious and infected the youngster.

The Parker article continues:

> Serial killings were all but unheard of 50 years ago. Could it be a coincidence that this tactic of "disengagement" appeared at about the same time? A sampling of the most notable snipers shows a clear connection between military training and the propensity to take innocent lives. Timothy McVeigh, the Oklahoma City bomber, and Robert Flores, a 41-year-old nursing student who recently opened fire on several professors and classmates before killing himself in Tucson, Ariz., were both Gulf War veterans, like John Muhammad.

McVeigh was motivated by a combination of paranoia and race hatred. The army trained him as a Bradley mechanized-infantry crewman, but his weapon in Oklahoma was the same low-yield, expedient explosive that Michigan farmers use to remove stumps. He just made a lot of it. He had joined the army to get Special Operations experience to carry out his mad, neo-Nazi fantasies, but he couldn't survive the selection and assessment process for Special Forces, so he ended up in "mech" infantry.[2]

Parker again:

> According to David Grossman, a former U.S. military psychologist, soldiers are taught to remove themselves from human suffering by a process called "disengagement." This process breaks down the natural human aversion to kill. The military increased these training tactics in reaction to soldiers' hesitancy to kill when commanded. The military implemented this training specifically to increase the "trigger pull ratio." This training is specifically designed for infantry soldiers, snipers and other military personnel who may have to kill people up close . . .

Flores was a mechanic who never saw a day of combat and who snapped out in response to a very hostile, high-stress academic atmosphere in the nursing school he attended. He used a handgun, on which the military had never given him a day of training. The only thing he was trained by the military to "disengage" was a clutch.

For that matter, in over two decades of being in combat arms, including in the role of sniper, I never received my "disengagement training." Perhaps I should write and ask why. It didn't seem to affect my "trigger-pull ratio," but one never can tell. There are still a few people I *want* to shoot, but since they are all unlikely to ever personally provoke me in a way that could construe my act as self-defense, I'll probably have to take these and a host of other unfulfilled fantasies to my grave.

We were subjected to extensive psychological testing prior to Delta selection to determine if we might have anything resembling "Texas Tower Syndrome," any hint of which immediately *disqualifies* a candidate.

Jeffrey Dahmer, David Berkowitz—dubbed by the press the Son of Sam—and Charles Whitman, who killed sixteen people and injured thirty-one others in a 1961 sniper shooting rampage from the top of a tower in Austin, Texas, were all military veterans . . . In fact, the very first documented serial killer, Howard Unruh, was a twenty-eight-year-old veteran of World War II who shot thirteen of his New Jersey neighbors in 1949 . . .

Jeffery Dahmer had sex with corpses, ate his victims, and kept their decomposing heads in the fridge as trophies. These tasks are not listed in the soldier's manual. He committed his first killing and dismemberment when he was fourteen, well before he was eligible to join the armed forces.

David "Son of Sam" Berkowitz—well, here's an interesting one, too—began hiding in the closet for hours between bouts of irrational and aggressive behavior when he was a child, well before his one tour in the army, where his most notable accomplishment was catching the clap from a prostitute in Korea—possibly his single sexual encounter. He was an adequate marksman, but when the centuries-old dog of his schizophrenic netherworld began to order the assassination of young lovers, Berkowitz selected a civilian revolver.

Whitman was a former Marine, and he did learn how to fire a rifle in the Marine Corps. But Whitman was stationed in Guantanamo Bay, where the biggest threat is stepping on a sea urchin, and he was reputed to have adapted poorly to military life and life in general, since he grew up under the discipline of a vicious father who battered his mother and him and once even attempted to drown Whitman in a fit of fury. Dad, it seems, was "disengaging" the lad long before Uncle Sam got hold of him.

Unruh was a disturbed child as well, and was subject to hallucinations prior to his shooting spree in a New Jersey neighborhood. He has been institutionalized and on psychiatric medication ever since.

The federal government was allegedly so anxious to try the case that a federal agent interrupted an interrogation by county prosecutors and whisked Muhammad off to Baltimore. Which raises another question: were these investigators getting Muhammad to talk about his motive for the shootings? And might that be embarrassing to the military?

I don't know, but this article certainly embarrassed me as a leftist.

I hate how facts keep making me go back and reassess my assumptions, but since easy answers never make for very persuasive arguments, I have to seek and account for the pesky things. Those of us in social movements bear a special responsibility because when we say silly things, that silliness is not simply attributed to the person who says them. It is transferred to the whole movement.

There is no doubt that combat experience—or even military experience—that involves *no* combat or special danger for the vast majority of troops (construction work is far more dangerous than most military service)—has a formative influence on people, some of it positive and some negative. I'm not dismissive of that. But stereotyping, conflating correlation with causation, and manipulating facts does nothing to tell us what those influences are. Demagogy discredits us.

We have way too much at stake to go for easy answers.

Fact is, many on the left have refused to take the leap from generalized moral judgments and theoretical pigeon-holing to study and criticism—alas, symptomatic of a larger malaise on the left that it has taken the rise of George Dubya Bush's crazed clique to begin to overcome. People rely on impressions about "the military," largely gained from secondhand polemics or entertainment media. And we miss much. Shortcut thinking always misses much.

The military is a violent macho culture. Surely that's no surprise. So are many team sports. Warfare did much to shape the gender roles that now dominate our culture, even those aspects of the male script that are no longer recognizable as martial.[3] Military institutions exist as the primary external armed body of the state, and in many countries as the internal armed body as well. All true. Military organizations are bureaucratic and they cover up their crimes and mistakes. Well and good. So do corporations, and there are workers there, too.

While reductionism as an interpretive method has run its purveyors into many a ditch over the last few decades, the left still clings to it on the subject of the armed forces.

How many on the left will acknowledge that the institution with the most effective affirmative action program in the country, at least with regard to race, is the United States Army? Interracial marriage is far more common in the military than the civil sector. How many on the left recognize that on a military base there resides a community that is more socialist than capitalist?

Every resident of a U.S. military base has come to expect high-quality schools, a plentitude of commons—including libraries, parks, recreation centers, gymnasiums, stadiums, swimming pools, cinemas, craft shops, hiking trails, community centers, and nature preserves—a three-tiered universal health care system, counseling centers, and safe, well-designed residential neighborhoods where housing, maintenance, and utilities are provided free. The disparity between the highest and lowest pay in the military is less than thirteen to one, compared to an average of four hundred and fifty-eight to one in the civil sector.[4]

That's being eroded very quickly as Bush & Company rush to pay for their patrons and their wars out of the bleeding public treasury, but it's still marginally true.

The majority of those who remain in military service remain for these reasons. It never occurs to them that what they like about the military is socialist. They frequently hate the deployments, the very occasional violence in which only a small minority actually participate, the bureaucratic backbiting, and the ubiquitous incompetence. They put up with all these negatives because they and their families enjoy some modicum of security and well-being. Soldiers know the concrete possibilities of socialism better than the rest of us. They've lived them.

When we refuse to take up the issue of women or gays in the military—masking contradictions by saying we are "against" the military anyway—we are missing the point that this is an issue of gender equality in federal employment. Queer people are isolated altogether, and women are legally excluded from the majority of positions (not specialties, that is different), and from those career tracks within which advancement is the fastest, and we just wrote them off because they weren't evolved enough to know better than joining the armed forces. As an organizer, I can only think of one word for this kind of self-righteousness. Stupid.

Little understood outside the military is the peculiar negrophobia of the Special Operations-subset within the otherwise thoroughly integrated armed forces. Here too is a wedge, a teachable moment for Black soldiers when we might begin to organize. Instead, the infantile left wants to badger them to revolt (now!) or write them off altogether. At the end of the day, these soldiers are just abstractions.

Every successful revolution requires either the neutralization or active participation of military people. It's really time to factor that into our thinking. It's time we thought about organizing within the military. And organizing is not helping out a handful of conscientious objectors (though that is important) or dropping into Fayetteville with antiwar petitions for GIs to sign. Organizing is getting to know them, listening to them, building relationships with them, and standing alongside them when they confront their own institution.

My vision is not that we beat our swords into plowshares. I am not a pacifist.

There are enough criminals like those who are our political leaders right now to ensure *we* will need the armed forces. Let's not forget that those anti-imperialist movements making the most headway in Latin America these days—in Colombia, Venezuela, and Ecuador—all have significant armed forces behind them. In Colombia the resistance has a viable armed insurgent force, and in the other two, the rebellious governments have the majority of their officially recognized armed forces behind them.

My vision is that the American armed forces, when they are harshly taught as the current conjuncture will teach them, will unite with the people, and that sections of it will break away and become the defenders of their families, and thereby a liberatory force. As America's political class becomes ever more lawless, ever more compelled to scrap bourgeois democracy and slouch toward fascism, we shall need them and they shall need us.

STRATEGY, CHAOS, AND AGILITY

Suddenly, when it comes to defending itself, America's streamlined warships, cruise missiles and F-16 jets look like obsolete, lumbering things. As deterrence, its arsenal of nuclear bombs is no longer worth its weight in scrap. Box-cutters, penknives, and cold anger are the weapons with which the wars of the new century will be waged. Anger is the lock pick. It slips through customs unnoticed. Doesn't show up in baggage checks.

—Arundhati Roy

The greatest paradox, in my opinion, of the left's failure to grasp any but the most superficial aspects of military reality is the left's adoption of an anachronistic military episteme of strategy in its own struggles.

The most fundamental weakness latent in the dominant way of "knowing" is Cartesian—the treasured fallacy that we can both grasp and control reality as something external to ourselves. With this Cartesian error, there is the metaphysical fallacy of believing that patterns we observe now will continue to repeat themselves indefinitely without any fundamental change. We interpret our experience of the world through signs and categories and gestalts with which we have prior experience, or which we have been taught, often metaphorically.

With my occasionally sharp critiques of Marx-*ism*, as a practice developed after Marx himself died, it is important to highlight one of Marx's most valuable contributions, his contribution to understanding epistemology, the way we know. His method of seeking out contradictions in appearances and then attempting to go below the surface of the appearance to resolve the contradiction led him to identify the dynamic interrelationship between what we do and how we think.

Our actions and the contexts for our actions that form the larger part of daily experience are constructed around us largely by individual economic necessity confined within the actual possibilities and limitations of society-as-it-is. The technologies and relationships that form the basis of the daily reproduction of a specific form of society are taken for granted as almost natural, so habituated to them do we become. But these technologies and the relationships developed in concert with these technologies structure our active lives.

An automobile is a technology, but it also implies a whole set of social relations that incorporate private automobiles, rules for driving, automobile manufactories with both bosses and workers, Departments of Transportation, Food Lions instead of nearby greengrocers, jobs that are farther and farther away, Code Red ozone days, gas stations with bad coffee for the road, and so forth. Thinking of it this way, it is easy to understand that this technology, which is so much a part of the everyday scenery of our lives that we pay little attention to its implications, in reality has an enormous impact on our experience and thereby on how we "know" the world.

In turn, how we "know" defines the possibilities and limits of our actions and thereby sustains and stabilizes the system. It is a self-reinforcing feedback loop. It is also a system in which one class of white men who own or control the most important institutions in the society (motivated by their own self-interest, but certainly as trapped in some ways as all of us *within* the system) actually decide what gets produced. One of the things they control the production of, along with electricity, cars, food, designer jeans, cheap toys to sell hamburgers, etc., is knowledge, including their own.

One of the most difficult conceptual leaps to take, and certainly the most important, is to take what we experience every day and conduct a rigorous interrogation of it. To do this, we need to critically examine every category, every premise, every assumption that underwrites what we think we know; then identify the contradictions we find; and begin the intellectual detective work to resolve the contradictions by going below the surface of our dominant way of knowing.

Even as Marx struggled to understand capitalism using this going below method of inquiry, it was only toward the end of his life that he began to identify a Western Cartesian bias in his description of human beings as organisms that conquer or dominate something called nature.

Unfortunately, leftists ever since then have failed to interrogate the premises of their own notions of strategy, and that failure to ask the right questions has led them to accept the "background," that is, the dominant episteme, while they are preoccupied with the foreground of current issues.

Developing the ability to conduct this interrogation is the essential first step for getting out of the dominant feedback loop of daily practice and understanding and positioning oneself to really challenge the system. This is also true of strategy, especially in the current conjuncture where the entire global system is undergoing a period of extreme disequilibrium.

Falling back on my own experience as a member of the armed forces and the combat arms, I can conclude that every failure of strategy is at bottom a failure of plans to conform to reality. In effect, every strategic failure is a failure of intelligence—intelligence being information that is interpreted to make sense of an overall situation.

If our environment itself is chaotic, any strategy that fails to take unpredictability into account is bound to be a strategy that encounters what military theorists have long called "friction." Translation, not to put too fine a pint on it: shit happens.

Maverick military theorist John Boyd, who developed the warfighting theory that drove nearly all systems development for U.S. fighter aircraft for the last two decades, studied chaos theory, entropy and dialectics, and dabbled significantly in epistemology. In 1959, he challenged all conventional wisdom on air combat. Boyd challenged any comers to simulated air combat, wherein he would defeat them within forty seconds of engagement. He was never beaten. His theories have been distorted both by the military itself—which was characteristically unable to escape its own bureaucratic and mechanistic culture—and the corporate sector, which is constantly hawking Sun Tzu, Boyd, and other war theory as an analogue to economic theory. This practice is certainly interesting, if misguided.

Boyd's own worldview was pretty social-Darwinist and consequently he never fully grasped the political character of war. But his contribution to a general theory of combat strategy was brilliant. Just as Marx teased the genius of the dialectic out of Hegel's idealism and integrated it with philosophical materialism, Boyd's theory needs to be extricated from his Nietzschean worldview and integrated with revolutionary insight into the political character of war.

Boyd critiqued Clausewitz and others for the notion that one can "overcome" chaos with planning and centralized command and control. He saw that as flying in the face of reality itself. Reality is nonlinear and dynamic, he reiterated again and again. This is the ABC of chaos theory. What we need to comprehend strategically is not what is under the chaos, but that the chaos (shorthand for nonlinear and dynamic) *is* the reality with which we must ally ourselves.

Part of that reality is our adversary and our adversary's psychological limitations. That reality as a totality—as a kind of strategic gestalt—"unfolds" according to Boyd, "forming, dissolving, and reforming." Boyd was enamored of both mathematician Kurt Godel's thesis that no single system of logic is adequate on its own—his Incompleteness Theorem—and Werner Heisenberg's "Uncertainty Principle." Boyd determined that any attempt to impose a "consistent" system of logic on a chaotic situation created a "mismatch" between reality and perception.[1]

Boyd:

> To comprehend and cope with our environment we develop mental patterns or concepts of meaning . . . we destroy and create these patterns to permit us to both shape and be shaped by a changing environment . . . [W]e cannot avoid this kind of activity if we intend to survive on our own terms. [Boyd is referring here to "initiative," which he calls "independence of action." —SG] The activity is dialectic in nature, generating both disorder and order that emerges as a changing and expanding universe of mental concepts matched to a changing and expanding universe of observed reality.[2]

Boyd refers constantly to creation and destruction, by which he means—from the standpoint of perception and consciousness—the recognition of significant patterns by shifting back and forth between inductive and deductive strategies. The only way, according to Boyd, to conform one's own actions to chaos is to develop the capacity to recognize and respond through constant reorientation, which he called an OODA loop—observe, orient, decide, act. The latter is, even by Boyd's admission, a gross simplification. Implicit in Boyd's thesis is that the patterns change, and each time we act, we disrupt and transform patterns in unpredictable ways, whereupon we have to re-orient for the next decision cycle. In adversarial strategy, then, Boyd recognizes no formulas. Schematic solutions are anathemas if one is trying to make an ally of chaos—nonlinear, dynamic, and therefore unpredictable situations.

Boyd's focus, then—and I think it is valid—is on developing this strategic intuition in leaders, not selecting from a playbook of formulas and subordinating leadership to them. This quest for "agility" recognizes the paramount importance of time in any conflict. Speed matters. A lot.

In *Modern Strategy*, Colin Gray notes:

> Boyd's theory claims that the key to success in conflict is to operate inside the opponent's decision cycle. Advantages in observation and orientation enable a tempo in decision making and execution that outpaces the ability of the foe to react effectively in time. This seemingly simple tactical formula was duly explained and copiously illustrated historically by Boyd in many briefings within the U.S. defense community over the course of twenty years. The OODA loop may appear too humble to merit categorization as a grand theory, but that is what it is. It has an elegant simplicity, an extensive domain of applicability, and contains a high quality of insight about strategic essentials . . .

The centerpiece of Boyd's theory is that one's adversary is always human. The counterposition of two set-piece strategies, especially in modern warfare, is a recipe for a bloodbath of attrition. To defeat the leadership (a perceiving human) is the goal, according to Boyd, and that is accomplished by maintaining the initiative through audacious, often uncoordinated, rapid actions until the adversary is overwhelmed by the "mismatches" between perception and reality. These mismatches are not the result of your "plan." They are an outcome of your agility— your superior ability to accept chaos and adapt rapidly to changing patterns. Improvisation.

Yet even the U.S. military, which studies Boyd incessantly, cannot reconcile the core insights of Boyd's theory with its own doctrine. This type of agility can only be achieved in a decentralized milieu, and the bureaucratic character of the U.S. military leviathan can't handle that.

For social change organizers, this is no excuse. What they share with the U.S. military, and what the left has traditionally shared with the U.S. military, is schematicism. We want the system. We want the formula. We adopt long-term plans through whatever process, then flog the hell out of them (long after the situation has changed) until the next reevaluation period.

In direct action organizing (as defined by the Midwest Academy in *Organizing for Social Change* [Bobo, Kendall, & Max]), for example, we have *the* three motivating goals (addresses a real need, gives participants a sense of their own power, changes the relations of power), a matrix for choosing an issue, a strategy development chart, a checklist for actions, and a playbook of tactics. In political formations, we see something called "democratic centralism" practiced in many of the same ways it was in the post-Lenin Soviet Union. Aside from its inherent sectarianism from the imposition of ideological conformity (a practice dating to the Comintern), there is an assumption that what may have worked in one place and period is transferable, and is idealized, becoming kind of doctrine. But reality is holding still for none of it. These are plodding models, deliberative, and often without a shred of tactical agility.

I'm not suggesting that these should be thrown out like a baby with the bathwater. But in many cases, it seems, we have thrown out the baby and kept the bathwater. Organization is important, but as a vehicle for action. Some deliberation is necessary for orientation. Plans are necessary for accountability. But grand long-term strategies will mismatch every time unless they are responses to grand long-term realities. It is a non sequitur to assume that a long-term goal necessarily requires a long-term strategy. The opposite is actually true. Over time, unfolding chaos is paradoxically the only certainty, and failure to develop organizational forms that can quickly and accurately adapt to disruptions of equilibrium create ineffective fighting organizations.

Constants in any adversarial struggle—be it a community issue fight or guerrilla warfare—include effective logistics, well-developed intelligence (which is information plus analysis), and a culture of self-discipline and leadership development. Organizational forms must adapt. There is no one-size-fits-all.

The twin focus must be on developing leaders who can inspire cooperation for action, and have well-developed tactical skills (the bag of tricks), but most of all, finely honed strategic intuition combined with the ability to quickly and seamlessly adapt to change and to be decisive about what trick to pull out of her bag.

In most cases, ten actions against one adversary in ten weeks—each designed to disorient one's adversary, even if they are not perfect actions—will be more effective than one action in ten weeks that is part of a highly formal strategic scheme. This puts us inside the "decision cycle" of the human beings against whom we are taking action and strips them of the most important intangible in any conflict—initiative.

In the initial phase of development of the Iraqi guerrilla resistance, for example, many of the actions seemed uncoordinated—which they may or may not have been. But the tempo of the hit-and-run attacks on U.S. occupation troops—averaging one attack almost every day—served to disorient the occupation commanders, compelling them in many cases—like Operation Desert Scorpion, et al.—to launch blind operations that served to drive more people into resistance. It was not the scope of the guerrilla attacks or even the strategic importance of the targets that was most significant in creating a qualitative shift in the situation, creating confusion among occupying commanders. It was the tempo.

Sometimes the best thing to do is just stir things up and see what happens. Then take advantage. As long as you are doing the stirring, you have the initiative.

The most important quality in a leader is the aggressive tenacity that never loses sight of the mission, combined with the creativity to achieve it in chaos—indeed, to make an ally of chaos. One of the qualities that seems to define so many so-called progressives is their utter lack of aggression and their constant moral hand-wringing. This is in large part responsible for their failure to mobilize masses. They only know how to mobilize fear that demoralizes people, instead of mobilizing rage that drives through fear and seizes the initiative. When the masses mobilize, they seek leaders who fight. The left has to quit demobilizing them with dithering disguised as sensitivity.

I'm going to again critique a favored organizational fetish among leftists, too. Democratic centralism. This was an organizational form that began agile. The pre-Revolution Bolsheviks were not a conformist sect. They were an extremely, sometimes wildly, creative and decentralized organization. Democratic centralism was the principle that after a period of intense discussion and debate, the organization would enter a period of intense activity based on a democratically arrived at determination of the strategic direction of the organization.

Analagously, today all our activities for the next period, based on our current analysis, should be connected to and directed toward the delegitimation of the government. That is an overarching goal, but not one that is constricted within a formula about how to do it. People in North Carolina's eastern Black Belt will have to figure out how to do that in a way that builds on the conditions there, and people in Silicon Valley will have to determine completely different ways to move things in this direction, based on the realities of Silicon Valley.

There is a democratic process to determine the central direction of organizational effort. In periods of relatively permissive organizing, communications flow freely and wide latitude is given to various components of an organization.

The Bolsheviks loosened and tightened their organizational process—and with it the degree of decentralized decision making—based on the level of repression they faced from the Czar's secret police. Heightened security needs call for underground forms of organization that emphasize operational security and compartmentalization of information—appropriate, I might add, when mistakes can land people in prison or before a firing squad. After the revolution, this underground form was translated into the organizational form for the ruling party by a situation in which civil war followed by incessant external conspiracy and attack fomented a garrison state—the Soviet Union. Lenin himself in his latter days, consumed with the business of leading a new nation through perilous straits, supported the formation of the Comintern, an international formation of revolutionaries that attempted to centralize the struggles of multiple nations using an organizational form that was suited only to a specific time and place in history.

Zinoviev codified it. Lenin—ever the agile tactician, but still capable of making mistakes like anyone else—died.[3] This organizational form was then consolidated by a vast state administrative structure and bent to the task of transforming an entire young revolutionary federation into a military formation to defend itself, which then commanded an entire international movement. Underwriting this whole notion of the Comintern—probably the biggest mistake the communist movement ever made—was a schematic, mechanistic theory of strategy.

Zinoviev, who formalized Bolshevik structures of war communism into the international organizational form, had tacitly accepted that organization (and therefore strategy) can be reduced to a schematic formulation that works the same in all times and all places. This is a metaphysical fallacy. The same dynamics are not extant in all situations, and to behave otherwise is to attempt the reduction of reality. In practice, the organizational attempt to reduce reality to a set of formulas leads to repetitive application of schematic tactics long past the time when those tactics are any longer appropriate. In theory, it leads to outrageous ideological conformity based on the delusion that these formulas define the "vanguard" of revolution. The common denominator among the whole range of Marxoid cults hawking their newspapers at demonstrations is the schematic notion of strategy that democratic centralism has become. That is why each will castigate the other for various blasphemies for exactly the same reasons. They have become arcane debating societies with little connection to real mass movements, based on a twin organizational and strategic fallacy: the implicit Cartesian belief that they can control situations, and the corresponding idea that this control is exercised by throwing all resources into some kind of mythical "main blow."

I believe in revolutionary vanguards. But they have been given a bad name by all these pretenders. A revolutionary vanguard is an organization that can mobilize mass movements, using a mass line (from the people, to the people), and win victories. The proof is in the pudding. Fidel Castro's 1950s guerrilla army was a real vanguard. A sect that indoctrinates its new members on a college campus and obliges them to hawk newspapers no one wants is not.

There is a conflation that occurs with the fallacy of identifying discipline with rigidity, which assumes we can act on a situation when the reality is that we act within situations. Discipline is essential in the execution of a strategy. Rigidity is an open wound.

In war, this rigidity raises body counts, often unnecessarily. A guerrilla struggle against an overwhelming power, for example, would do well to prioritize not high-attrition actions against its enemy, but actions that force the enemy to focus inward to reorganize—snipers, harassing ambushes, and other hit-and-run tactics, combined with a well-developed underground logistical network. Urban environments are now more advantageous for guerrilla warfare since war technology has been developed with an eye to identifying and isolating targets in rural terrain—heavy population has now become the ultimate camouflage as rural areas disappear and observation technology like night vision and infared have pulled the covers off of rural terrain. Urban terrain is now a place where guerrilla forces can potentially combine for quick strikes, then just as quickly rediffuse into cities and reassume noncombatant identities. And the majority of the world now lives in cities.

Units of three to five people can operate autonomously while coordinating directions through non-tech communications (tradecraft) networks. Skill sets include nontechnical communications like dead drops, live drops, brief contacts, and other cut-outs; basic urban tactics; and a strong emphasis on plain old marksmanship. Precision bolt-action rifles for snipers (along with sniper tactical skills) combined with short-gun proficiency (pistols and shotguns). Improvised explosives and mechanical ambushes. Pinprick strikes of high frequency to disrupt the enemy decision-cycle. These are the skill sets in the bag of tricks required for underground work and insurgency.

The enemy also requires intelligence, logistics, and discipline to be effective. These and not the enemy's strong forces will be the targets of effective guerrilla action. The most important source of reliable intelligence for a large conventional force outside its own country is a network of indigenous "trusted agents." Collaborators. They are vulnerable (and comparatively easy) targets, and their ruthless elimination will effectively blind the conventional force, whose own intelligence is frequently delusional based on its own institutional, political, and cultural biases. Logistical lines of communication are the lifelines of any conventional force and always more vulnerable than the force itself. These are a high-intelligence priority. Where can they be targeted? How? These are the questions an unconventional weak force must ask itself when facing a powerful conventional one.

The most important question is how to stay inside the adversary's decision cycle.

On the question of skill sets, people might ask the hypothetical question, How can we, in Developed Country A, prepare ourselves for the eventuality of heightened repression, deepening misery, and civil war? Well, the answer has nothing to do with colonizing workplaces to distribute literature or getting yet another Ph.D. There are vocations and avocations that will strengthen the basic skills as well as collective capacity. Hypothetically, there would be a need for paramedics, printers, machinists, mechanics, gunsmiths, and the like. And hypothetical hobbies that might help are chess and Go (strategic games, one of maneuver, the other of positions) for bad weather days; and bird watching, orienteering, and shooting during good weather. Bird watching sharpens reconnaissance-like skills (observations, optics, photography, stalking, camouflage, and concealment). Orienteering advances spatial and navigation skills as well as familiarizes people with a topographical map, protractor, and compass—and develops good motor skills for fast overland travel. Shooting speaks for itself, and the air rifle has a lot to be said for it as a tool that can be used to practice quietly in urban environments to keep shooting fundamentals sharp. Ultimate Frisbee is a superlative game for sharpening teamwork while getting a killer workout.

But that's all hypothetical.

HOMO FABER SAPIENS

When one distinguishes between intellectuals and non-intellectuals, one is referring in reality only to the immediate social function of the professional category of the intellectuals, that is, one has in mind the direction in which their specific professional activity is weighted, whether towards intellectual elaboration or towards muscular-nervous effort. This means that, although one can speak of intellectuals, one cannot speak of non-intellectuals, because non-intellectuals do not exist. But even the relationship between efforts of intellectual-cerebral elaboration and muscular-nervous effort is not always the same, so that there are varying degrees of specific intellectual activity. There is no human activity from which every form of intellectual participation can be excluded: homo faber cannot be separated from homo sapiens. Each man, finally, outside his professional activity, carries on some form of intellectual activity, that is, he is a "philosopher," an artist, a man of taste, he participates in a particular conception of the world, has a conscious line of moral conduct, and therefore contributes to sustain a conception of the world or to modify it, that is, to bring into being new modes of thought . . . The traditional and vulgarized type of the intellectual is given by the man of letters, the philosopher, the artist. Therefore journalists, who claim to be men of letters, philosophers, artists, also regard themselves as the "true" intellectuals. In the modern world, technical education, closely bound to industrial labor even at the most primitive and unqualified level, must form the basis of the new type of intellectual.

—Antonio Gramsci

I was roaming through a Barnes & Noble bookstore in February 2003 when I ran across a book written by my old team leader from 1st Special Forces Operational Detachment–D (Delta Force). The book, oddly enough, was entitled Inside Delta Force.1 The author, my old team leader, is Eric Haney.

Paging through the book, I found a photograph of our team, a team that got the shit shot out of it on the "Chalk 4" helicopter during Operation Urgent Fury, the invasion of Grenada. In the photograph, we had been posed by who-knows-who in a cluster, apparently preparing for our departure from the island. The grime and the funk of the operation was still on us, and we were wide-eyed with fatigue and stale adrenaline.

I flipped over to page 291, where Eric described the whole debacle in dramatic detail. He'd changed a few names for whatever reason, and mine had been changed to Stan Johnson.

It all made me feel strangely nostalgic, not about being shot at, but about having grown so much older, I think, and about how far I've journeyed since then, twenty years ago.

Later that day I stopped for coffee at a much better, non-corporate-franchise bookstore, the Regulator in Durham, where I saw a volume in the military history section called *American Soldier: Stories of Special Forces from Iraq to Afghanistan*, edited by Nate Hardcastle and Clint Willis.2

On a reluctant impulse, I pulled it down, and there on the cover of this anthology was my name. My publisher for *Hideous Dream* had given permission to include a substantial portion of my book. Eric's book had an excerpt in there, too. There were accounts going all the way back to Vietnam, mostly written by the actual participants.

What struck me about this coincidence of books was that most of what I had run into was written by former enlisted men—sergeants like me.

Memories started to itch.

In 1986, I started having problems at Delta. I'd begun quarreling with and alienating the Masonic inner circle there a year earlier, when I had "embarrassed" them in an exercise in Panama where—playing the role of an enemy—I had defeated my own squadron. That same year, the unit was embroiled in a fraud scandal that implicated virtually all of Delta Force, and the investigations had started an orgy of finger-pointing and betrayal that wrecked morale and ignited a purge.

On Thanksgiving Day 1986, I was called into Sergeant Major Mel Wick's office and summarily relieved; my security clearance was suspended, and I was told to start looking for a job. The rumor upon which my relief was predicated was that I had, while in El Salvador in late '85, taken a woman who was a former FMLN guerrillera into Ambassador Edwin Corr's bedroom at his palatial residence in Colonia San Benito while he was away and shared carnal pleasures with her on the presidential representative's very sheets.

In a way, I would have liked to have claimed the rumor—if for nothing else than its iconoclasm—but alas, it is not true. That didn't matter. I was purged.

Pending the reinstatement of my security clearance, I had to look for an assignment where an airborne ranger infantry sergeant first class could work without access to classified material. That's how I happened to get assigned, as a military science instructor, to the Department of Military Instruction at the United States Military Academy at West Point, New York.

At West Point, during the first freshman semester of military science, dismayed baby-faced plebes file into the classroom expecting to be instructed in the ways of warriors.

Instead, they are subjected to a highly selective version of U.S. military history that tracks the development of the U.S. Army officer corps through the funhouse lens of something called Huntington's model of military professionalism.

At first, having reviewed my course material thoroughly to ensure that *my* cadets could survive the gauntlet of examinations, I thought the semester was just another sadistic extension of the "fourth-class system," that mindless tradition of sleep deprivation, generalized subjugation, and hazing that West Point freshmen endure for their first nine months.

I was wrong.

All U.S. would-be military officers are indoctrinated in Huntington's model. It is the canon.

Samuel P. Huntington, the great cultural racist and intellectual Cold

Warrior, developed a creepy theory of "military professionalism" and the "civil-military relationship" that was decades ago adopted as the official "theory" for the U.S. Armed Forces officer corps.

At West Point, this indoctrination is almost a Skull and Bones–like, semi-hypnotic brainwashing because it is inflicted on cadets who enter the classroom in a post-traumatic somnambulant state. Unlike the Bush boys, however, no cadet is ever forced to lay in a coffin and recite his sexual history to his fellows while he whacks off.[3]

Huntington's model, which I promise not to belabor overmuch here, describes the ideal military officer as a kind of Prussianized version of doctors, lawyers, and corporate managers—"professionals"—with professional*ism* mechanically defined by three attributes: specialized technical knowledge, a "sense of corporateness," and a broad, liberal education.

The latter means a college degree.

Huntington also makes the patently absurd claim that the professional military must be apolitical, a bizarre assertion from a man who claims to have been influenced by the great Prussian military theorist Carl von Clausewitz. Clausewitz begins his theory of war with the premise that "war is politics continued by other means."

Huntington's model provides a theoretical justification for the reproduction of a class system in the military, a system and a justification uniquely fitted to the post–World War II U.S. military.

Looking at his criteria for a "professional," it becomes immediately apparent that experienced enlisted people in the military meet two of those criteria. They have technical acumen on par with most officers and they share fully in the military culture—the sense of corporateness. The distinction, then, rests on a formal university degree, a credential described by Huntington as a "broad, liberal education."

There are some very practical reasons, based on pure military logic, for hierarchy in the armed forces. The most obvious is that the defining activity—though not by far the most prevalent activity—of an armed force includes killing, dying, maiming, being maimed, and destroying property. These are, to put it mildly, counterintuitive behaviors, often committed in pursuit of a political objective that is little more than an abstraction for those obliged to do all the mayhem. The more removed from the experience of the soldier that objective is (as is most often the case for soldiers fighting in *foreign* lands), the more difficult it is to convince the soldier of its merits once he (and occasionally she) is confronted with a credible enemy who gives as much as s/he gets. So, along with an ideology of militarism that in modern times also leverages deeply irrational male sexual terrors, a system of draconian discipline has to be established to ensure that the majority of the troops will fight instead of flee or shoot their officers—perfectly rational behaviors in many cases—when the shit hits the proverbial fan.

But Huntington was working on his military professional model in the 1950s, and by then hard discipline for the military had been axiomatic for centuries. Huntington's "contribution" was, in fact, to develop a theory specifically suited to the needs of America's first full-fledged standing imperial post–World War II military.

Why would he be so keen on this definition of professionalization for the armed forces?

He expresses open admiration of the Prussians, but notes that feudal customs (which, by the way, infect all large military organizations around the world to this day) had been adapted and modified to reinforce a sense of tradition (not practice) and maintained a kind of cultural continuity through the many technological, doctrinal, and structural changes in the conduct of war. These changes are reflective of the society in which these military organizations are embedded. Only the military ethos is Prussian.

That ethos cannot be confused with the practical needs of a vast, modern, mechanized (and now computerized) military force, designed to project itself internationally across a spectrum of conflict from minor police actions to reassure a few pasty-faced bankers to something called total war, in which the objective is the destruction of an entire society.[4]

The clue to the riddle of Huntington's model is what the model calls the military officer: "a manager of violence." Emphasis on manager.

A standing military organization consisting of hundreds of thousands of people and hundreds of billions of dollars worth of equipment and supplies, employing state-of-the-art technologies, and spreading itself across five continents has many of the characteristics of, say, a multinational corporation. This magnitude of size and complexity carries with it a complex and highly specialized division of labor, which in turn requires a vast administrative apparatus to keep it synchronized.

This is at least part of the definition of bureaucracy.

Bureaucrats do not need leaders in the Homeric warrior-hero sense, or even in the plain wisdom and initiative sense. They need managers.

Bureaucratized class societies like ours reproduce themselves, that is, maintain their own structures and relations. An important mechanism for this social and institutional class reproduction in the civil and military sectors is credentialing.

Once those West Point freshmen finish pinging through the gauntlet of their plebe year, they spend the next three years being indoctrinated in how to maintain control over untrustworthy, dissembling, sly and treacherous enlisted swine—all this coded now in the co-opted language of right-wing PC: "backbone of the Army," "Soldiers first!", and so forth. Included among the sly and treacherous are those enlisted people upon whom these officers will utterly depend for their success, the noncommissioned officers (NCOs), sergeants of various ranks.

The tiny handful of senior enlisted people with whom I taught at West Point were a kind of bold, experimental excursion to expose the cadets to the "good" NCOs. In most cases, though, the perverse cadets preferred us to the tight-assed officers and so that experiment has long since been terminated.

This points us to an important arena of class struggle, I think.

From this stroll through Delta and West Point, I need to reorient the reader back to Eric Haney's book. *Inside Delta Force* is a paean to Special Operations and militarism, glossing over the masculinist-racism of the unit, engaging in some execrable Muslim-bashing, and even hinting at deeply cherished blood-and-soil white supremacy stirred into Eric's latent populism. But in places Eric also raises uncomfortable questions about U.S. foreign policy and describes—as my own book did—the actual experience of the people behind the wretched Special Ops mystique. In our case, these are the experiences of enlisted people who in many ways transgressed the invisible boundary between enlisted people and the credentialed "managers of violence."

And it's well written.

Both of us, in our time on active duty, became people upon whom officers would rely, but found worrisome and hard to control.

The real point I want to emphasize is that Eric Haney and I wrote books at all. And that they were published.

Nothing so contributes to the reproduction of class in our society, aside from property relations, as the institutionally enforced intellectual division of labor. It dissects knowledge into academic ghettos and attempts to freeze working-class people out of the intelligentsia altogether. Credentials!

Capitalism needs its credentialed mandarins, and the mandarins often define even who the "legitimate" critics of capitalism are. Specialization and credentialing are the keys to this legitimation, and to the exclusion of would-be transgressors.

Those of us who lack the credentials must be excluded from the intelligentsia because the inclusion of our voices, the legitimation of our voices, calls into question the legitimacy of the whole system.

I feel this personally, both as a former enlisted man and as a leftist. As a leftist, I have sometimes encountered powerful pressure to circumscribe my own role and to limit my own public discourse to criticism of U.S. military policy, to serve the revolution only as a witness.

Leave theory to the experts. Just like the military.

Working-class people can and must become intellectuals. We can and must study diligently, debate, self-criticize, restudy, and continually sharpen our ability to play intellectual hardball.

We can't be lazy about it. It's always easier to pretend you know something than it is to learn about it. It's always easier to be cute than it is to be rigorous. It is easier to talk trash than to practice the humility of the serious student. We have to work, harder than the bourgeoisie, because we are at war. Perhaps the biggest "war lie" of all right now in the United States is that our ruling class is at war only with external enemies. Look around.

"United we stand." Who the fuck is "we?" Is the general facing the same situation as the private? Are the moguls of agribusiness sharing hardship with the people whose communities they pollute? Is the vicious preppy prez sharing his privileges with the South Asian family running a fleabag motel for a corporate chain? Is John Ashcroft getting personally involved to gain justice for the community of Tulia, Texas, where dozens of Black families were railroaded into prison by racist cops and judges?

We who are doing that labor to become working-class intellectuals can *never* allow ourselves to be intimidated by advanced degrees—just as we cannot become anti-intellectuals. We can never afford to contain ourselves within predetermined specializations. The experience of working-class intellectuals will enrich theory. Our stories will keep things real. Our practice will define the future.

And we deserve to be heard.

FULL-SPECTRUM ENTROPY: OUR PERIOD OF DISORDER

> *We can of course quote other social bifur-
> cations related to fossil energy: coal, oil,
> which lead to the industrial society. Now
> we have the information technology, which
> leads to the networked society. What will be
> the effect of the present bifurcation?
> Because of the scales involved we can
> expect a larger role of non linear terms
> therefore larger fluctuations and increased
> instability.*
> —Ilya Prigogine, 1999

> *People say, how can I help in this war on
> terror? How can I fight evil? You can do so
> by mentoring a child, by going into a shut-
> in's house and say I love you.*
> —George W. Bush, 2001

The web dictionary of cybernetics and systems says:

> A system that exits far from thermodynamic equilibrium,
> hence efficiently dissipates the heat generated to sustain it,
> and has the capacity of changing to higher levels of orderli-
> ness . . . contain[s] subsystems that continuously fluctuate.
> At times a single fluctuation or a combination of them may
> become so magnified by possible feedback, that it shatters
> the pre-existing organisation. At such revolutionary
> moments or "bifurcation points", . . . it is impossible to
> determine in advance whether the system will disintegrate
> into "chaos" or leap to a new, more differentiated, higher
> level of "order".
>
> The latter case defines dissipative structures so termed
> because they need more energy to sustain them than the sim-
> pler structures they replace and are limited in growth by the
> amount of heat they are able to disperse.

Ever since I was a kid, I've been preoccupied by this kind of stuff. Time. Infinity. Systems. Existence.

I am not a scientist, and in fact my first real foray into science—aside from that crap that passes for it in school—was the year-long Special Forces medical course, where I was captivated not by its abstractness but by its tangibility. During the course and afterward as a Special Forces medic, I worked in labs, hospitals, ambulances, and the field. I did CPR on codes, performed a cricothyroidotomy on a human being (who died anyway but not on my account), studied blood and urine and stool like a detective for clues, treated injuries and disease, pulled teeth, treated domestic animals, developed field sanitation and preventative medicine annexes to operations orders, and even caught nine babies (my very favorite thing) in three days at the OB-GYN wing of Claremore Indian Hospital in Oklahoma.

Precision long-range shooting is about applied Newtonian physics.

Overland navigation is applied geometry.

Explosives are about chemistry and physics.

It's pretty practical, but I think everything is practical. I'm very suspicious of abstractions. I was extremely suspicious of Marx when I read *Capital*, all that about labor-in-the-abstract, until I figured out what he was talking about, and then I gained a new insight: tendential laws. Left alone, systems *tend* toward disorder. Without intervention, the rate of profit *tends* to fall. These are laws that assert themselves over time, a very underappreciated dimension.

When I was in the field during training exercises at Fort Bragg, I was surrounded with long leaf pines. I occasionally had lots of time to kill, and when you start to actually think about anything you are seeing, there are mysteries there.

I'm still working these things out. Once I got hold of the notion of fractals, I started seeing them everywhere. Patterns. Tendencies. Repetitions and bifurcations.

Einstein once petulantly asserted that "God does not play dice with the universe" against quantum physicists who were asserting that God does play dice with the universe. Complexity and chaos theory are saying that "God plays dice with the universe, but the dice are loaded."

There are billions of long-leaf pine needles in North Carolina.

Billions. And every single one of them is conclusively identifiable as a long-leaf pine needle. And yet every single one of them is different. Loaded dice. Variation combined with order, holding things together, but giving us constant change, and evolution aboard the irreversible arrow of time.

Nothing, absolutely nothing in the entire universe is reducible. Because everything exists in and is partly defined by its relations to everything else, and not a single one of those relations is holding still. It was this epiphany that led me to dialectics. How I can be whatever it is I am, but whatever that is, is changing from instance to instance, along with everything else.

Like the sight of one's own blood, this gives some people vertigo.

I can't resist it.

I don't need anything other-worldly like religion. The material universe holds more than enough fascination to keep me occupied. I read something a few years back on thermodynamics and caught that bug.

Thermodynamics, Sustainababble, and War

What is thermodynamics?

Well, it's the study of something I don't understand very well: energy. The force that moves things. Not even that, because at some level the things and the force are united. Matter/energy.

Everyone who knows me has heard me ranting for four years about fossil fuel. I've even been accused of having an obsessive-compulsive disorder. But paranoids might have real enemies and obsessives might obsess about really important stuff.

Overdevelopment (as in capitalist core-infrastructure) and underdevelopment (as in lack of autonomous infrastructure in the exploited global periphery) are interdependent polarities on a shared social axis, where value is drained from the latter into the former for the purpose of maintaining a ceaselessly expanding accumulation regime. It's a relation—not two things, one thing.

Think colonizer and colonized. Think parasite and host. Interdependent polarities, like left is not left without a right, and up is not up without a down. Their existence is defined in and by a relation.

The ceaselessly expanding accumulation regime that defines the global structure of society has a shorter definition. Capitalism. Like a shark, it can never stop doing what it does or it will die. What it does is accumulate and expand value. What it eats are workers, and women, and colonies, and the biosphere.

It is not only environmentally unsustainable, it is economically and socially unsustainable, and that's how we are in this fix. All these are related within the system itself, of which each is merely a facet, and the system is unsustainable—or rather, based on increasing disequilibrium. It is a social, and therefore a political, system.

Politics is economics by other means, and war is politics by other means.

I have to detour here.

Radical economists know that "value," that is, exchange value, is a social transfer of embodied labor (including unremunerated labor largely from women). Let's think about that same social transfer as the transfer of energy, just to put this on a strictly physical basis. Later, I will reiterate why and how the separation of economics (and therefore war) from ecology is completely arbitrary.

Now we need to understand entropy. The tendency toward disorder. Put a hot bowl of water on the table, and the heat drifts out of that nice, neat bowl and ends up dissipated all over the room. You can't even get your oatmeal to swell up in it. The bowl of water is showing you thermodynamic entropy.

In the biosphere there are two predominant counterentropic processes: gravity and photosynthesis. I want to focus on photosynthesis. Think of entropy as the level of dissipation of energy, with dissipated energy being that energy that is less able to move matter, or do "work." Most of our energy originates from the sun.

Energy, just like society, has a history.

Photosynthetic plant life is a self-reproducing set of structures that "capture" that energy and store it in chemical form (as sugars and proteins and lipids and so forth). So plants concentrate energy into low-entropy forms (low entropy = more work potential, high-entropy = less work potential). We actually measure that energy in heat equivalents like BTUs or calories or even joules. Even when plants die, they keep a lot of their stored energy. It's locked into molecules. That's why we can pick up a piece of dead wood, set it on fire, and it releases a lot of heat. Every time that energy is transferred, there is some wasted or "dissipated." So a bug eats a leaf and gets energy, but some of that energy is lost during the metabolic process of the bug. So the bug is a higher (more complex) net-entropy phenomenon than the leaf. It represents, in the larger scheme of things, more order in itself and more disorder external to itself, unless developing complexity and redundancy in the biosphere outruns the disorder. And the chicken that eats the bug is still getting energy that originated from the sun, but the chicken is warm-blooded and is giving off dissipated heat constantly. She "wastes" more energy or heat, so she is higher-entropy than the bug. Then the large predator, like the human, eats the chicken for energy.

In fact, we are very high-entropy forms, because we do something none of the rest of these species do. Not only do we exploit energy inside our bodies through metabolism, like the other critters do, but we also exploit energy (and dissipate it) outside our bodies. No other species does that.

We burn things.

Wood. Coal. Oil.

Work is energy dissipation. Humans have always dissipated a lot of energy. We boost our work output by using heat (energy) from out-of-body sources. We also hang out in places where metabolism alone is insufficient to keep us at a viable internal temperature. Like Maine or Tierra del Fuego. We use up photosynthetically stored solar energy by releasing it through combustion of wood, coal, oil, etc., just to stay alive in places like that.

We are entropy's best friends here on earth. When we make things that work, like machines, these are (energy) dissipative structures. When we use machines that require very low-entropy inputs, like fossil fuels that are the end result of about millions of years of patient photosynthesis (remember, we have no technology that can replace photosynthesis for counterdissipation), we are dissipating energy at breakneck speed.

Here's the rub. Price (monetized value) is based on embodied socially necessary abstract labor in the production process (as well as "invisible" unremunerated labor mostly from women). But in a growth-driven economy (capitalist or socialist that is forced into growth through competition with capitalists), where technology becomes an ever-increasing set of dissipative structures (more buildings and machines and vehicles and gadgets), the energetic base of that very same economy is undermined. The same process that generates "growth" or "wealth" generates thermodynamic entropy and concurrently system disorder. For that more general disorder, thermodynamic entropy is a correlative and a marker. The order generated by "work" (product) goes somewhere, and the correlative disorder created by the production process goes somewhere. Where this order and disorder "goes" is determined within a social system.

Energy itself is productive potential if it can be directed by human energy (and socially constructed consciousness operating in a specific social system). But something unique is added to the accumulation process when energy is traded as a commodity, with a price. At one time, one form of that work-energy was slaves with force multiplied by animal power. Now the work-energy is wage labor, but just as significantly, fuel—that technologically directed force-multiplier of the worker's output. We even measure it, harkening back to history, as horsepower.

Orthodox leftists will insist that work and energy are not the same things. They are quite correct in asserting that social systems based on specific forms of technology are an outcome of history and social struggle. And I'm certainly not here to claim that a gallon of gasoline is the same thing as a human being. But human labor is not only a social phenomenon; it is also a physical phenomenon. It is an expenditure of energy: a thermodynamically entropic process. The human is distinguished by her subjectivity as well as how she is constructed by a specific society. She has the capacity to reflect and intervene in the social system that gives these entropic processes a specific historical character.

The non-subject here—and the key force-multiplier upon which industrial, globally networked, capitalist civilization is built—is out-of-body, super low-entropy fossil fuel. The average American home uses the equivalent physical energy of dozens of people should they be unaided by fossil-powered energy. We won't even begin to calculate transportation. So this "commodity" is far more than a commodity. It is a "force-multiplier" of production, but conversely, it is also a hugely energy-dissipative and disordering process. It is not only disordering thermodynamically, as in heat being released from fuel and used up; it is disordering the dynamic structures of a socially impacted biosphere.

This process goes somewhere. It is temporal and cumulative.

To know where, we can not get caught in either of two traps. One trap is to think of this process as purely technical. Machines and cars and gadgets are neither asocial nor apolitical. They did not appear and evolve outside of history. They were and are parts and outcomes of social systems, developed by and within the logic of those systems.

What is the per-capita energy use for an average American as opposed to an average Haitian? What political reality underwrites this ratio? If we're not asking this question, we are reifying. This is not a natural order, but a set of relations that are enforced.

The way we use technology is inextricable from the social system in which it gets used. Conversely, the social system cannot be designed to overcome certain inherent characteristics of specific technologies.

People who claim, for example, that capitalism can overcome its dependence on fossil fuel have either not researched the question or they are on mescaline. Bourgeois economics has the same disorienting effect. And socialists who claim we can simply reorganize politically to overcome our current entropic dilemmas are eating the same cactus.

Where we are all going together, very fast, is toward a clear and unbreachable thermodynamic wall. As we approach it, the more generalized disorder, of which that thermodynamic disorder is only one part, will surface in one crisis after another.

Those crises will not appear as a single cataclysmic event, some form of Armageddon. They will appear as a lowered level of maintenance of the commons, as uncut weeds along the highway. They will appear as budget cuts, as strikes, as the reorganization of extended families to cope with economic contractions. They will appear as empty offices, as outbreaks of goofy religion, as water shortages. They will appear as new diseases, disruptive weather patterns, species extinctions, crime waves, ever more craven pandering by entertainment media. They will appear over time, in many guises, with plenty of time for establishment ideologues to define what is happening to us and try to lead us back to superficiality, tribalism, and war.

There is no existing technology that is not dissipative, and nothing replaces photosynthesis as the fundamentally essential counterentropic process for energy in our biosphere. Neither is there any technology that is not structurally dissipative, that is, disordering. Order created by technology at its locus corresponds to a higher level of net disorder away from its locus.

We, as a planet and species, are running out of fossil fuel, and oil has already reached peak production.[1] In the meantime, we are using that energy force-multiplier to create disorder faster, and are basing ourselves—especially in the developed world—on ever more unstable, technologically dependent forms of organization. This is not a crisis, as simple input models would have it, that will show itself first through blackouts and finally in collective hypothermia. On the surface of things, this reality is apparent in ways seemingly unrelated to carbon: currencies, diplomacies, job losses, race-baiting, and the names of the places written on the tags in your clothes.

The biosphere is a vast, self-organized counterentropic system of matter/energy, and it is the material basis for all life and therefore humanity as a species and society. In a sense, a sustainable society (which must be socialist, as I will explain later) will have to somehow take into account a ratio between (entropic) technomass and (counter-entropic) biomass. Sustainability will be determined, in the last instance, by the ability to reduce aggregate dissipation below the aggregate photosynthetic "capture" as it pertains to energy—and reduce dissipative structures (technological, but also social) below some yet unmeasurable threshold of disorder.

Of course, aggregations and disaggregations don't tell the whole story. I can count the houses in my neighborhood, but that doesn't tell me much about the complex dramas going on inside them.

Alf Hornborg explains that if we stay with an aggregate-disaggregate analysis, we are reducing our interpretation to an input-output model and are therefore victims of false consciousness, bad epistemology. Machines and technology are commodities, socially constructed but sitting in front of us as if independent—outside of social history—in their existence, seen as a combination of material and knowledge with social relations concealed. Old timers call this the fetishization of the commodity.[2] I look at my bathrobe in the store and I see its utility and its price. Unless I do some research, beginning with the tag on the back of the neck that says, "Made in Turkey," I don't see the American directors of the company that profit from it, I don't see the proletarian Turkish women in the sweatshop where it is produced, I don't see the Turkish comprador who collects an export fee, or the army, etc. There is a history embodied in this bathrobe that is concealed beneath its appearance—an appearance I take for granted, as if it were natural, as if this bathrobe grew on a bathrobe tree. This concealment of social relations within the commodity is fetishization. It allows the working woman who bought it for me in the United States—in her role within the international division of labor as consumer—to conduct the transaction with no awareness of the working women half a world away, who worked all day for pauper's wages to produce these robes, and thereby concealed is the whole international structure in which the U.S. produces dollars and Turkey is producing things-to-get-dollars.

Similarly, energy forms can be fetishized, not just as a failure to apprehend the concealed social relations, but as a failure to see their concealed entropic history.

Oil, for example, which has taken hundreds of millions of years to concentrate energy has had half of its total energy dissipated by combustion in just over a century. I have a beat up Chevrolet Prism outside that is made of metal and plastic and paint and rubber, etc., each of which went through some process of extraction (conducted by laborers) that disordered the biosphere, some process of refinement (conducted by laborers) that disordered the biosphere, some process of transport (conducted by laborers) that disordered the biosphere, and some process of assembly, based on other technologies, and so on. That Chevrolet uses up gasoline, oil, parts, and contributes to wear on roads that themselves represent the disordering of significant sections of biosphere.

Marx said that false consciousness is largely based on reification, our predominant epistemological error.[3] We think of abstractions like they are material things, or treat a transient historically specific category as if it is universal (human nature is my favorite). Think about terms like "the market," for example. Is that a real thing that exists outside of history? Social constructions, like growth-development and technological forms, are now treated like God-given material parameters, irreducible and inescapable. I can forget that the bathrobe or the Chevrolet have histories that reveal some very specific social relations because I am trained by society to interpret things in a different way—as "market forces," as "growth," as ahistorical technology. I can gain the impression that appearances that are temporary within history are somehow and forever universal.

Roy Bhaskar called this the confusion of transitive with intransitive realities.[4] The speed of light is an intransitive reality. On the other hand, everyone knows what a "family" is. Most Americans have an idea what that is and they regard it as some eternality. But, in fact, our current "family" structure is a very recent, very historically contingent form, which would have been unrecognizable a hundred years ago here, and remains unrecognizable in many places around the world today. It is a transitive reality.

So is U.S. global power.

Conflating the transitive with the intransitive serves current social power relations by closing off deeper ways of knowing and understanding the social structures that perpetuate those power relations. And the observation of aggregation (looking at how much of this or that there is in the world, without specifically looking at how it is distributed and used) conceals the reality of techno-mass concentration in urban, especially core-urban, centers, which are energy sinks, dissipative concentrations, the equivalent of economic/ecological black holes that suck in minerals, fossil energy, and biomass (often through labor itself) from the periphery—and export the consequent disorder.

The urban-sinks disorder is thus conveniently kept out of sight in the imperial metropoles but exists side by side with it in the various colonies. In Haiti, the mansions are surrounded by squalor, separated only by a security wall. Even within the United States, even here in my own state of North Carolina, the shiny metropolis does not want to be reminded of its material basis or the consequences of its actions, so it ships its enormous wastes into the colonized communities of poverty and color. As I write this, the overflowing trash of upscale Wake County has exceeded the low-income space available for landfills, and its political bosses have targeted a Black community in adjacent Lee County for construction of a new ranch-sized trash heap. It's an export of disorder.

But it was precisely the order in the periphery that was exploitable as value, and so there is a fundamental erosion of the basis for accumulation, like eating next year's seed corn. America was first seen as a "virgin continent," and I won't even digress to explore the gendered implications of its "penetration."

There is a material analogue for this physical disorder as social disorder because society has a physical basis. This is what I am calling social entropy.

Under this new epistemological light, "sustainable development" is exposed as a grim oxymoron. It's a cosmic rescue fantasy, a superstitious technological optimism. But capitalism cannot ultimately be rescued from its own consequences.

And "growth-development," it must be said, was an external imperative for encircled-garrison socialism (and still is!). But it was external. Trotsky correctly commented once that the failures of socialist states were partly caused by "value . . . chattering at the borders." Moreover, Marxists themselves were deluded by cornucopian fantasies of modernity, beginning with Marx's youthful, off-the-cuff reference to "rural idiocy."

But "growth-development" is not an external (military) imperative for capitalism. It is a defining characteristic of it. No system with property and profit as its bases can escape this. Capitalism is a system of self-expanding value based on property. It has, from its very first stirrings hundreds of years ago to its current malignancy been based on enforcement by arms.

No alternative system that fails to rationalize the whole system in accordance with needs in a self-reproducing way can hope to prevent humanity from racing over the edge of an abrupt cascade of disorder as the latent social entropy of technology-dependence, which is consuming its own material bases builds toward one system collapse after another. And in the long run, we might charge over the bluff of an energy step-change that will result in a massive die-off of humanity. Inside these entropic boundaries, we are trapped in a deadly zero-sum situation, which Hornborg says we deny and call a cornucopia.

Ordering the economy based on use and not value is socialism. But the garrison socialism that depends on development has exhausted itself. The next social transformation will have to be based on the primary principle of the physician: First, do no harm. Everything will have to be measured not only by its benefit upon appropriation, but also against its impact on the biosphere and within a protracted project of ecological and social repair. It will not be economic. It will not be profitable.

We as individuals may not perceive our current process of collapse as an apocalypse. For individuals, five years can seem an eternity, and massive changes within that timespan have plenty of time for humans to accommodate them. But five years ago, I can remember when shit jobs were offering health benefits because we were almost one hundred percent employed at the peak of the dotcom party. George W. Bush was an ignorant, rich-boy upstart, whom we hadn't yet really imagined being in control of the world's largest nuclear arsenal.

The Soviet Union was an economic powerhouse for a time, but without a genuine periphery to exploit, it collapsed. "Growth" is only compatible with an exploitable periphery. With that collapse, Russia was not transformed into a core industrial state, but into yet another economic colony. The war in Chechnya is a scramble for spoils, but Chechnya does not now (nor will it ever) constitute an adequate exploitable periphery to launch a project of broad capital accumulation that can pacify a whole Russian working class. Russia is fighting against being the latest addition to the periphery and a die-off of historic proportions is still underway there now, with the population reduced by as much as eleven million since the end of the Soviet Union—768,000 in 1998 alone—and life expectancy dropping to that of Guatemala.[5] The rest of us aren't as far behind as we may think.

With an entropic material foundation, society itself is now organized in a way that can only increase disorder. This is the dialectic behind sustainababble, the urban idiocy of reformist "greens" and the cornucopian orthodox left. This is also the foundation for understanding disorder more generally in order to gain a deeper understanding of the profound danger of our current period in history. Entropy is generally seen as a thermodynamic phenomenon, but no one logic is ever sufficient to explain anything, and heat is just one facet of "order and chaos."

Social disorder is related to and will precede our thermodynamic crisis. Social entropy is here now, and the epitome of social entropy is war.

I am writing about the military, but to provide the context for understanding both the current historical conjuncture, which has moved the military center stage again, and the relationship between political economy, armed bodies, military doctrine, and conflict itself, I have to back up.

I was just getting grounded in historical materialism and the labor theory of value, the key components, along with class struggle, of the Marxist challenge to the bourgeois episteme.[6] That was reforged by the feminist challenge and recreated in the light of national liberation (particularly, for me, Black nationalism).

Then along came thermodynamics. As philosophical materialists, socialists ignore the science associated with thermodynamics and the epistemological challenges it presents when combined with historical materialism, at our peril.

World System theorists like Andre Gunder Frank, Immanuel Wallerstein, and Samir Amin have studied imperialism as a centerperiphery dynamic, and with this perspective raise the question of material unsustainability on a global scale.

It was Lenin who claimed that socialism would be constructed on a foundation of electrification. Lenin was familiar with the Second Law of Thermodynamics, but geology was not very technologically advanced then. And that law had much to do, which is still unacknowledged, with the eventual collapse of the heroic and tragic Soviet experiment.[7]

The world is now running out of oil. Some say sooner and some say later, but the thermodynamic lifeblood of industrial, globally networked capitalism is on an inevitable decline (it is finite) while the very nature of industrial, globally networked capitalism is to "expand" value—which will require more, not fewer, thermodynamic inputs.

We have achieved peak production globally and will begin to see permanent production declines against increasing population and demand immediately. This is an empirical thermodynamic wall we are approaching, and it is unmovable. Human society can accelerate or slow its approach to that wall, voluntarily (only possible in the context of a socialist reorganization of society) or through economic crisis (like depressions, where demand falls with economic collapse). But that wall is there, and it will not move. There is no escape from the fact that the entire organization of society across the planet is now utterly dependent on fossil fuel inputs.

Moreover, there is no alternative to them that can generate even a fraction of the energy we currently use from combustion of hydrocarbons. It is important to explore and develop alternatives to fossil energy, but the reality is that maximum use of alternatives after decades of research and development (in which the ruling class has to date shown no serious interest), all the feasible alternatives combined cannot generate but a fraction of the energy we currently use in fossil fuels. Growth-driven economics, furthermore, mean our demand is continuing to rise. The physical reality is that "sustainable growth" is an oxymoron. A soft energy landing from the last two hundred years of development will require massive conservation, especially by the overdeveloped countries, and that can happen only in a nongrowth (and therefore noncapitalist) society.

Energy questions are only a window on the larger dilemma, which includes finite resources like iron and bauxite, androgenic climate change, water shortages, and how these resource constraints will interact with class struggles embedded within an international division of labor. Social systems are not abstractions, but real relations of real people and things, and social order is a transitive reality.

We now have the scientific understanding necessary, if we are willing to confront it squarely, to flesh out this question of sustainability, and to expand and improve our understanding of the materialism in historical materialism. Marx glimpsed the sustainability issue as well with his questions about soil degradation and capitalist agriculture raised by his study of Liebeg.[8]

In fact, it is Marx still who forces us back to a dialectical consciousness, to a critique of the Cartesian separation of subject and object (a real issue for ecologists and feminists as well), to the questions of reification and mystification (that is, epistemology and ideology).

One place where misdirection (in the sense of magic tricks) seemed to often plague both ecologists and (variously orthodox) socialists was this self-same Cartesianism—human/subject, nature/object—which quietly led us to ucritically accept a notion of technology as somehow separated from nature, and as existing independently as it were from social relations: a fundamental rejection of the most valuable insights of dialectical materialism.

This error is also at the root of the naive faith of many socialists in some yet unexamined and undefined "alternatives" to fossil fuel that will rescue our now obsolete Cornucopian models of socialism.

Hornborg states:

> It is not enough to say that the specific forms of technology are socially constructed; ultimately, the whole idea of a technological "realm", so to speak, rests on social relationships of exchange. This implies that what is technologically feasible cannot be distinguished from what is socially, i.e. economically, feasible. If, since Newton, the machine has served as a root metaphor for the universe, an advocate of a less mechanistic world view might begin by demonstrating that even the machine is an organic phenomenon.[9]

The machine is an organic phenomenon.

It is this understanding that helps clarify the interpenetrating relation between an independent material universe, our interpretations of "reality" generally, our technical knowledge and its applications, our social relations, and the whole notion of "development." There is a value judgment implicit in the notion of "development," if it can mean anything at all. To simply reduce it to evolution is tautological. Development is evolution and evolution is development. We are chasing our tails.

There is a subtext in the connotation of the term that implies "improvement," and this introduces the question of, for whom?

Radical critiques of political economy have done a creditable job of partially resolving this issue by demonstrating that capitalist development, at least, is based significantly on the material exploitation of people's labor power. They have also identified the predominant role of specific technology (instruments of production) in development understood as social evolution.

We haven't done such a great job of escaping dogmatic interpretations of Marx et al. that ignore the role of unremunerated (women's) labor and nonmonetized, finite resources from the natural world, but we're getting better. Here is that Cartesian subject-object relation, wherein men subjugate women and powerful men subjugate nature and colonies.

"Sustainability," as a concept, requires us to understand accumulation and development globally, as a physical phenomenon, and relate that understanding of matter and energy to our social organization. The most popular understanding of the term sustainability appears to be willfully ignorant of the most axiomatic forces in the physical universe and how those forces respond to "development" as a social process. The question is not one of sustainability, but of relative equilibrium—of socio-ecologic homeostasis. Capitalist technology is based on continual disequilibrium.

While failure to grasp the insufficiency of sustainability as a theoretical category is forgivable in the general population, where the mass intellect is still so thoroughly commodified and mystified that educated people in advanced societies still watch televangelists and believe that Saddam Hussein planned 9/11, it is downright cynical when this willful ignorance is deployed by the ruling class and altogether astonishing when it is tacitly accepted by "scientific" socialists and other putative materialists.

It is also an epistemological problem—a failure to question our own assumptions—if we don't account for Hornborg's point that there is no such thing as a technological "realm." Not only do we need to extend our theory more deeply into materialism in order to understand our period, we also need to retroject this insight into an analysis of the collapse of eastern European and Asian socialism, which in different ways (Soviet and Maoist) adopted an approach to technology that was fundamentally undifferentiated from that of capital.

The original Maoist orientation, in fact, privileged the countryside over the highly dissipative urban structures, though for strategic reasons. This may have actually demonstrated a deeper, if still vague, understanding of these issues. But the trajectory of Chinese socialism, under both internal and external pressure, shifted toward "market socialism," which has now transformed China into a massive and growing urban energy-sink. Just like the Soviet Union, China will not have a global periphery to which it can export its entropy, and it will ultimately abandon its current course or fail. As we have seen earlier, this is a central issue in the current and dangerous geopolitical period. At the center of our current world system is not only an international division of labor, but also a net transfer of physical and social entropy to the hinterlands; the very same hinterlands upon which the metropoles depend absolutely.

There were predictions of collapse in the sixties and seventies based on orthodox readings of political economy. They focused on the contradictions at the level of production—economic contradictions, which in fact came to pass. By the early seventies, global capitalism entered a deep accumulation crisis and has through a process of trial and error since then managed to offset that economic crisis through a vast credit scam—now reified as globalization—backed up by immense military force. It has shipped its crisis to the periphery, not resolved it. It is only metropolitan self-centeredness that allows us to ignore (while we still take hot showers and watch television) that for the majority of the world, the collapse has already happened.

The same practices that led most of the world into that collapse will envelop the metropoles, because the world itself is physical, and at the end of the day, these are material contradictions—real entropy. You cannot eat money. You cannot even boil a cup of rice in a treasury bond, though you might add it to the fuel under the pot.

If by sustainability, we mean something akin to systemic inputs equaling systemic outputs—a kind of ecologic/economic perpetual motion machine—then we have fallen into a trap. Nature does not act that way. Nature itself over geologic time is not in a state of equilibrium, not in some cosmic homeostasis. Contrary to the proverb in Ecclesiastes, there is nothing not new under the sun. If we are to survive, we will have to learn how to dance with the biosphere, not conquer it—because all we shall conquer is our existence.

Matter/energy changes form constantly, sometimes gradually, sometimes violently, in ways that will never be perfectly penetrable by human consciousness and in very nonlinear ways. And in our little cranny of the universe, there has been a dialectical development between our environment, our social development within it, and our consciousness.

To be meaningful at all, we have to alter that conception a bit and arrive at some approximation of socioecologic equilibrium as ensuring some life-essential matter/energy forms are reproduced indefinitely in this biosphere, a massive counterentropic system of which we and our grandchildren are a part.

Just as I warned earlier against tautology, we have to have something against which to measure a concept like disorder.

The Organic Architecture of Order

There is a deeper material relationship, in my unschooled opinion, between the conversion of low-entropy potential into high-entropy commodities (and wastes) and the social chaos we are now witnessing. This deeper relationship has something to say about both the military and its current employment as the mailed fist of imperialism in deep economic crisis.

The transfer of disorder to the social from the physical is very material. In fact it is not a transfer at all, but the same thing, separated only in discourse. The obstacle to even describing this relationship is that we are held hostage by the language of a Cartesian way of knowing.

All production is a dissipative process (thermodynamically). That's why magic bullets, like hydrogen-fusion-telepathic channeling, are so much alchemy as they are currently conceptualized. There really is a "carrying capacity" to the earth, a physical one and therefore inescapable. There is a material basis of production and it never deviates from physical law, which unlike human law is not breakable. So while we see human agency determined within a structure of social relations that is based on capital accumulation and incessant expansion, the only separation between a law of value and a law of physics is conceptual. I don't say they are the same thing, but that they cannot be separated. Fetishization conceals social relations, in this case those of imperialism, but it also conceals the role of the physical bases of social relations. Imperialism has irreversible physical outcomes.

The appropriation of low-entropy (high-productive potential) is inextricable from the appropriation of surplus value. Not the same themselves, they are inseparable aspects of a deeper phenomenon that is the same.

Example: the great protein stores that were oceanic fisheries are about to collapse.[10] The capacity to exploit them as capitalists do now is based completely on technology that uses hydrocarbon combustion. The incentive to exploit these fisheries is not the fish itself because the owners of the corporations are not taking the fish home to eat. They are selling them. The incentive is profit, that is, the expansion of value. Money prime.

The development of industrial capitalism was inextricably based on hydrocarbon combustion. The factory trawlers now scoop out salable and non-salable sea life by the millions of tons, ripping over and destroying the reefs and other structures upon which these species depend for their future. The production of ever-higher quantities of food-as-commodity in the short run is the predicate for the expansion of the reserve army of labor (people to work and to provide the market for the food)—which increases the working and buying population—and there is no solution in sight, even as we can conclusively prove that this is a non-sustainable activity. The system is one that is politico-economically based on the self-expansion of exchange-value. And the same system is thermodynamically dependent on increasing inputs of fossil energy. This is emblematic of the runaway train we are now on.

The capitalist imperative to expand is an inescapable imperative to accelerate entropy, and the "order" that accrues to ruling class centers is the product of "disorder" (extractive destruction, social disruption, and waste) in the peripheries.

The order that is the biosphere developed within a material architecture with quantity and quality inextricable from one another, the disruption of which—in any way—constitutes an additive dissipative process, and at some point crosses a point of no return beyond which the wounds are no longer self-healing.

When a perfect marble block is used to build an apparently orderly structure in one place, it is the direct result of the more violent and penetrative extractive process elsewhere that constitutes a disruption of that "natural" organic architecture and a net expenditure of energy. A piece of the geologic-organic-biospheric architecture—one that was dialectically developed over eons—is ripped up to get at the stone. Energy is burned to get it out. Soil is ripped off the surface and left to run down streams, where it changes the pH of the water and introduces nutrients that change the net chemical composition of the waterway. Roads are built to transport the marble, destroying more of the organic architecture, the topsoil and the trees. And the wastes of this whole process are shipped off somewhere, creating yet more disruption to the energy-order architecture.

It is additive because the disruption of this architecture undermines the overall "counterentropic" process itself.

Marx took us below the surface of exchange relations to production and demystified things like "the market." We are at a conjuncture, I think, where we have to go under the surface of production to social reproduction, where women are no longer "invisible," and deeper still to its physical basis—because socialism must be, above all, about consciously securing our future and that of our children and grandchildren. And just as exterminist imperialism eats up its own social basis, it is eating up the biosphere, our very physical basis.

Revolution is not a choice between capitalism and socialism. It is a choice between the violent overthrow of the existing order or our exermination by that order. Is that clear enough? Do we need a little sugar with that?

Imperialism overcame its own early limitations through the generalization of war and plunder. But as a form of capitalism it must expand value, and to do that it has to expand the basis of value and the market for it, and that is the expansion of population beyond the carrying capacity of the earth. Marx called it the General Law of Population and said that it is a fundamental law of capitalist expansion.[11] This should not be confused with Malthusian Sierra Club racism and immigrant bashing.

That expansion now threatens two-thirds of humanity (the optimistic estimate) within a couple of decades, and it is tortuously killing us off in the peripheries right now.

The metropoles will not experience this crisis directly in the near-term, but in a mediated way through social relations in extreme crisis.

The forms of crisis we will experience will be felt on our skins as unemployment, repression, deflation, economic collapse, and right now, as war. The price of gasoline might actually fall for a while, and production rise for a while. Politicoeconomically it will be experienced as an impasse of profit—as unproductive and excess capital—that requires an attempt to restructure by the only method still available— war and metastatic economic malaise.

We are not destined to smash into the thermodynamic wall unless it is some lemming-like and irresistible genetic command. I admit that in my darker moments I wonder if there is some unbreachable limit to mass consciousness that can not overcome collectively the kinds of chaos we can set into motion against ourselves. But that is fatigue and frustration talking.

I have not one iota of doubt that America—as it is now politically constituted—will self-destruct.

There is no good news here. These are real problems, and symptomatic of a larger problem, the most dramatic ecocide since the extinction of the dinosaurs. The rate of species extinctions right now is far more rapid than the Triassic-Jurassic extinctions. And energy deposited in the form of biomass on the earth is being consumed at more than one hundred thousand times that rate of deposit. This is not a phenomenon that is in our genetic code, as the Malthusians insist, but one that has a specific social form that relies on self-expanding value: monetized exploitation of wage-workers and semifeudal peasants, based on non-monetized social reproductive labor (over ninety percent done by women), which expansion is absolutely dependent on the rape of the biosphere.[12] That self-expansion of value is the raison d'etre of that system, and that system either exists or it doesn't. The choice is now becoming either capitalism or humanity.

Its consequences will continue or they won't depending on whether we cleave to that system or overthrow it. There is not a reform program within capitalism that can correct this because capitalism is self-expanding value, and value is based on material inputs, not least of which are biomass, fossil energy, and human labor—all of which are inextricably linked in a single interdependent physical reality. We are inextricably and utterly dependent upon and embedded within that reality. No economy based on "growth" can continue indefinitely and that is an inescapable fact. Root and branch, it has to go . . . capitalism, patriarchy, and entropic technologies. Or not. Homo sapiens were not issued an indefinite guarantee, and we never got a waiver from nature. The conquest of nature may be the most dangerous myth we ever subscribed to in our Cartesian delusions.

The reason it is hard for people to see any hopeful alternative to our present self-destructive course is that we are still resisting the implication: revolution. These destructive processes are not an outcome of a selfish gene. They are an outcome of a system that has led us at last to Rosa Luxemberg's choice: socialism or barbarism. But the surprise is, the barbarism that was left behind by development is waiting for us more horribly at the end of development's road. This barbarism will happen not in a world of yet unexploited habitats with new human niches yet to be filled, but on a shattered, toxic heap of rusting detritus.

There is one more hypothesis I want to state here. We see social entropy in events around us all the time. There is an increasing potential for social disorder growing out of technological dependence that is analogous to (and materially related to) Marx's organic composition of capital, which leads to similar consequences. Just as the increasing utilization of technology and exhaustion of resources (constant capital) in capitalist development—which replaces the human beings (variable capital) whose labor contributions are the source of profit—serves to undermine and destabilize capital accumulation, a social system's dependence on more and more complex and interdependent technology increases it potential for abrupt and sometimes catastrophic destabilization. In other words, increasingly complex technological systems become stronger and stronger . . . until they don't. Then they become destabilized.

Cybernetics: the most volatile element of a system has the most influence over the other parts of the system and over the system as a whole.

The U.S. security state with its military is just such a system.

The generalized interdependency of technologically complex systems employed to rescue the ruling class and its capital accumulation regime carries with it an increasing potential for generalized disorder catalyzed by disruptions that, in themselves, may seem inconsequential.

One man rushes for his plane. Thousands of people delayed, millions of dollars lost, exponential chaos. Remember Hartsfield Airport.

JESSIE

> *Soldiers have a specific way of relating to the truth: it matters to them. It is a matter of life and death to them.*
>
> *So they judge people by a different standard of truth. And they judge politics differently. They are the first to know what kind of power comes from the barrel of a gun.*
>
> *That is why soldiers make good revolutionaries, and that is why revolutions always acquire their most turbulent force and active expression among the men and women of the armed forces, the workers in uniform.*
>
> *Soldiers are political scientists. No-one is more interested than they are, in what they are asked to die for. For this reason, no-one is closer to the heart of the people than soldiers are. When the people are rotten, soldiers cannot fight. When the people rise up, it is the soldiers who are always first to the front ranks.*
>
> *We must learn to work amongst the armed forces.*
>
> —Mark Jones

My eldest stepson, Jessie, whom I first met when I picked up his mother for a date more than twelve years ago and have watched grow from a corpulent, chattering little boy into a clean-limbed, handsome, twenty-year-old man with his own son, joined the army in July 2002. Children grow up and they make their own decisions. And we don't abandon them when those decisions fail to conform to our wishes.

He met me when I was assigned to 7th Special Forces Group in Fort Bragg. His mother, Sherry, my partner-in-life to this day, was working as a civilian medical records clerk at one of the troop medical clinics. She was holding down, heroically (in my view), this and another job at night to feed, care for, and otherwise sustain three small children alone.

The first thing Jessie asked me when I came by to take his mom to a movie was if I jumped out of airplanes.

I did. He even came out to watch one of my free fall jumps at Raeford drop zone when he was eleven. I didn't know then where that shine in his eyes—watching me descend under canopy to land ten feet from him in the pea gravel pit—would take him.

In February 2003, Sherry and I drove to Fort Benning, Georgia, and watched Jessie's fourth, then fifth and final qualifying static-line parachute jump. The next day we attended his graduation from the U.S. Army's Airborne School, where, like me almost thirty-three years ago, he had silver wings pinned over his left breast pocket. An hour later, he secured his orders for assignment to the 82nd Airborne Division at Fort Bragg—the very same division to which I was assigned in 1971 after returning from Vietnam.

I feared that he would soon be issued his desert camouflage uniforms and in short order be sent apart from his then eight-week-old child, Jaydin, for so long that by the time our grandson walked, he would not know his father.

There I was. Flying in the face of my sometimes self-assured facade, Jessie had not done as I said, but did as I did, and I was feeling very helpless.

That was my second trip to Fort Benning in the span of five months. I went there the prior September to visit Jessie when he graduated from basic training.

That first visit was a hard experience to describe. Any time I am on an army post, I am seized by a sense of both sadness and belonging. I lived a pretty nomadic childhood, and I never developed that sense of place that many people reserve for home.

I'd be the last person to romanticize my own past—how trapped I often felt on active duty, how enraged I could become with the whole shadow army of bureaucrats, or how I lived in a kind of subclinical state of dread thanks to the physical risks of the career track I had taken.

But it's *my* past, and that's where I have my sense of place, no matter the paradoxes.

I know an army post. I know its social architecture. I know its energy ebbs and flows. I know its tendencies, its rules, its personality. I know where its advantages are hidden like treasures. I know its traps. I know what's edible and what's poisonous. I can navigate there. I know the language. My retirement ID is almost a diplomatic passport. I recognize all the hieroglyphics.

When, in September, I waited in the Sand Hills area at Fort Benning for Jessie to get a local pass, I strolled past the manicured grounds, the idle obstacle courses, the PT tracks, the classrooms, the barracks, the motor pools, the mess halls, the clinics, all the orderliness that contains not an ounce of anything commercial, that fits together coherently, coordinated to some singular purpose.

Gaudiness and commercialism are confined to the Shopette, a combination convenience store/video arcade/fast food joint in a single building with its single outside sign—isolated, so the anarchy of outside society is kept cleanly separated from the utilitarian beauty of the rest of post. Inside, the trainees, who are on some two-hour respite, gaggle in the lines to buy shoe polish and razors, wolf down pizza, play the video games, and carry on slightly furtive conversations with a watchful eye ever-trained for NCOs, especially drill sergeants. Absolute authority is ubiquitous.

Since I had gone through basic training some thirty-three years ago, much had changed. There was a draft then. Antibiotics could handle every known sexually transmitted disease. There was a Black Power movement gaining ground. The Cold War defined us. The scrambled eggs in the mess hall were a green mass reconstituted from some powder. Half the drill sergeants were bona fide sadists who stole from recruits, beat down recalcitrants behind closed doors, and referred to trainees as maggots, shitbirds, and dickheads. The pay was shamefully low, and a quarter of it was taken back in the pay line for various army scams.

The old cruelties had morphed into a kind of humorously benign authoritarianism, as conscious as any physician's office of the potential for litigation. The physical brutality, direct and indirect, that trapped us on one side, with the exotic, fatal mystery of Vietnam on the other, is gone. Tobacco, our truest friend and pacifier, is now banned. As I said, a lot had changed.

But there is an essence there—seeing these hairless, pimply lads trying to fit themselves to a new and as yet unformed identities—which made me deeply sad. Not out of empathy for the young men so much as self-pity associated with plain, garden-variety mortality. I felt old.

That was me once, just as young and real and unformed and charged up on ignorance, hormones, and unknowably remote possibility.

I saw those boys and I became overwhelmingly aware of how unlike my postadolescent expectations my future had become. I looked at these shaved-down youngsters in their cherry uniforms and all I could see was how little they understood that every passing day was further circumscribing some of their own potentialities, and opening up others—many they might fear to welcome.

I'd have never seen the inside of a college classroom had it not been for the Army. I'd have never traveled to Guatemala or England. I also doubt that I'd have ever taken from another human being the one thing I can never give back—life.

I could not know the first time I received post privileges in basic training, when I rushed down to the PX to get half-pissed with my associates on 3.2 percent beer, that in a very few months I was to become a witness to murder, that I would be strung out on opium-laced marijuana, and that that I would learn to close myself off from my own actions, my own brutality, and don a hard shell that would never completely come off. I was to become infected with a shapeless covert rage that would bury the fearful, bright-eyed, expectant boy from basic training for good.

I saw those kids at Fort Benning. I mourned the buried boy. And I felt old.

I wrote something to an email list about my emotional reaction to Jessie's military service, and a self-righteous shit wrote me back that Jessie had chosen his course of action, he had made his decision, and if he is lost in this gangster's project of international plunder, oh fucking well . . .

I didn't bother to tell him that I was as concerned with the possibility that Jessie would learn xenophobia, that Jessie would be called upon to kill, that Jessie would have his human trust buried, as I was with the prospect of Jessie being killed in action—a dreadful possibility to be sure, but one I considered more remote than the others. Things are just never simple enough for an ideologue who still believes that soldiers are all robot killers and that the world is divided into good and evil.

I remembered a passage from *Grundrisse*, a startling declaration by Marx, that "society does not consist of individuals." Some people have taken comfort from religion. Some people from therapy. I found mine, and the way out of the morass of my own past, in these forbidden texts.

"Society does not consist of individuals."

My initial confusion about this statement was based on my fixation on nouns and my inattention to verbs. "Society does not consist of INDIVIDUALS." Absurd. Of course it does. But my stroll through Fort Benning and the sealed porches of my own memory reminded me that "Society does not CONSIST of individuals . . . but EXPRESSES the sum of connections, relations, in which these individuals stand with respect to each other."

I don't need to get off the hook, to be morally absolved. But the truth is, you are just as much a part of this system if you work at a scented candle boutique as you are if you are a soldier. You can't burrow into your little niche and look down on anyone, because we are all in this system together. And I figured out a long time ago that we can't rewind and re-record life. The role of soldier existed long before I took it, and it exists now as Jessie occupies it. I reproduced that role in my time, and now I am transforming that role in the context of a politics of resistance. Hope, as Brecht said, is hidden in contradictions.

There is hope for Jessie. It's the same hope we have to hold for humanity—that we can transform our roles, roles constructed like so many doors for us to go through by history, and by and by transform the whole edifice of human relations.

Meanwhile, I will love my son. I will wish as fervently and vainly as anyone else. And I will continue to fight for the political destruction of these posturing, caviar-and-cocktail-fed Washington thugs and the liquidation of their class. That's what we do when we are awake.

If we want simple, we'd best avoid life.

EPILOGUE

Here it is, October 2003. The final draft of everything that has gone before was submitted on July 1, and since then we have witnessed much.

On August 14, there was an electricity failure that plunged fifty million people into darkness, and made my Atlanta airport cautionary tale seem almost quaint.

It immediately occurred to me that sixteen nuclear plants automatically shut down in the U.S. and Canada during that little episode. I imagined the worst that lay within the possibilities of our technological interdependence and the criminal negligence of the capitalist state.

Nuclear power plants run on offsite power, not their own reactors.

If the electrical grid fails, reactors are designed to automatically close down. One or more diesel generators, with the capacity to power basic safety equipment including the cooling system, are supposed to start up. If generators fail, the reactor cannot be restarted without offsite power: another wonder of fanatic technological optimism.

Well. Attacks, ice, or windstorms can also knock out transmission lines to nuclear plants for extended periods. Nuclear plants that lose all power can quickly be converted into giant "dirty bombs," wind-driven clouds of radioactive isotopes.

Something has to continually pump circulating cooling water to the reactor and to the giant, densely packed waste-fuel pools, or those fuel rods, active and spent, will catch fire and reproduce Chernobyl or worse. Restoring offsite power to the sixteen nuclear plants during the blackout—long before reactors powered back up—was a high priority in order to restore safety and security systems.

On April 26, 1986, a complex of four nuclear reactors in the Ukrainian town of Chernobyl ran a safety test. The Soviet nuclear power program wanted to find out if it could bypass the cost of an expensive system that would crank up emergency diesel generators within seconds in the event of a loss of external power—a loss like that which just shut down sixteen nuclear reactors in the northeastern United States and parts of Canada.

Just as those nuclear plants automatically shut down during the blackout, Soviet nuclear plants were designed to automatically shut down because nuclear plants can become very unstable if they slow down. At Chernobyl, they wanted to see if they could provide enough backup cooling to the reactor with their own remaining nuclear-generated power as the reactor wound down, at least for a few minutes, while they manually brought the diesel back-up generators on line.

That experiment failed spectacularly and created the biggest nuclear power disaster on record. The reactor quickly heated up and exploded, contaminating over six thousand square kilometers with dangerous isotopes for centuries and triggering the forced resettlement of four hundred towns. Again, the goal of this tragic experiment was to delay the use of emergency diesel generators in the event of a grid shutdown. Operators ran a test to see if they could wait a few minutes before starting emergency diesel generators (EDG)—in case of loss of offsite power like that in the U.S. and Canada.

Not enough of a cautionary tale?

In some cases, a reactor core might last up to eight hours without backup generators—although deteriorating conditions like a tornado or hurricane could damage safety systems and impair workers' ability to protect the core.

At the Fermi plant near Detroit, all four backup generators were found inoperable on February 1, 2003. Had the regional blackout happened at that time, there could have been a full-scale evacuation called for the Detroit area, further complicated because sirens to alert citizens within ten miles would not have worked because the electricity was off. Reportedly, the sirens at all sixteen nuclear plants affected by the latest blackout were rendered inoperable.

In June 1998, a tornado downed all external transmission lines at Ohio's Davis-Besse plant. The diesel generators ran for twenty-six hours until they overheated and failed. The air outside was 93 degrees. One of the outside transmission lines had been restored one hour prior to the EDG failure. Oh entropy!

There were fifteen instances in the twelve months leading up to the blackout in which emergency generators had either malfunctioned or failed to operate at all, in certain cases leading to plant shutdowns. On several occasions all backup generators failed at once.

The Brunswick I unit in Southport, North Carolina, where Sherry and I used to fish, lost offsite power for nine hours in March 2000, during which time both emergency generators failed simultaneously. One was restarted in eighteen minutes, after the temperature of the water surrounding the core had risen several degrees.

Failures of emergency diesel generators occur frequently—one hundred and thirty-eight have been recorded since 1985, the majority discovered during tests when there was no emergency requiring their immediate use. Fifty-nine of these failures were failures to start, and seventy-nine were failures to run. Causes of failure ranged from design error to manufacturing error, construction or installation error, design modification error, accidental actions, incorrect procedure or failure to follow procedure, inadequate training, inadequate maintenance, fire or smoke, humidity, high or low temperature, electromagnetic disruption, radiation, bio-organisms, dirt, bad weather, and calibration failures.

This wide spectrum of error-variables for a system upon which the reactor core and spent fuel pools depend during a blackout creates an incalculable number of unforeseen consequences. This is comparable to having a vehicle upon which your life may depend sitting unused in a parking lot for a year at a time, then depending on it to take you out of harm's way at one hundred miles per hour.

Just add intent, and all probabilistic risk analyses are moot.

And this is not merely technology; it is capitalist technology, as even Soviet technology was. The twentieth-century socialist states were, above all, phenomena within a capitalist world system. Not technology alone, but technology developed and operated organically within capitalist social relations. Nuclear plants are now subsidized and regulated by institutions of the hegemonic capitalist state, the ultimate guarantor of property.

The Nuclear Regulatory Commission (NRC) regularly allows nuclear plant operators to violate safety regulations.

Since 2000, the NRC has issued 106 Notices of Enforcement Discretion (NOED), which allow utilities to continue operations even while in violation of regulations that require it to shut down for safety purposes. This is like the police allowing drivers to skip vision tests or drive while under the influence. NOEDs have been issued to plants regarding their faulty diesel generators.

Due to industry and NRC secrecy, paradoxically invoked with security as a justification, the people may never know the extent of problems experienced with diesel generators at the sixteen plants affected by the recent blackout. As the capitalist state would have it. The Bush administration wants to license a hundred more of these things.

"The massive failure that knocked out power to the Northeast and Midwest U.S. and Canada looks like the disastrous blackouts of 1965 and 1977," said Lloyd Dumas, author of *Lethal Arrogance: Human Fallibility and Dangerous Technologies*. "Once again we are reminded of our technological vulnerability and the impossibility of eliminating failure. Electric systems were connected together to make blackouts a thing of the past. In 1965, when part of the grid failed and the rest took over, the strain caused more to fail. The system designed to prevent blackouts triggered a progressive collapse that blacked out the entire Northeast United States."

"Technology," Hornborg reminds us, "is a social phenomenon." There is no way to understand how technological successes and failures occur without looking at social relations.

This is but one example of what might have been. Entropic cascades are real, and as the frantic drive to preserve accumulation regimes accelerates the accumulation of latent disorder, we shall see more and more of them.

There was a massive blackout in Italy on September 27.

Of course, should one martyrdom-seeking asymmetric warrior decide to fly an ultralight plane over a nuclear power control building with a barrel of cyanide, or one team penetrate the maintenance space beneath the spent fuel pools with a rucksack full of explosives, that latent disorder can be unleashed by design, like it was in September 2001. There is no equation for intent. And the international provocations of Bushfeld continue to career out of control.

As regards the question of military overreach, I needn't say a lot. The United States is losing the war in Iraq. It has already lost in Afghanistan.

At morning formation on July 23, Jessie and the rest of his company were told to get their affairs in order. They were going to replace the 3rd Infantry Division in Iraq.

His mother and I were scrupulously "normal" for the next few weeks, self-consciously so. We showed great attention to detail in our day-to-day activities. We stayed busy.

I reassured her and myself that he is a light wheeled vehicle mechanic; that he wouldn't be participating in convoys when his unit went to Iraq in August; that Baghdad airport, where the motor pool probably was, had by then been turned into an impregnable fortress (I was way wrong on this one); that perhaps there wasn't as much depleted uranium fired there as in some Baghdad neighborhoods; that he wouldn't be obliged to take lives and lose that little piece of his soul; that he wouldn't fall into the habit of calling Iraqis ragheads or hajjis; that he could just save some money, do his job, and stay busy and out of harm's way. This is what people who are in that position say to each other. There is no alternative way to think and still go to work, still attend to the needs of other children, still manage relationships, and still maintain some modicum of self-control.

Now look at me.

Everywhere I turn—past, present, and future—I am inside imperialism, and not just positioned somewhere in it, but slipped like a little plastic dust cover over the barrel of its gun. Former instrument of it, enemy of it, parent of one of its fresh tools—unable to rejoice at either its advances or setbacks in this new Vietnam.

I can't even be a pacifist. I just have to settle for being an uncomfortable revolutionary. Pacifism is a reflection of decency and good will, but it blinds us.

I have to live with my nightmares. Maybe we all do. Maybe we all have to accept our post-traumatic stress disorders as the price of life if we have any intention of participating. Even if our period is one lived at gunpoint, what are we to do? Pretend the guns aren't there?

And the only way to fight guns—all ahistorical nonsense to the contrary aside—is with guns. That is the essence of the conjuncture that it is U.S. military power that must be defeated, and that—for us in the metropoles—the armed forces are contested terrain. This is our fight back: to midwife another post-Vietnam military malaise born of Iraq and Afghanistan, and many small rebellions in the periphery. And our job is to reclaim the American armed forces as an instrument of the people, no matter the obstacles, no matter the difficulty.

In Iraq, all doctrine has now shattered like Humpty Dumpty. Powell Doctrine is buried under a steady stream of casualties, flown back under cover of darkness to Dover Air Force Base and Walter Reed Army Medical Center. Rumsfeld's toys are rendered irrelevant by platter charges—child's play in the world of improvised explosives—that deliver Armageddon one vehicle at a time. Now the American military is adrift in Iraq, impotent in Afghanistan, doctrine-less as they seem to find themselves in every war. In the past, they were thrown into the mix with obsolete doctrine, and this time with a doctrine attempting to leap over history.

Bolivia has become a firestorm and part of the continental drift that is the global rebellion against neoliberalism. The U.S. has resorted to using Israel to attack Syria, relentless in the pursuit of its own failure.

The dialectical movement of economics, politics, and military power is folding and swirling like weather. Politics is being reshaped by military failure. Military failure is being shaped by economics.

When the dollar falls, as it inevitably will, the U.S. will become ill but the rest of the world will also collapse. This is the frightening deadend we have been driven into—not by Bush (who is just overseeing this phase of collapse), but by capitalism. It is a cul-de-sac where the financial architecture crumbles, the oil begins to run out, women are hurled back toward atavistic subjugation, the fisheries collapse, the aquifers run dry, the forests fall, arable land is desertified or salinized, weather patterns destabilize, prisons burst at the seams, the swelling human numbers concentrate into hopeless megalopolises, and the world fragments into armed camps. This prognosis will neither be legislated nor reformed away. These are the most wicked delusions of all, putting the brakes on the masses when they desperately need to be in motion.

Elections? These are not conjectural things, these are processes in motion, and demonstrably so. If the measures required for self-defense in the twentieth century were considered extreme, wait and see what is in store now at the end of hydrocarbon capitalism. It won't be the industrial nirvana, and it won't be some stateless Druid paradise. It will be war, and war without quarter. And like it or not, everyone will become combatants.

As I put this polemic to bed, Bushfeld is encountering international recalcitrance—teasing at time, blunt at others. Germany plays coy. France snubs. Turkey's oligarchs, in exchange for providing much needed troops strength in Iraq, which will only turn up the heat on that pressure cooker, has accepted a fool's bribe, another loan to further indebt its stricken economy and put off for a year or two its own Argentine comeuppance. The glowering Kurds warn their American allies that Turkish occupation will not stand, but deafness still reigns over Washington. Russia is playing the coquette between Europe and the U.S. China places its next stone on the Go grid.

George W. Mouth was at it again on October 9, telling National Guard troops in Portsmouth, New Hampshire, that "Americans are not the running kind." Just when we thought—in the wake of the outrage at his "Bring 'em on" remark some months earler—he might be chastened enough to refrain from shit-talking! What's worse was that this time it seemed the line was crafted by the junta's weird spin staff, because Paul Wolfowitz said exactly the same thing elsewhere on the same day.

The longer this thing goes on, the more it seems we have all stepped through the looking glass. George and his cabinet ministers transformed into *Taxi Driver* Travis Bickles, practicing armed confrontation lines on the other side of the mirror. California, the world's seventh largest economy, in a bout of steroid psychosis, selected yet another mediocre actor to govern, this time the Narcissist King.

That hoary euphemism for left-wing homophobia, "bourgeois decadence," suddenly finds its true substance in our new millennium. The post-nineties politics of megalomaniacal machismo has been dressed up as statecraft, like putting sunglasses on a pig. Soon those New Hampshire National Guards, along with thousands of others, will face the reality outside the looking glass, where a schoolyard challenge-line has been drawn from the comfort of Washington, and people in Iraq and Afghanistan willingly step across it with rocket propelled grenades and improvised explosives.

Not the running kind, indeed!

The old official masculinity, enduring, quiet, emotionally distant, and unconcerned with its coiffure—illusory and oppressive as it was— now looks almost attractive in the face of the new one—immodest, loud, and fascistic—vicariously played out on stages and in studios by a lumpen-bourgeoisie with its own gangster aesthetic. Found attractive by the nazifying anti-intellectual sector of the American white "middle" class as its standard of living comes under attack from some mystifying force and is itself blinded to the origins of its fatal malady by a culture of huckster anticommunism and commodified resistance, the new machismo of George W. Bush is politics as low performance art by those who have the freedom to indulge *l'imaginaire*, that habit of consciousness that Sartre characterized as an escape from social reality.

There is certainly plenty from which to escape for our intrepid neo-con adventurers, and for the pitiful cowering Democrats (who will almost certainly replace them), as the private school thugs atop the world's hierarchy thrash this way, then that, seeking a way out. But they cannot escape from value, only make it ever more top heavy, and they cannot leap over the Grand Canyon of ecological collapse that lies ahead.

They are not only presiding over the breakdown of their own delusions, they are faced with the more terrifying realities of a world reaching its limits: of an approaching precipice over which their accelerating stampede of accumulation is about to plummet. Caught in the tar baby of Iraq, the administration rails louder against its international subalterns and competitors, who are now cautiously watching—and hoping—that here at last is their opportunity to escape from the immense gravitational pull of the rotting dollar.

I see my little grandson, ten months old now, and I know the meaning of responsibility, and that it begins with truth telling and it ends with necessity.

He is not growing up at the end of history. He has inherited a global Palestine.

On October 12, 2003, even as Donald Rumsfeld was finally being eased out of the driver's seat in Iraq, the *Independent* (UK) published a story by Patrick Cockburn about American troops in central Iraq retaliating against Iraqi farmers who were perceived to be withholding information about the guerrillas. Retaliation took the form of using bulldozers to plow up centuries-old groves of date palms and fruit trees. One woman threw herself in front of the bulldozer only to be dragged off crying. In the same week, Israel was violating Syrian sovereignty— acting as a surrogate for the overstretched U.S. armed forces—by bombing an alleged "terrorist training camp" thereby throwing gasoline on the fires of Arab resentment against the U.S.–Israel Axis. With the bulldozing crops, the Bush administration had finally achieved the Palestinization of the region, and in some sense the Palestinization of the planet. We are all Palestinian now.

When in Palestine, we do what Palestinians do. We learn the lesson of the rocks.

Intifada.

NOTES

Chapter 1: Haiti

1 Paul DeRienzo, "Haiti's Nightmare: The CIA Coup and the Cocaine Connection," *Shadow* (April/June 1994).

2 Jen Sullivan, "More from the Exile Files: The life of ex-despots isn't all jail and frozen assets," *Mojo Wire* (September 1997), http://www.motherjones.com/news_wire/sullivan.html

3 Robert Fisk, interviewed by Amy Goodman, *Democracy Now*, June 2003.

Chapter 3: Latin America

1 Seymour Hersch, the journalist who broke the story of the My Lai massacre n Vietnam (for which Colin Powell was eventually to oversee PR damage control), broke the story in the May 22, 2000, edition of the *New Yorker*. General McCaffrey, who as the Division Commander for the 24th Infantry Division ordered an unprovoked attack on retreating Iraqi columns on March 2, 1991, two days after the ceasefire was in effect. Hersch writes, "Apache attack helicopters, Bradley fighting vehicles, and artillery units from the 24th Division pummeled the five-mile-long Iraqi column for hours, destroying some 700 Iraqi tanks, armored cars, and trucks, and killing not only Iraqi soldiers but civilians and children as well." This is a violation of the Geneva and Hague Conventions and the Law of Land Warfare. For his actions, McCaffrey was rewarded with the U.S. Armed Forces Latin American Theater Command at Southcom, and later became President Clinton's drug tzar. A very good web account of this war crime by Major Glenn MacDonald (Retired) U.S. Air Force, can be found at http://www.militarycorruption.com/barry.htm.

2 Mark Cook, "Colombia: The Politics of Escalation," *Covert Action Quarterly* (Spring–Summer 1999), http://www.covertaction.org/full_text_68_01a.htm.

3 Ibid.

4 Ibid.

5 "Colombia's Killer Networks: The Military-Paramilitary Partnership and the United States," *Human Rights Watch*, November 1996, http://www.hrw.org/summaries/s.colombia9611.html.

6 Samia Montalvo, "Paramilitaries, Drug Trafficking, and U.S. Policy in Colombia," *Dollars and Sense* (July/August, 2000): 9–11.

7 Alfred McCoy, "Drug Fallout," *Progressive*, August 1997, http://www.thirdworldtraveler.com/CIA/CIAdrug_fallout.html.

Chapter 4: Moral Imperialism & the Iron Logic of War

1 Amnesty International, *The Acteal Massacre* (Mexico: December 1998): Index AMR 41-43-98.

2 International Commission of the FARC-EP, *FARC-EP: Historical Outline* (2000). $14.00 payable to "Historical Outline" to PO Box 69051, Toronto, Ontario, M4T 3A1. In Canada this includes shipping. U.S. orders in U.S. dollars.

3 Mao Tse-tung, "Report on an Investigation of the Peasant Movement in Hunan,"in *Selected Works of Mao Tse-tung* (Peking: Foreign Languages Press, 1975), 1: 23-29.

4 International Commission of the FARC-EP, *Historical Outline*.

5 Ricardo Vargas Meza, *The Revolutionary Armed Forces of Colombia (FARC) and the Illicit Drug Trade* (Washington Office on Latin America, June 1999).

6 Javier Giraldo, *Colombia: The Genocidal Democracy* (Monroe, Maine: Common Courage Press, 1996), 68.

7 "Army, Paramilitaries Implicated in Bojaya Tragedy," Colombia Watch, May 2002.

8 Amilcar Cabral, *Unity and Struggle* (New York: Monthly Review Press, 1979.)

Chapter 5: Somalia

1 I differentiate "political faction" from simple faction, adhering to Marx's (still valid in my opinion) assertion that various sectors of the ruling class are like character masks that get changed for the same

group of actors as an adaptive mechanism. But political factions do emerge, and this is precisely what Republicans and Democrats are, variant political factions within the same U.S. ruling class. There are even factions within factions, but any challenge from lower classes is met with the utmost solidarity. The exception to this, which is important in this period, is an international one: inter-imperialist rivalry.

2 Ridley Scott's film received unprecedented cooperation from the Bush administration's Department of Defense, to include bringing cast and crew into contact with top secret military units, allowing them to observe and practice tactics and techniques that are classified, and allowing the military to exercise veto power over virtually every aspect of the film. The bizarre combination of direct wag-the-dog collaboration between Hollywood and the Department of Defense along with the privatization-commodification of official propaganda is a reflection of the desperate degeneracy of this period and this political establishment.

3 See: www.fas.org/man/dod-101/ops/docs/97-0364.pdf

4 These kinds of arguments assume that all variables are independent, when the opposite is true. If the "enemy" in this case had observed heavy armor as part of the Task Force, they would have altered their tactics appropriately. If the intelligence environment had been different, then what it observed would have been different. Still, this kind of superficial and fallacious thinking is ubiquitous among the officer corps of the U.S. military.

5 Interview with Zbigniew Brzezinski about how the U.S. provoked the Soviet Union into invading Afghanistan. See: Le Nouvel Observateur, January 15–21, 1998, http://members.aol.com/bblum6/brz.htm.

6 The author also participated in Operation Uphold Democracy (in Haiti), a year after the catastrophic denouement of Operation Restore Hope (in Somalia). He provides an extensive critique of Special Forces and the U.S. military there in his book, *Hideous Dream: A Soldier's Memoir of the U.S. Invasion of Haiti* (Soft Skull Press, 2000). Hope was not restored in Somalia. Democracy was not upheld in Haiti.

7 Robert Parry and Norman Solomon, "Behind Colin Powell's

Legend," *Consortium* (1996), http://www.thirdworldtraveler.com/
Political/Collin%20Powell_Legend.html.

8 "Proportionality" is the idea that the military action is proportional
to the need. As a principle of war, this is called "economy of force,"
and it is preached from the pulpits of service academies, like West
Point where I taught military science for three semesters. But when
civilians are blamed, using the "independent variables" retrojection
analysis referred to earlier, "proportionality" is transformed into the
civilian heresy that subverts military success. In other words, Powell
believes that defeat in Vietnam was a consequence, in part, of the failure to be willing to escalate to whatever means necessary, including
nuclear weapons.

9 The Day paper also accurately portrays the absurdity of employing
a crew of white CIA agents to gather human intelligence in a black
nation like Somalia.

10 Ahmed Rashid, "Afghan Warlords Kill at Will, Says UN Envoy,"
Telegraph (UK), January 31, 2003.

11 Sarah Left, "U.S. Troops kill 13 Iraqi Protesters", *Guardian* (UK),
April 29, 2003.

12 Jonathan Steele, "The Pentagon's One-size-fits-all 'Liberation' Is a
Disaster in Iraq," *Guardian* (UK), May 6, 2003.

Chapter 6: Full-Spectrum Fuckup

1 The dilemma, if it is even recognized by the middling intelligence of
George W. Bush and Donald Rumsfeld, is that this intensely complexi-
fied technocentric doctrine is now the keystone of an entire geopolitical strategy with the singular goal of imposing order on a highly
unstable world situation. The systemic potential for entropy means
that something will inevitably disrupt that system and create "the cascade of disorder." Remember the Atlanta airport. Remember
September 11.

2 Leon Hadar, "Cakewalk? What Cakewalk?" *Straits Times*
(Singapore), March 28, 2003.

Chapter 7: Iraq

1 Dexter Filkins, "We Killed a Lot of People", *New York Times*, March 29, 2003.

2 Ole Rothenborg, "U.S. Forces Encourage Looting," *Dagens Nyheter* (Stockholm), April 11, 2003.

3 Goodman, Peter S., "Workers' Frustrations Mount in South as Operations Remain Stalled," *Washington Post Foreign Service*, May 1, 2003.

4 Steele, "'Liberation' is a Disaster in Iraq."

5 "Americans Are Being Hunted," *Lebanon Daily Star*, June 8, 2003.

6 Michael R.Gordon, "G.I.'s in Iraqi City Are Stalked by Faceless Enemies at Night," *New York Times*, July 10, 2003.

7 Laura J.Winter, "No Ticket Home," *Daily News* (New York), May 31, 2003.

8 David Rohde and Michael Gordon, "U.S. Forces Move Against Iraqi Resistance," *New York Times*, June 12, 2003.

9 Andrew Marshall, "Troops Battle Iraqis at 'Terrorist' Camp," Reuters, June 12, 2003. Interestingly, Marshall put quotation marks on "terrorist," an indication that even members of the mainstream press were willing to question official U.S. credibility by June 2003 .

10 Associated Press, "U.S. Military: Insurgents in Afghanistan stepping up attacks on Coalition," June 14, 2003.

Chapter 9: Special Operations in a Special Period

1 Black soldiers have largely not been interested in army selection programs that emphasize abuse and humiliation. For many white soldiers, it's perceived as a kind of rite of passage into manhood, a one-shot novelty. Blacks are also weeded out of Special Forces and the Rangers by racists who wield subjective evaluations like weapons throughout the courses and phases of training and selection.

2 If any. I don't know right now. When I was at Delta, there were two Black operators over a period of almost four years. In Seal Team 6, with whom we occasionally worked, I never saw a single Black operator, and they openly referred to their thirty-six-hour defense of the governor's mansion in Grenada, after they were trapped there, as a

"nigger shoot."

3 Jerry White, "More Evidence of U.S. War Crimes in Afghanistan," *World Socialist* (December 13, 2001), http://www.wsws.org/articles/2001/dec2001/pows-d13.shtml.

4 One of the most important things I can point out, as a veteran of more than two decades in the military, is that the Department of Defense is a bureaucracy. This point puts things into perspective. Bureaucracies are intrinsically incapable of admitting wrongdoing. The ABC of bureaucrats is CYA (cover your ass). What is going on here is a cover-up.

5 "Operation Anaconda: Questionable Outcomes for the United States," Stratfor, March 11, 2002.

Chapter 10: Hangul: Korea

1 Joon Kim, "Court Finds Soldiers Not Guilty," Chosun (Seoul) Ilbo, November 20, 2002.

2 "Soldiers Commit 600 Crimes a Year," *Ohmy News*, October, 2002, http://www.kimsoft.com/2002/us_sofa.htm.

3 William Steuk, *The Korean War* (Princeton, NJ: Princeton University Press, 1995), 47–54.

4 Michael M. Sheng, "China's Decision to Enter the Korean War," *Korea and World Affairs* (Summer 1995).

5 Lee Wha Rang, "Anti-U.S. Sentiment in South Korea: Root Causes," *Koera Web Weekly,* December 16, 2002, http://www.kimsoft.com/2002/anti-uslwr.htm.

6 Gregory Elich, "Targeting North Korea," *Center for Research on Globalization*, December, 31 2002, http://www.globalresearch.ca/articles/ELI212A.html.

7 Nick Mamatas, "Carter Hounded by Kwangju Massacre," *Village Voice*, October 11, 2002.

8 "Soldiers Commit 600 Crimes a Year."

9 Ashton B. Carter and William J.Perry, "Back to the Brink," *Washington Post*, October 20, 2002, http://www.ksg.harvard.edu /news/opeds/2002/carter_korea_wp_102102.htm.

10 Ibid.

11 Leon V. Sigal, "Jimmy Carter," *Bulletin of the Atomic Scientists* (January–February 1998).

Chapter 11: Overreach

1 Gowan, Peter, *The Globalization Gamble: The Dollar-Wall Street Regime*, 1999, www.gre.ac.uk/~fa03/iwgvt/files/9-gowan.rtf.
2 Standard Shaefer, "Duck, Duck, Goose: An Interview with Michael Hudson," *Counterpunch*, April 23, 2003, http://www.counterpunch.org/shaefer04232003.html.

Chapter 13: The Left

1 *Homefront, A Military City and the American 20th Century* (Boston: Beacon Press, 2001) is anthropologist Catherine Lutz's study of Fayetteville, North Carolina, the city adjacent to Fort Bragg. It is well-written, very readable, and a very important work.
2 "Timothy McVeigh: Convicted Oklahoma City Bomber," CNN, March 29, 2001.
3 In late 2004, Soft Skull Press will release my next book, *Sex & War*, which will explore the complicated relationship between gender and the military.
4 Stacey Garnett, "Shareholders Urge Honeywell to Link CEO to Worker Pay," *United for a Fair Economy*, April 26, 2000.

Chapter 14: Strategy, Chaos and Agility

1 John Boyd, "Destruction and Creation," September, 1976. Archived online at http://www.belisarius.com/modern_business_strategy/boyd/destruction/destruction_and_creation.htm.
2 Ibid.
3 Louis Proyect, *The Comintern and the German Communist Party* (2001). Online at http://www.columbia.edu/~lnp3/mydocs/organization/comintern_and_germany.htm.

Chapter 15: Homo Faber Sapiens

1 Eric L. Haney, *Inside Delta Force* (New York: Delacorte Press, 2002).

2 Nate Hardcastle, *American Soldier: Stories of Special Forces from Grenada to Afghanistan* (New York: Thunder's Mouth Press, 2002).

3 Skull and Bones began at Yale. In 1832, General William Huntington Russell and Alphonso Taft put together a secret society for the elite children of the Anglo-American Wall Street banking establishment. William Huntington Russell's step-brother Samuel Russell ran "Russell & Co.", the world's largest opium smuggling operation in the world at the time. Alphonso Taft is the grandfather of our ex-president William Howard Taft, the creator of the forerunner to the United Nations. Only fifteen seniors are picked to join each year by the former graduating class. They are required as a part of their initiation ceremony to lie naked in a coffin, holding their dicks and reciting their sexual history. This method allows other members to control the individual by threatening to reveal their innermost secrets if they do not "go along." George Bush's father as well as George W. Bush were members of Skull and Bones.

4 "Spectrum of conflict" is the term used to describe a graduation of conflicts on continuums of intensity and scope.

Chapter 16: Full-Spectrum Entropy

1 Albert A. Bartlett, "An Analysis of U.S. and World Oil Production Patterns Using Hubbert-Style Curves," *Mathematical Geology* Vol. 32, No 1, (2000): http://www.dieoff.org/page187.htm.

2 "A commodity appears, at first sight, a very trivial thing, and easily understood. Its analysis shows that it is, in reality, a very queer thing, abounding in metaphysical subtleties and theological niceties. So far as it is a value in use, there is nothing mysterious about it, whether we consider it from the point of view that by its properties it is capable of satisfying human wants, or from the point that those properties are the product of human labour. It is as clear as noon-day, that man, by his industry, changes the forms of the materials furnished by Nature, in such a way as to make them useful to him. . . .

"Whence, then, arises the enigmatical character of the product of labour, so soon as it assumes the form of commodities? Clearly from this form itself. The equality of all sorts of human labour is expressed objectively by their products all being equally values; the measure of the expenditure of labour-power by the duration of that expenditure, takes the form of the quantity of value of the products of labour; and finally the mutual relations of the producers, within which the social character of their labour affirms itself, take the form of a social relation between the products.

"A commodity is therefore a mysterious thing, simply because in it the social character of men's labour appears to them as an objective character stamped upon the product of that labour; because the relation of the producers to the sum total of their own labour is presented to them as a social relation, existing not between themselves, but between the products of their labour. This is the reason why the products of labour become commodities, social things whose qualities are at the same time perceptible and imperceptible by the senses. In the same way the light from an object is perceived by us not as the subjective excitation of our optic nerve, but as the objective form of something outside the eye itself. But, in the act of seeing, there is at all events, an actual passage of light from one thing to another, from the external object to the eye. There is a physical relation between physical things. But it is different with commodities. There, the existence of the things qua commodities, and the value-relation between the products of labour which stamps them as commodities, have absolutely no connection with their physical properties and with the material relations arising therefrom. There it is a definite social relation between men, that assumes, in their eyes, the fantastic form of a relation between things. In order, therefore, to find an analogy, we must have recourse to the mist-enveloped regions of the religious world. In that world the productions of the human brain appear as independent beings endowed with life, and entering into relation both with one another and the human race. So it is in the world of commodities with the products of men's hands. This I call the Fetishism which attaches itself to the products of labour, so soon as they are produced as commodities, and which is therefore inseparable from the production of commodities. . . ." Karl Marx, *Capital*, vol. 1, http://csf.colorado.edu/psn/marx/Archive/1867-C1/.

Fetishism is a form of *reification*.

3 The transformation of social relations into an objective existence. Reification is often used to describe imagining that *abstracted* relations exist in Nature, rather than being products of human thought. *New World Dictionary*: "Reify: To treat an abstraction as substantially existing, or as a concrete material object."

4 "[Roy Bhaskar] distinguished the transitive or epistemological dimension of reality from its intransitive dimension. The transitive dimension is essentially our perception of reality, whereas the intransitive dimension is the actual underlying structure of reality. It is important to point out that Bhaskar is mainly concerned with ontology not epistemology, and that he is confusing the conditions of possibility of science with the conditions of its intelligibility." Fadhel Khaboub, "Roy Bhaskar's Critical Realism: A Brief Overview and a Critical Evaluation," December 2001, http://f.students.umkc.edu/fkfc8/BhaskarCR.htm.

5 Natalia Rimasheveskaya, "There Will Be Only 55 Million of Us," *Institute of the Socio-Economic Problems of Demography* (May 2001).

6The following lengthy quotes, including citations, are taken from the glossary archived online at http://www.marxists.org/glossary/terms/h/i.htm. Specific citations for Marx's works can also be found there:

> Historical Materialism: This conception of history depends on our ability to expound the real process of production, starting out from the material production of life itself, and to comprehend the form of intercourse connected with this and created by this mode of production (i.e. civil society in its various stages), as the basis of all history; describing it in its action as the state, and to explain all the different theoretical products and forms of consciousness, religion, philosophy, ethics, etc. etc. arise from it, and trace their origins and growth from that basis. Thus the whole thing can, of course, be depicted in its totality (and therefore, too, the reciprocal action of these various sides on one another).

It has not, like the idealistic view of history, in every period to look for a category [eg. measuring periods of history in accordance to certain ideas], but remains constantly on the real ground of history; it does not explain practice from the idea but explains the formation of ideas from material practice. Accordingly it comes to the conclusion that all forms and products of consciousness cannot be dissolved by mental criticism, by resolution into "self-consciousness" or transformation into "apparitions," "spectres," "whims," etc. but only by the practical overthrow of the actual social relations which gave rise to this idealistic humbug; that not criticism but revolution is the driving force of history, also of religion, of philosophy and all other types of theory.

It shows that history does not end by being resolved into "self-consciousness as spirit of the spirit," but that in it at each stage there is found a material result: a sum of productive forces, an historically created relation of individuals to nature and to one another, which is handed down to each generation from its predecessor; a mass of productive forces, capital funds and conditions, which, on the one hand, is indeed modified by the new generation, but also on the other prescribes for it its conditions of life and gives it a definite development, a special character. It shows that circumstances make men just as much as men make circumstances. (Karl Marx, The German Ideology)

The first premise of all human history is, of course, the existence of living human individuals. Thus the first fact to be established is the physical organisation of these individuals and their consequent relation to the rest of nature.

Men can be distinguished from animals by consciousness, by religion or anything else you like. They themselves begin to distinguish themselves from animals as soon as they begin to produce their means of subsistence, a step which is conditioned by their physical organisation. By producing their means of subsistence men are indirectly producing their actual material life.

The way in which men produce their means of subsistence depends first of all on the nature of the actual means of subsistence they find in existence and have to reproduce. This mode of production must not be considered simply as being the production of the physical existence of the individuals. Rather it is a definite form of activity of these individuals, a definite form of expressing their life, a definite mode of life on their part. As individuals express their life, so they are. What they are, therefore, coincides with their production, both with what they produce and with how they produce. The nature of individuals thus depends on the material conditions determining their production." (Karl Marx, The German Ideology)

At a certain stage of their development, the material productive forces of society come into conflict with the existing relations of production, or—what is but a legal expression for the same thing—with the property relations within which they have been at work hitherto. From forms of development of the productive forces these relations turn into their fetters.

No social order ever perishes before all the productive forces for which there is room in it have developed; and new, higher relations of production never appear before the material conditions of their existence have matured in the womb of the old society itself. Therefore mankind always sets itself only such tasks as it can solve; since, looking at the matter more closely, it will always be found that the tasks itself arises only when the material conditions of its solution already exist or are at least in the process of formation. (Karl Marx, Contribution to the Critique of Political Economy)

This concept is founded on Dialectical Materialism applied to history. Another name for the 'materialist conception of history' formulated by Marx and Engels, 'Historical Materialism' was coined by Engels, and later popularized by Kautsky and Plekhanov."

From http://www.marxists.org/glossary/terms/l/a.htm: "The labour theory of value is the proposition that the value of a commodity is equal the quantity of socially necessary labour-time required for its production.

"The 'germ' of bourgeois society is the commodity relation, by means of which the labour of one person is brought into relation with that of another person and exchanged. The quantitative aspect of that act of measuring the labour of one against the labour of another is the determination of value. A central part of Marx's study of bourgeois society was his study of this value-relation:

> that which determines the magnitude of the value of any article is the . . . the labour-time socially necessary for its production. Each individual commodity, in this connection, is to be considered as an average sample of its class. Commodities, therefore, in which equal quantities of labour are embodied, or which can be produced in the same time, have the same value. The value of one commodity is to the value of any other, as the labour-time necessary for the production of the one is to that necessary for the production of the other. 'As values, all commodities are only definite masses of congealed labour-time.' [*Capital*, Chapter 1]

"That it is the quantity of labour-time required to produce a commodity which determines its value (or "natural price") in bourgeois society was by *no means* a discovery of Marx, but was an observation dating back to ancient times. Adam Smith formulated it as follows:

> The value of any commodity, therefore, to the person who possesses it, and who means not to use or consume it himself, but to exchange it for other commodities, is equal to the quantity of labour which it enables him to purchase or command. Labour, therefore, is the real measure of the exchangeable value of all commodities.
>
> The *real price* of everything, what everything really costs to the man who wants to acquire it, is the toil and trouble of acquiring it. What everything is really worth to the man who has acquired it, and who wants to dispose of it or exchange it for something else, is the toil and trouble which it

can save to himself, and which it can impose upon other people. [*Wealth of Nations*, Chapter 5]

"There can be no doubt that the labour theory of value tells us important things about the way people relate to one another in bourgeois society and the growth of these relations into entities which take on the appearance of objective laws of nature. Nevertheless, it should not be thought that Marx shared the view of the political economists that the labour theory of value constituted such a law of nature or eternal law of society or that in that sense, that Marx was developing a branch of social science in the writing of *Capital*. Marx studied the 'social science' writing of the political economists as the more consistent and worked out formulations of the same forms of consciousness that they claimed to study.

"Thus, for Marx, the labour theory of value is a form of consciousness which is 'natural' on the basis of social relations founded on commodity production. It is itself a 'fetishism' of exactly the kind described in Section 4, Chapter 1 of *Capital*:

Whence, then, arises the enigmatical character of the product of labour, so soon as it assumes the form of commodities? Clearly from this form itself. The equality of all sorts of human labour is expressed objectively by their products all being equally values; the measure of the expenditure of labour-power by the duration of that expenditure, takes the form of the quantity of value of the products of labour; and finally the mutual relations of the producers, within which the social character of their labour affirms itself, take the form of a social relation between the products."

Marxist/ism: This term requires clarification. It has been subjected to many uses and abuses over the years. The word itself has named many straw men. In this context, however, it means I adhere to an interpretive methodology that takes dialectical materialism as its philosophical axiom and historical materialism as the application of dialectical materialism to questions of social development. It does not imply, and in fact rejects, the conversion of some version of "Marxism" into a quasi-religious doctrine, complete with infallible prophets and holy texts, nor does it imply either wholesale endorsement or rejection of the practices, including the exercise of state power, by Marxists in the past or present. Marxism, as both critical method and political practice, is still evolving, and this book is partly intended as a small contribution to that evolution.

7 The Second Law of Thermodynamics is the law of entropy, which states that in the absence of intervening structures, and in a closed system, energy will tend to dissipate. This is a vast oversimplification of the law and its implications. In fact, the popular variant, alluding to the tendency toward disorder, is Murphy's Law: anything that can go wrong will go wrong. There are some important qualifications to the Second Law. It is a tendential law, not a strictly causative one. It asserts itself over time and in the face of seeming exceptions. One of those key exceptions is life. Life forms are counterentropic (intervening) structures.

8 John Bellamy Foster, "Marx's Ecology in Historical Perspective," *International Socialism Journal* (Winter 2002), http://pubs.socialist-reviewindex.org.uk/isj96/foster.htm.

9 Alf Hornborg, "Technology and Unequal Exchange," paper presented to the INES 2000 workshop C3, June 16, 2000, http://www.ines-global.org/hornborg.html.

10 "Great Fish Going the Way of the Dinosaurs," Environmental News Service, May 14, 2003.

11 Martha Gimenez, "The Population Issue: Marx vs Malthus," *Den Ny Verdun* (Denmark) (1973): http://csf.colorado.edu/authors/Gimenez.Martha/popissue.html.

12 Maria Mies, *Patriarchy and Accumulation on a World Scale* (London: Zed Press,1998).